CULTUR

A Survival Guide to

CW00968764

SAUDI ARABIA

Peter North
Harvey Tripp

Marshall Cavendish
Editions

Photo Credits:
All photos from alt.TYPE/REUTERS except pages 59, 117 (Ian Blain);
page 7 (Focus Team, Italy); page 181 (Angela Jackson); pages 13, 153
(Photolibrary.com). ▪ Cover photo: Photolibrary.com

All illustrations by TRIGG

First published in 2003
Copyright © 2006 Marshall Cavendish International (Asia) Private Limited

This edition published in 2006 by:
Marshall Cavendish Limited
119 Wardour Street
London W1F 0UW
E-mail: enquiries@marshallcavendish.co.uk

Other Marshall Cavendish Offices:
Marshall Cavendish International (Asia) Private Limited. 1 New Industrial Road,
Singapore 536196 ▪ Marshall Cavendish Corporation. 99 White Plains Road,
Tarrytown NY 10591-9001, USA ▪ Marshall Cavendish International (Thailand) Co
Ltd. 253 Asoke, 12th Flr, Sukhumvit 21 Road, Klongtoey Nua, Wattana, Bangkok
10110, Thailand ▪ Marshall Cavendish (Malaysia) Sdn Bhd, Times Subang, Lot
46, Subang Hi-Tech Industrial Park, Batu Tiga, 40000 Shah Alam, Selangor Darul
Ehsan, Malaysia

Marshall Cavendish is a trademark of Times Publishing Limited

ISBN 10: 0-462-00628-X
ISBN 13: 978-0-462-00628-4

Printed in Singapore by Times Graphics Pte Ltd

ABOUT THE SERIES

Culture shock is a state of disorientation that can come over anyone who has been thrust into unknown surroundings, away from one's comfort zone. *CultureShock!* is a series of trusted and reputed guides which has, for decades, been helping expatriates and long-term visitors to cushion the impact of culture shock whenever they move to a new country.

Written by people who have lived in the country and experienced culture shock themselves, the authors share all the information necessary for anyone to cope with these feelings of disorientation more effectively. The guides are written in a style that is easy to read and covers a range of topics that will arm readers with enough advice, hints and tips to make their lives as normal as possible again.

Each book is structured in the same manner. It begins with the first impressions that visitors will have of that city or country. To understand a culture, one must first understand the people—where they came from, who they are, the values and traditions they live by, as well as their customs and etiquette. This is covered in the first half of the book.

Then on with the practical aspects—how to settle in with the greatest of ease. Authors walk readers through topics such as how to find accommodation, get the utilities and telecommunications up and running, enrol the children in school and keep in the pink of health. But that's not all. Once the essentials are out of the way, venture out and try the food, enjoy more of the culture and travel to other areas. Then be immersed in the language of the country before discovering more about the business side of things.

To round off, snippets of basic information are offered before readers are 'tested' on customs and etiquette of the country. Useful words and phrases, a comprehensive resource guide and list of books for further research are also included for easy reference.

CONTENTS

FOREWORD

In his book *The 100: A Ranking of the Most Influential Persons in History*, author Michael H Hart judged that the world's most influential person of all time was an Arab trader who lived at the turn of the 6th and 7th centuries in Mecca in present day Saudi Arabia. The name of this individual was Muhammad, the founder of the Muslim religion. To Muslims, presently 20 per cent of the global population, Muhammad was the Prophet who delivered God's word to the world. To non-Muslims, Muhammad was the man who delivered the Muslim religion to the world. Either way, Muhammad's effect on global human affairs since his own time has been profound.

The other major influence, in terms of recent global interest in Saudi Arabia, was the discovery on the Arabian Peninsula of the world's biggest oil deposits. The development of the Saudi oil fields after the 1940s cast Saudi Arabia as the swing supplier of the world's energy and the most influential member of OPEC (Organisation of Petroleum Exporting Countries). The interaction of these two factors, Islam and oil, have made Saudi Arabia one of the most pivotal countries on the planet.

Oil and the income it has generated has had a profound effect on the Saudi culture in this once dirt-poor country of limited interest to the rest of the world. In the modern era, Saudi Arabia's economic prospects have varied with the oil price. In 1940s and 1950s, as the the first oil revenue flowed into the country, the Saudi Royal family first experimented with conspicuous consumption in its most extreme form—nearly driving the country bankrupt in the process. After the first big oil price increase in 1973, Saudi Arabia spent some of its petrodollars on national development and invested some in Western banks. The Western banks in turn invested in Latin American countries, which subsequently announced an inability to repay their debts. Laundered through various countries, these petrodollars found themselves in the accounts of Swiss banks in the name of various unsavoury Third World dictators—well beyond the reach of the Treasury of Saudi Arabia, the ostensible owner of the money. The price of oil peaked again in 1979 during the Iranian Revolution, but then slumped over the 1980s and 1990s when Saudi Arabia survived by deficit financing, building up a massive overseas debt. Since the oil price spike that started in around

2002, Saudi Arabia has applied the bulk of its funds from the booming oil price into paying off its accumulated debt and increasing its rate of development. At time of writing, the country is once more in good financial shape. In 2006, the World Bank ranked Saudi Arabia as the best place in the region to do business because the cost of living, shipping and warehouse charges as well as licence fees were substantially lower than the surrounding Gulf countries. In addition, with a projected population of 33 million in 2020, it is not only the fastest growing regional market, but the largest.

To implement its social and physical development programme, Saudi Arabia has, for many years, imported from other countries a guest workforce of skilled and unskilled labour. Saudi Arabia has a guest labour force five to six million strong in a total population of 26 million. Opportunities are many for guest workers inside Saudi Arabia to undertake an enormous variety of labour contracts, occupations and industries.

This book is principally written as an information guide to Saudi's army of guest workers. It also offers advice and information for those visiting the kingdom to do business, visit family members of guest workers and many other reasons. While the major viewpoint taken is that of the Western visitor who has accepted employment in Saudi Arabia, or is considering doing so, the book also contains helpful hints for guest workers from other countries. It offers thumbnail sketches of important historical accounts that have created present-day cultural attitudes, and includes information of day-to-day events within Saudi Arabia.

As the title of the book suggests, an assignment in Saudi Arabia is an experience in the clash of cultures. Saudi Arabia is located in a part of the world where the cultural mix is pronounced. Three of the world's dominant religions—Islam, Christianity and Judaism—originated in these ancient lands. In this region, Islam, Christianity, Judaism, Buddhism, Taoism and various other 'isms' uneasily rub shoulders against each other on a daily basis. Culture shock is a part of life in Saudi Arabia, both for the guest workers and the indigenous population. Avoiding the pitfalls of culture shock and getting the best out of your time in Saudi Arabia are two of the main themes of this book.

ACKNOWLEDGEMENTS

With thanks for contributions, advice and proof-reading from Margaret Tripp, Charles Jamieson, Anton Mayer, Joseph Elkhorne, Ian Blain, Angela Jackson and Len Tripp.

Central Riyadh, Saudi Arabia, seen through mirrors from Faisaliah Towers.

MAP OF SAUDI ARABIA

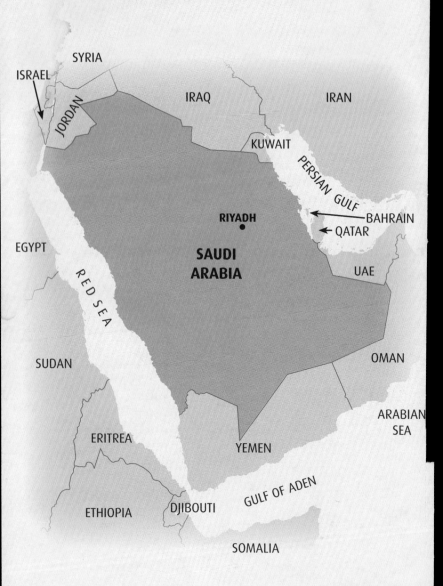

FIRST IMPRESSIONS

CHAPTER 1

'The real meaning of travel, like that of
a conversation by the fireside, is the discovery of
oneself through contact with other people...'
—Paul Tournier, *The Meaning of Persons*

WHEN I, ONE OF THE AUTHORS OF THIS BOOK, was first assigned to a project in Saudi Arabia, the personnel agent dealing with my paperwork jokingly referred to Saudi Arabia as a 'sandpit'. My mental impression, and I guess his too, of Saudi Arabia was an austere barren strip of land peopled by men in flowing robes and women in black *abayas*. In addition to vast expanses of sand, I visualised oil wells, oil pipelines, big landscapes, big skies, stifling heat and occasional camels strolling by.

When I arrived, that's pretty much the way I found it—at least so far as the countryside was concerned. But missing

Riyadh—modern skyline to an ancient town.

from this mental picture were the ubiquitous features of the modern world, the cosmopolitan cities of high rise buildings, the extraordinary airports, the spectacular eastern architectural features in mosques and public buildings, the freeways, the traffic snarls and the shopping centres.

Most of the physical infrastructure you will see in Saudi Arabia is modern for no better reason than almost all the country's infrastructure has been built in the last 50 years. This appearance contrasts starkly with attitudes, some of which haven't changed greatly since the 7th century AD.

Saudi Arabia is a modern country with some very ancient ways. Therein lies Saudi Arabia's culture shock.

GETTING THERE

It is just possible to enter Saudi Arabia by surface transport. The border with Iraq is closed until the political climate improves, but most of the other land borders are open. Access is possible, with various degrees of difficulty, through most of the countries with which Saudi Arabia shares land borders, Kuwait, Jordan, Yemen, Oman, the United Arab Emirates (UAE) and the island kingdom of Bahrain which is now connected to Saudi Arabia by causeway. People have even been known to make landfall on Saudi Arabia by *dhow*, one of the preferred methods of travel of previous eras and still operating today. But overland and seaborne entry to and from the country is unusual, attempted only by the more intrepid explorers. Most people arrive and leave by air.

Almost all visitors to Saudi Arabia enter through one of three airports: one on the Red Sea Coast, one in the centre of the country and one on the Persian Gulf coast.

The 'Persian Gulf' as it is denoted on most maps of the Middle East is more widely known in Saudi Arabia as the 'Arabian Gulf'. Alternatively it is often referred to merely as 'The Gulf'. All three terms describe the same body of sea water between the Arabian Peninsula on its western coast and Iran on its eastern coast. In this book, we are using the term 'Persian Gulf' throughout.

It was through the last of these airports, the one at Dhahran, that I first entered the country. From air and at night, my first impression on flying over the oil bearing parts of Saudi

Arabia was of a scene from Dante's *Inferno*. Down below flickered the orange flares from a thousand oil wells stretching from one horizon to the other, and out into the Persian Gulf. Even in these times of increasing energy consciousness and concerns for global warming, much of the waste gas associated with oil is simply flared at the wellhead of each oil well.

On flights by day, added to the same scene is the acrid black smoke from burning this dirty gas. Usually, a robust north-west wind carries these fumes away, spreading them across the northern waters of the Indian Ocean. But in still weather, the gulf coast may be wreathed in a grey canopy of sulphurous fumes.

Further west, over the land of the interior and away from the oil fields on the east coast, the orange desert vista stretches mostly uninterrupted from one horizon to another. Occasionally, dusty towns and a few large cities pass under wings. From the air, most of Saudi Arabia appears hot, hostile and featureless desert terrain as it truly is at ground level.

Flying In

Saudi Arabian Airlines, also known as Saudia, is the Kingdom's domestic and international carrier. A number of Asian, European and US airlines service the three major Saudi Airports to the two coastlines and the central region. Saudi Arabia can also be reached via hub airlines from the smaller Gulf states like Bahrain, Dubai and other UAE airports.

Along the western edge of the Arabian Peninsula is a mountain range running parallell to the Red Sea coast. The highest part of this range, in the south-west corner of the peninsula near Saudi's border with Yemen, is the Asir region—the wettest part of the country. Sufficient rain falls here to plant and harvest vegetables. From the air, by Saudi standards, the Asir countryside looks uncharacteristically green.

The Immigration Card

Like most places, entry to Saudi Arabia starts with flight attendants distributing immigration cards shortly before arrival. By the standards of immigration cards worldwide, Saudi Arabia's are remarkably user-unfriendly. An idea of how Saudis think can be gleaned from the fact that the smallest field width on the form is the one requiring the most letters—your address in Saudi Arabia. If you are staying somewhere like the Hilton, the form will allow just enough room to provide a brief address; otherwise you will have to abbreviate or attach a microchip.

The other field of major interest on the card is that asking you to state your religion. While back home one's religion may be a secret about which others are not legally entitled to ask, Saudi Arabia is one of the few countries in the world which asks you to declare your religious allegiances on arrival. This might immediately suggest to you, should you have been unaware of it, that in this place, religion matters. In reaching this view, you will be absolutely right. Only in few countries is religion quite as prominent in day-to-day affairs as it is in Saudi Arabia.

Saudis, like most religious people, consider their own religion the one true faith. Though Saudi Muslim clergy may come down hard on alternative religions, Islam does afford some respect for the older religions, such as Christianity to which it is related. Saudis tend to believe that everyone has a religion of some sort. Since they pray at least five times a day, most Saudis can't quite get their heads around belief systems based on the absence of any god at all.

Presented with the choice on the immigration card, that asks you to summarise the state of your religious beliefs in a space with room for about ten letters, you might be unwise to write 'atheist' in this field. It is better to declare one's faith in a false prophet than in no prophet at all. On the other hand, Saudis are unlikely to be interested in the fine print of your religious beliefs. Saudi Arabia doesn't really need to know, for example, whether you are a Seventh Day Adventist or a Member of the Church of the New Order. The best response, unless you happen to be a Muslim, is something brief like 'Christian', 'Hindu' or 'Taoist'. It almost goes without saying that 'Judaism' is not the appropriate word to enter in this field.

On the Ground

Disembarking from the plane, your first taste of the exotic delights of the Middle East will be the airport itself. *Sheiks*, kings, *emirs*, *sultans* and presidents of the Middle East tend to rival each other in expending public money (which, under their system of government, is effectively their own money) on extravagant public buildings. Modern-day Middle East potentates attempt to outdo each other in the grandeur of their airports, seemingly driven by the need to keep up with the Joneses, or in the case of the movers and *sheiks* of the Middle East, the Al Sauds. The lavish airports of the Middle East have enabled architects of renown to design and construct some of the modern world's most impressive major public buildings.

The Middle Eastern countries of the Arabian Peninsula are extraordinarily over-serviced by airports. For example, five of the seven emirates of the United Arab Emirates (UAE)—Abu Dhabi, Dubai, Fujairah, Sharjah and Ras al Khaimah—have international airports; Abu Dhabi now having two with its second airport at Al Ain. The maximum distance between any two airports of the single nation of the UAE is 180 km, with the airports at Dubai and Sharjah within 20 km of each other.

The three major airports in Saudi Arabia are King Abdulaziz International Airport in Jeddah, King Khaled International Airport in Riyadh and King Fahd International Airport in Dammam. All three of these airports have at least one feature that ranks as the biggest in the world.

King Abdulaziz International Airport services the western side of the country, including Mecca, and is ranked by at least one authority as the world's most beautiful airport. It includes a special terminal, the Hajj Terminal, used for handling Mecca's annual influx of pilgrims. The Hajj Terminal, open only for one month of the year during the pilgrim season, is the world's biggest single terminal by area, capable of handling 80,000 travellers per day.

When it was built in the early 1980s, King Khaled Airport in Riyadh was the world's biggest airport. It can still lay claim to the world's biggest airport mosque, a building capable of holding 5,000 worshippers, with room for another

The cavernous duty-free shopping area of the King Khaled Airport in Riyadh.

5,000 in balconies adjacent to the building. King Khaled serves travellers to the centre of the country. The airport was built bigger than it needed to be. One third of Riyadh Airport has not been used since it was first opened.

King Fahd Airport at Damman, opened in 1999 to replace the run-down Dhahran International Airport, is, at time of writing, the world's biggest airport by area. This airport serves the eastern seaboard of Saudi Arabia, including the main oil producing areas and Aramco, Saudi Arabia's state-owned oil company.

At the Immigration Desk

Entering Saudi Arabia is likely to be more arduous than in most places. Of course experiences vary from visit to visit and from one immigration official to the next. But by and large, Saudi Arabia would have to be one of the more nerve-wracking countries in which to clear immigration and customs.

Any number of stories can be told regarded the demeanour of Saudi immigration officials who might seem, to the traveller, to have been hand-picked for their brusqueness and lack of humour. Entering the country, you may queue up for an hour to clear immigration, and take another hour to depart the airport. You will be told to form orderly lines (something that Saudis themselves are not very good at) then continually be shifted to different lines. When you reach the head of the line, having perhaps been moved from one line or another, you may be told you are in the wrong line, and told to head back to the top of a different line. Needless to say, the correct procedure is not to remonstrate. You'll clear immigration eventually.

Having received a passport stamp, the next step in the entry procedure is to pass through customs. This, once again, is more testing in Saudi Arabia than in most places. Not only does Saudi Arabia have an extensive list of prohibited imports, its customs officials are proportionately more diligent at finding them. Customs officials in Saudi Arabia are more to likely to ask you to open your bags than most places. Alcohol, if found in anyone's luggage, is a coup for the official. The bottle is taken with a great flourish, to disappear in a desk some place, to be returned (as far as the official record is concerned) to its maker. You will be issued countless warnings not to carry alcohol into Saudi Arabia, but people who habitually carry bottles of whisky wherever they go sometimes overlook this rule and are regularly apprehended to face their fate, typically a few days in jail.

Do The Crime, Do The Time

Carrying products into Saudi Arabia that are obviously intended to brew alcoholic beverages is also not a good idea. A friend of one of the authors lost a debate with a customs official that a packet of champagne yeast in his bag (perhaps packed by someone else without his knowledge or permission) was really for making bread. A couple of nights in the slammer was the penalty for this offence.

Plus loss of yeast.

Porno photos, defined as naked flesh anywhere between neck and knees, are also not advisable imports. (If you really need alcohol, porno pictures and champagne yeast, getting them inside Saudi Arabia on the black market is a better method of procurement rather than bringing them in yourself.)

Magazines with dubious political content are also looked at with disfavour, in particular those containing articles that could possibly be interpreted as critical of the host country. Video tapes and DVD's are likely to be taken away for on-the-spot inspection. The contents of laptop computers may also be subject to scrutiny. Importing contraceptives is also banned, though they are obtainable over the counter in the kingdom. For a while after they were introduced, cell phones with cameras were also illegal. At time of writing, we believe this rule has now been relaxed.

Knowing all this (because you bought this book), you will not be carrying any of these items. When challenged, you will able to tell the customs official you have nothing to declare. In theory you should then pass through customs, possibly after a bag inspection, and escape into the countryside, thinking to yourself, "From here, things can only get better."

The chances are, they will!

LAND AND HISTORY OF SAUDI ARABIA

CHAPTER 2

'Come O men of Riyadh, Here I am,
Abdulazziz ibn Abdulrahman of
the House of Saud, Your rightful ruler.'
—Battle cry of Ibn Saud on defeating the
Al Rashid tribe at Riyadh in 1901

THE BEGINNINGS

According to most historians, human civilisation started when the first settlements based on permanent agriculture replaced preceding hunter gatherer societies. Sometime around 3000–4000 BC, in an area around present-day Kuwait and northern Saudi Arabia, a tribe of people known as the Sumerians arose, moved north and settled in a then-fertile region between the Tigris and Euphrates rivers in present-day Iraq.

Arguably, Sumeria was the world's first civilisation—the first place in which people in the world formed a self sufficient city state. The settlement endured and developed. Over a period of about one thousand years, the Sumerians invented advances such as writing, the wheel, the calendar, the seven day week, the 24-hour day and the 360-degree circle. The Sumerian tongue—unrelated to any language of the modern world—was probably the world's first written language.

That civilisations rise and fall has been the mark of history. Sumerian society stayed more or less intact for a long time, but eventually succumbed to an invading race: the Akkadians based in Akkad, the city that later became Babylon. Culturally and administratively, the Sumerians were far more advanced than their conquerors. As the two societies merged, the Akkadians adopted most of the Sumerian customs, culture and knowledge with the exception of the Sumerian language.

For a while, the Akkadians and Sumerians maintained a fractious relationship within their mixed society, reminiscent of the disharmonies between Arabs and Jews in the present day. The Akkadians spoke a Semitic tongue that is probably the genesis of the present-day languages of Hebrew and Arabic. As an identifiable race, the Sumerians, along with their language, were absorbed into Akkadian culture and disappeared from the pages of history. But their great civilising advances in administration, law, written language, agriculture and science survived them.

Forces of nature rather than forces of man eventually put paid to early settlements in Mesopotamia. The history of many semi-arid regions has proved that one effect of long periods of irrigated agriculture is environmental degradation. Contaminated by salt, the Sumerian fields became increasingly unfertile. Forests disappeared, and along with them, the wildlife that Sumerians used to supplement their diet. Rainfall declined and Mesopotamia depopulated. Today's salt marshes of Iraq serve as a reminder of the long-term consequences of the process.

While the area north of the Arabian Peninsula, and the peninsula itself, fell into decline, similar agriculture-based societies advanced in places like Egypt, the Indus valley, China and even the Andes. With the decline of Sumeria, the Arabian Peninsula, being as desolate then as it is now, is thought to have been almost uninhabited over thousands of years. After their pivotal role in the foundation of human history, the lightly inhabited lands of the Arabian Peninsula became best known as trading routes between the Indies, the countries of the horn of Africa and the Gulf, to Asia Minor and Europe.

THE LIE OF THE LAND...
Saudi Arabia is the biggest country in the Middle East and the 13th biggest country in the world. About the size of Western Europe and one quarter the area of the USA, Saudi Arabia occupies approximately 80 per cent of the Arabian Peninsula—a large slab of land, roughly rectangular in shape that juts into the northern seas of the Indian Ocean.

Desert landscape is a common feature in Saudi Arabia.

Saudi Arabia is hot and dry, and water is scarce. Annual rainfall is low almost everywhere. The country has no permanent rivers or lakes. The desert to the north, the Nafud, extends as far as Syria and into Iraq. In the south-east, the Rub al'Khali—the 'Empty Quarter'—is one of the most arid regions on the planet. In Saudi parlance, the Empty Quarter is simply known as 'The Sands'. Between the deserts of the north and south, arid plains of gravelly sand stretch across the centre of the country. The eastern seaboard along the Persian Gulf is mainly flat with rolling dunes. To the west, a range of low mountains parallels the Red Sea coast, from Jordan in the north to the hill country of the Asir region in the far south-west. Only here, near the Yemen border, is there significant rainfall.

The total length of Saudi Arabia's land borders are 4,400 km (2,700 miles). Bordering countries are Jordan, Iraq, and Kuwait to the north, Qatar, the United Arab Emirates (UAE) and Oman to the south-east, and the Republic of Yemen to the south. Saudi Arabia is also joined by a 24-km (15.5-mile) causeway/bridge to the island kingdom of Bahrain in the Persian Gulf (called the 'Arabian Gulf' by the Saudis!) The official border between these two states is set at 8 km along the causeway from Bahrain, and 16 km from Saudi Arabia. In addition to its land borders, Saudi Arabia has a total of 2,500 km (1,550 miles) of coastline on two different waterways. Egypt, Sudan and Somalia lie to the west across the Red Sea. Iran lies to the east across the Persian Gulf.

Winston's Hiccup

In the tradition of shifting lifestyles from Bedouin times, locations of boundaries are, for the most part, not precisely defined nor completely agreed. The most intriguing piece of haphazard cartography in Saudi Arabian recent history is its boundary with Jordan. At this point, Saudi Arabia seems to intrude into Jordan and out again for no apparent reason. According to contemporary legend, possibly apocryphal, this kink was due to some inaccurate drafting by the British wartime prime minister, Winston Churchill who was establishing the boundaries of the world one afternoon after a very pleasant lunch. According to this story, Churchill's hand slipped after he hiccupped from too much brandy, thereby bequeathing to Saudi Arabia several thousand square kilometres of not very valuable Jordanian land. From then on this tract of desert was termed by some as 'Winston's Hiccup'. No one has yet gone to war to right this wrong.

TRADING WITH THE WORLD

With its parched and burning sands, for much of its history Saudi Arabia has been a harsh country that offered little and received little in return. At times, as its history unfolded, it could take advantage of its strategic position between east and west. At other times, it seemed a worthless piece of real estate, a desert peninsula leading to nowhere—a vast mass of desolate empty land sticking out like a blunt finger into the Arabian Sea.

Despite the harsh environment, a small population did make a living on the Arabian Peninsula, built towns, and practised limited agriculture. In addition, the Arabs were traders. For over a thousand years until around AD 1500, Arabia provided a major trading route from India and Africa to Europe. Spices were landed on the west coast of the Persian Gulf, loaded onto camels and hauled to present-day Syria to join ancient Phoenician trading routes to the Mediterranean. Goods were also shipped across the narrow straits at the bottom of the Red Sea between modern-day Yemen and eastern Africa. In addition, the Arabian Peninsula produced a few of its own products that were also shipped to European markets—pearls from the Persian Gulf and frankincense from the gnarled grey trees of present-day Oman.

The period between the 7th–10th centuries was the most powerful era of Arab history. This was a golden age of Arab literature, astronomy, mathematics and influence. Inspired by the exploits of Muhammad, the Islamic fundamentalists of the time spread the Islamic message as far west as Morocco and Spain, into Asia Minor, and to the Far East.

As its power waned after the Middle Ages, the Arab world fell under the influence of a number of conquerors, in particular the Ottoman Turks who stayed on the Arabian Peninsula until the end of the World War I. Meanwhile, events elsewhere in the world diminished the importance of the Arab trading routes. In 1497, the intrepid Portuguese navigator, Vasco de Gama, became the first European to round the Cape of Good Hope en route to India. After that, ocean-going sailing ships operated by the great European East India trading companies, and later steamships, bypassed overland trading routes through the Arabian Peninsula. A few centuries later, the Suez Canal, which opened in 1869, put an end to the traditional overland trade routes for all time.

In terms of its interest to the rest of the world, the Arabian Peninsula probably reached its lowest ebb during the 19th century. Curiosity rather than commercial interest tempted a handful of European explorers to Arabia, particularly a number of intrepid Englishmen who absorbed the Arab ways and reported their adventures back home. The best known of them was 19th century's Richard Burton, the indefatigable traveller of Africa who disguised himself as a pilgrim, learned Arabic (he mastered around 30 or so languages) and visited Mecca by passing himself off as an Arab. These were the salad days of the Royal Geographical Society. The adventures of returning travellers were of great interest to the aristocracy of London.

In the early 20th Century, this tradition continued. T E Lawrence, 'Pasha' Glubb, St John Philby and Captain William Shakespear, who all roamed the deserts with tribes of Arabia, were amongst other Englishmen who succumbed to the fascinations of the Arabian Peninsula. Typical of the breed, Shakespear was described in despatches as 'soldier by training; diplomat by profession; amateur photographer, botanist and geographer by inclination; and adventurer at heart'.

THE AL SAUDS

The modern state of Saudi Arabia had its origins in the Bedouin tribes that roamed the Arabian Peninsula. In 1774, Muhammad ibn Abd al-Wahhab, a fundamentalist religious leader formed an alliance with Muhammad bin Saud, a local ruler in the Najd area near Riyadh. Al Wahhab and the Al Sauds pledged to pool their religious and military resources to spread Wahhab's religious message and Al Saud military protection to surrounding tribes and settlements.

Wahhabism

Named after its founder Muhammad ibn Abd al-Wahab, Wahhabism is a fundamentalist religion that does not take kindly to new knowledge. It preached a puritanical approach to faith and its religious practices.

For a century and a half after the rise of Wahhabism, power in the area of present-day Saudi Arabia rested with three main family groups—the Al Sauds, the Rashids and the Hashemites—whose respective influence waxed and waned with the strength of their leaders. In 1802, Al Saud forces captured Mecca, which they subsequently lost, regained and lost again. By the end of the 19th century, the Al Saud's

fortunes reached their lowest ebb. The tribe had retreated to Kuwait where they were given refuge by the Al-Sabah family who rule Kuwait to this day. Tradition and debts of honour die slowly in the Arab world. The Al Sauds returned the 100-year-old favour to the Al Sabah family when Kuwait was invaded by Iraq in the Gulf War of 1991.

From its low point in the first days of the 20th century, the fortunes of the Al Sauds took a turn for the better. In 1901, 21-year-old Prince Abdul Aziz bin Abdul Rahman Al Saud (more commonly known as Ibn Saud) emerged from Kuwait to avenge the defeat of his father at the hands of the Rashids. Ibn Saud undertook an intrepid journey accompanied by about 40 adventurous companions, setting out by camel on a long trip to Riyadh with the object of reconquering the city. Against the odds, and greatly outnumbered by Rashid forces, Ibn Saud and his stalwarts crept into the walled city at night and overcame the defenders.

After reconquering Riyadh and consolidating for a while, Ibn Saud turned his attention to the garrisons of the Turks on the Arabian Peninsula's eastern seaboard. In the early 20th century, Ottoman influence was in general decline across the Middle East. In 1913, Ibn Saud's forces overcame Turkish resistance in the area around present-day Dhahran. At around the same time, the Hashemite family—associated with the enigmatic Briton T E Lawrence (aka Lawrence of Arabia)—was pushing the Turks out of regions on the Red Sea coast. The Ottoman cause was further undermined when Turkey aligned itself with the losing side in World War I. At the end of the war, with Franco-British troops in Istanbul, the 500-year-old Ottoman Empire was brought to a close. In the 1920s, preoccupied with defending its own borders from the Greeks in the west and the Armenians in the east, the newly installed government of the Republic of Turkey was not greatly interested in recapturing its dusty domains on the Arabian Peninsula.

The demise of the Turks left the Hashemites and Al Sauds as the two dominant forces on the Arabian Peninsula. Before too long, these two competing erstwhile British allies ended up fighting each other. Much to the chagrin of Lawrence, the

Hashemites were forced to retreat to Jordan, where the family established the monarchy that has continued to this day. By 1924, the Al Sauds had gained control of Mecca and by 1932, they controlled most of present-day Saudi Arabia. Ibn Saud then declared himself king of a new nation that he named Saudi Arabia, after himself.

A Mutual Alliance

The alliance between 'men of the pen' (the Wahhabi clerics) and 'men of the sword' (the Al Saud warriors) has endured to the present day. The alliance is symbolised on the Saudi coat of arms as a pair of crossed swords beneath a script that proclaims God as Allah and Muhammad as the Prophet. Each year, to celebrate this alliance, the now much dispersed Saudi Royal Family holds a reunion in Riyadh featuring, as its centrepiece, a ceremonial sword dance.

SAUDI ARABIA: THE EARLY DAYS

The new nation of Saudi Arabia was the size of Western Europe, stretching from Transjordan and Palestine in the north to the shores of the Arabian Sea to the south. From east to west, it spanned the Arabian Peninsula, from the Persian Gulf to the Red Sea. Only a few territories around the edges of the country—the present-day Qatar, Kuwait, the United Arab Emirates (UAE), Oman and Yemen—escaped absorption into the new kingdom. Other than the vastness of its territory, the new nation didn't have much going for it. It was two-thirds desert, and desperately poor. But it did occupy a strategic position in the world because it commanded two major sea routes: the Persian Gulf and the Red Sea.

Developed by British interests in Persia, the first commercial oil well in the Middle East was brought into production in 1908. To maintain the flow of Persian oil to market, and in particular to the Royal Navy, the British needed to secure its sea lanes in the Persian Gulf. Well before World War I, the British had forged an alliance with Ibn Saud. In return for keeping the western shores of the Persian Gulf secure for British shipping, Ibn Saud could, from time to time, cadge a little money from the British Treasury and arms from its armoury.

Oil prospecting in Saudi Arabia started in the 1920s when Britain's Eastern General Syndicate obtained a concession to explore for oil on the east coast of Saudi Arabia. They found oil. But having announced that oil had been 'discovered', the Eastern General Syndicate failed to develop the find and the concession lapsed.

In the first half of the 20th century, Arabia lived a subsistence lifestyle. A small amount of trading and pearling was conducted through the settlements on the Persian Gulf and the Red Sea coast. Riyadh, near the centre of the country, was based on its large oasis. But overall, the climate was too harsh and rainfall too erratic to support a large population. In much of the country, Bedouin tribes moved their meagre flocks of camels, goats and sheep from one patch of skimpy grass to another. Water was their most precious commodity and the Bedouins jealously guarded their waterholes.

Though Saudi Arabia was still desperately poor, unimaginable riches lay just around the corner or more precisely, a few hundred yards beneath the desert. Commercial oil production from the western side of the Persian Gulf first got underway in the 1930s, not in Saudi Arabia but in the offshore sheikdom of Bahrain, about 40 km from the Saudi Coast. As things turned out, the Bahrain oilfield was a small one by subsequent Middle East standards.

Ibn Saud tried to get the British to take his oil interests seriously. But the Great Depression was underway in the West and the British weren't interested in acquiring a country that the colonialists of the 19th century would have snapped up without hesitation. Undeterred, Ibn Saud approached the Americans—at the time the world leaders in the oil prospecting. In 1933, the Standard Oil Company of California acquired the concession to prospect for Saudi Arabian oil for the bargain basement price of US$ 250,000 plus royalties on oil produced. Aramco (the Arabian American Oil Company), a consortium of American oil companies, was established to find and develop Saudi oil. The world's largest, most productive and easiest to exploit oil fields were about to get underway, culminating in the Ghawar oil field discovered in 1948 and brought into commercial production in 1951. Approximately 280 km long and 25 km wide, the Ghawar field is the biggest oil field ever discovered and likely to remain so. Sixty years later, it is still in production, producing 5 million barrels of oil per day, or around 7 per cent of world oil supply.

For all his Bedouin background, Ibn Saud proved commercially astute. Typical was his position in World War II. Saudi Arabia's commercial allies, Britain and the US, were on the same side. In accordance with the traditional Bedouin practice of backing only winners, Ibn Saud bided his time, remaining neutral while he established which way the wind was blowing. Though Saudi Arabia allowed the US to build an air base in Dhahran, it remained uncommitted until the last days of the war. Then, in March 1945, with the allied victory in Europe only a month away, Saudi Arabia declared war on Germany and Japan—in time, the King no doubt hoped, to avoid the conflict but share the spoils of victory.

In Saudi Arabia, royalties went to royalty. Since the King had conquered the country, he owned the country. At first the Saudi aristocracy spent their newly won oil money, as they knew best: on themselves. They built luxurious palaces, played the gaming tables of Monte Carlo, took many wives and did little to develop their country or improve the lot of the community. The infrastructure of the country and the education of its people advanced little from its state under the collection of disparate sheikdoms of 50 years before.

The Kings of Saudi Arabia

In 1953, Ibn Saud died, leaving behind an enigmatic memory. To his admirers, he was the great uniting force of his country. To his detractors, he was a ruthless conqueror who was cruel to the vanquished, abused women, celebrated ignorance and wasted the country's resources in frivolous consumption. Whichever he was, after his death he left behind a country ill-equipped for the modern world.

The first king after the death of Ibn Saud was his eldest son, also called Saud. King Saud's rule was marked by extravagance, a declining economy, an increasing gap between rich and poor, and ultimately social unrest. Saudis travelling within and outside the kingdom during this period earned an enduring reputation for ostentatious wealth and wasteful expenditure.

After some years of Saud's erratic rule, the Saudi Royal Family progressively engineered his downfall. In 1958. King Saud was persuaded to transfer to his half brother, Crown Prince Faisal, executive powers in foreign and internal affairs. In 1959, Faisal introduced an austerity programme that, among other things, cut subsidies to the Royal Family, balanced the budget, and stabilised the currency. In 1962, Faisal was appointed prime minister. In 1964, King Saud was forced to abdicate and Faisal was crowned king.

During his reign, King Faisal strove to find the middle ground between his Western associates who urged him to increase the pace of modernisation and the Ulema—the Council of Senior Islamic Scholars—who urged him to maintain the status quo. Faisal cautiously introduced social reforms such as free community health care and the right of females to receive an education. Faisal's progressive agenda and fiscally responsible government received widespread support both within Saudi Arabia and outside his country. In 1974, *Time* magazine selected King Faisal as its 'Man of the Year'.

Though King Faisal had international support, inside Saudi Arabia his reforms were opposed by religious fundamentalists. One measure in particular that earned the reprobation of his critics was the introduction of television into Saudi Arabia in 1965. Religious fundamentalists considered TV salacious (perhaps with some cause). When opposition to TV was at its height, one of Faisal's nephews was shot and killed by police after leading an assault on a TV station. Nine years later, in a tit-for-tat killing, Faisal was himself shot and killed by the dead nephew's brother, who was publicly beheaded for his trouble.

After Faisal's assassination in 1975, another of Ibn Saud's sons, Faisal's half brother Khaled, was installed on the throne. After King Khaled died in 1979, the next monarch was King Fahd, another son of Ibn Saud. Fahd died in 2005 after suffering a stroke in 1995 and spending the last few years of his reign convalescing in a clinic in Switzerland. Fahd was succeeded by his half brother, King Abdullah. By that time Abdullah, in his role as crown prince, had already been the country's effective leader for ten years.

THE ORIGIN OF ISLAM

To understand what makes Saudi Arabia tick, one needs at least a background knowledge of Islam's history and beliefs. Beginning in the 7th century AD, Islam was the last of the world's great religions to get underway. No major world-sweeping religions have been founded since.

Like Christianity and Buddhism, Islam was the inspiration of a single individual—the prophet Muhammad—though later scholars and clerics also made their contributions. Muhammad was born in Mecca to a poor family in AD 570. At the time, Mecca was an important trading post for caravans travelling to Europe and throughout the Middle East. Muhammad started his working life as a shepherd. When he was about 15 years old, he was hired by a distant and older female cousin, Khadija, who ran a trading business into Asia

Minor. In this role, before the end of his teens, Muhammad travelled throughout Arabia as far afield as Damascus and impressed Khadija with his skills as a trader.

When he reached 25, Khadija, who was 40 years old and a widow, offered to marry him and he accepted. Muhammad was Khadija's third husband and she was his first wife. Muhammad and Khadija had two sons who died before they reached two years of age and one daughter, Fatima, who survived into adulthood. Fatima became an important historical figure after the Prophet's death in AD 632.

The Split of the Faith

Islam divided into two denominations immediately after Muhammad died and even before his funeral. The Shia or Shi'ite sect believed the first caliphate to be Ali, the husband of Muhammad's daughter Fatima, and reputed to be the second person to embrace Islam. Present-day Shi'ites believe the caliphate line runs only through direct descendants of Muhammad via Ali and Fatima. (Shia or Shi'ite derives from a shortening of Shiat Ali, meaning 'follower of Ali'.) The Sunni sect, by contrast, believed Ali to be the fourth caliphate, with the three caliphates who preceded him all dying in fairly short order. The third of Sunni's caliphs, Uthman (AD 644–656), was murdered while at prayer and Ali succeeded him to the caliphate under dubious circumstances, with Utham's supporters alleging that Ali was implicated in Uthman's death. The disputants turned to violence which has marked relations between Sunnis and Shi'ites before and since. Both sides of this argument held the Qur'an as sacrosanct. At the Battle of Suffin, when the Sunnis showed up with verses of the Qur'an stuck on the sharp end of their spears, the Shi'ites were too devout to join the fight. But later fighting, was resumed in and in 661, Ali was murdered in an internecine dispute. Later, at the Battle of Karbala in 680, Ali's son Hussein was also killed, but Hussein's own son survived, thus perpetuating the Shi'ite caliphate line.

To outsiders the differences of the two denominations may seem trivial, though probably no more so than the schisms of the Christian Church. Whatever the respective merits of these opposing claims to the caliphate, over the centuries, rivers of blood have been shed contesting the issues that separate these two Islamic sects.

Before marrying Muhammad, Khadija had already accumulated a significant fortune. By the time he was 30, by trading on his own account, Muhammad had already made himself a wealthy man. By that point in his life, he had the time and money to reflect on the meaning of life, and did so at considerable length. It was in these reflections, Islam had its origins.

The Islamic code of conduct that Muhammad drafted was much influenced by Christianity, Judaism and the pagan religions that vied for influence on the Arabian Peninsula at the time he lived. Muhammad's new religion amalgamated elements of these existing religions with some bold new ideas of its own. Islam adopted monotheism, the central idea of Christianity and Judaism that there was only one God, rather than the range of Gods for different purposes of the pagan religions. To Islamic scholars, both Christianity and Judaism compromised their monotheistic character by clouding the status of God with quasi-god figures. In this view, Christianity with its Holy Spirit, the Virgin Birth and the Son of God, enshrined interactions between God and humans in much the same way as the pagan religions of the Greeks and the Romans. Islam, by contrast, stripped religion down to its barest essentials: one God and one major prophet—Muhammad himself, not the Son of God, merely a man selected by God to pass his word on to the rest of mankind. Since Islam drew from Christianity which itself drew from Judaism, Islam recognised both Jesus Christ and Judaism's Abraham as Prophets of God, though not quite on the same rank as Muhammad himself.

Of all the established religions in Arabia in the 7th century, Christianity provided Muhammad with his strongest influences. The core idea of Lent, for example, was installed as Ramadan in the Islamic calendar. Both Lent and Ramadan are periods of abstinence and religious introspection. The method by which the two prophets, Christ and Muhammad, received their instructions from God was also similar. Christ retired in solitude to a mountain to communicate with the Almighty. Muhammad retreated to a cave near Mecca and received God's instruction through an intermediary, the Archangel Gabriel. Christ's experiences were recorded by his disciples and incorporated into the Bible. Muhammad (who is thought to have been illiterate) later related the messages of Archangel Gabriel to scribes who then passed them onto the rest of mankind through the Qur'an, the Holy Book of Islam.

Muhammad was undoubtedly a charismatic character who inspired loyalty and self-belief. The Islamic religion was simple and held appeal. Nevertheless, Muhammad's religious revival started unpromisingly. Like Christ before him, Muhammad found his life threatened by the establishment. The merchants of Mecca regarded Muhammad as a dangerous radical. But unlike Christ who paid for religious dissidence with his life, Muhammad retreated about 400 km (250 miles) north of Mecca to the city of Medina, where religious ideas were more fluid and the establishment less entrenched.

Muhammad arrived in Medina on 24 September 622 AD, the date that is now the first day of the Islamic calendar. He announced himself as God's Prophet and soon attracted a following. He stayed in Medina for seven years, building his strength and debilitating his enemies by plundering the caravans sent north by the merchants in Mecca as they passed by Medina en route to the Mediterranean and Asia Minor.

Muhammad was a capable desert fighter and military strategist. His military valour and religious zeal won over the local tribes around Medina. His conquests of the Meccans laid weight to his declarations that God was on his side. Every victory over his enemy rendered Muhammad's claims to be God's messenger more credible.

Muhammad established a religious power base in Medina but Mecca was the centre of religion in Arabia, and the most powerful settlement in the region. It was the place to which Muhammad had to return to if his religious ambitions were to be realised. In AD 630, Muhammad led his army to Mecca, captured the city and became Mecca's undisputed leader. Muhammad was clearly a winner and so was his new religion. Recruits flocked to the cause.

Though Islam adopted beliefs from other religions, it also incorporated its own unique features to suit Muhammad's own circumstances and those of the wider community.

Polygamy and promiscuity were common practices in pre-Islam Arabia. Times were violent, and there was a general shortage of men. After his wife Khadija died, Muhammad accumulated several wives, some of them widows from slain followers. Thus equipped with female companions, Muhammad decreed that in the new religion, men could take up to four wives at a time on the proviso that they could all be kept in reasonable comfort. Islam recognised the rights of both parties of the marriage to divorce, stipulating that divorce could not be allowed on frivolous grounds, such as lack of looks.

The religious day was set as Friday to distinguish the holy day of the new religion from Judaism (Saturday) and Christianity (Sunday).

In Judaism of the time, women veiled their faces and covered their limbs in public to protect women from the prying eyes of men. Muhammad's rules of Islam merely followed this practice.

A common belief of all the religions of the region—Christianity, Judaism, paganism and Islam—was that their gods dwelt in the sky above their heads rather than in the earth beneath their feet. Many religions have laid great store in objects that appear to arrive from the sky, as if cast down by gods. Meteorites, in particular, have been treasured as religious icons by a number of the world's religions. By the time Muhammad was developing the Muslim religion, a black glossy stone known as the Hajar ul Aswad had been sanctified for over 1,000 years as the most religious object in Arabia. It is possible that the Hajar ul Aswad is a meteorite that had been blistered by fire as it burned through the atmosphere in some distant era before coming to rest on the Arabian sands. Before Islam arrived on the scene, Mecca was already a destination for pilgrims who visited the city to pay homage to the Hajar ul Aswad. Pilgrimages had already become a mainstay of the Meccan economy. Today, the Hajar ul Aswad, residing atop a metre-high plinth built into a small stone structure called the Ka'bah, rates as Islam's holiest icon in its holiest temple, the Great Mosque of Mecca.

The Hajar ul Aswad is one of the holiest relics of Islam and resides within the Ka'abah.

Five Pillars of Islam

Muhammad laid down the rules of conduct that have survived to the present day as the five pillars of Islam:

- *shahadah* Bearing witness that there is no other God than Allah, and Muhammad is his prophet
- *salat* Everyone should pray five times a day
- *sawm* Fasting between sunrise to sunset during the month of Ramadan
- *zakat* Giving 2.5 per cent of one's assets to charity
- *hajj* Believers must try to make a pilgrimage to Mecca once in their lifetime

The rules had various origins and served various purposes.

Shahadah

According to Muhammad, the Archangel Gabriel declared that God had chosen him, Muhammad, as his messenger on earth for all mankind. That Allah is God, and that Muhammad is his prophet is the fundamental belief of the Muslim faith.

Salat

There are various accounts for the requirement to pray five times a day. One is that Muhammad introduced frequent praying as a disciplinary measure for his armies. Another is that, Gabriel took Muhammad to Paradise where God demanded Muhammad and his followers pray 500 times a day. But prodded by Moses, Muhammad bargained God down to five times a day.

Sawm
The idea of fasting for the month of Ramadan was borrowed from the Christian idea of Lent. Muhammad's proscribed the holy month of Ramadan—30 days in the 12-month, 354-day Islamic calendar—as the month for fasting, abstaining and religious reflection

Zakat
Saudi Arabia has no income tax, but *zakat* is a form of tax that looks, at first glance, to be a low impost (2.5 per cent), but really may be considerably higher since it is levied on assets rather than income. It is a tax of conscience that is meant to be paid by Muslims, and is not levied on guest workers.

Hajj
The procedure laid down by Muhammad was, and still is, that pilgrims make their once-per-lifetime *hajj* to Mecca where they are obliged to perform various rituals. The *hajj* has to be undertaken in the last month of the Muslim calendar, the month of Dhu al-Hijjah. This was, and still is, an economic measure to boost the Meccan economy. Those who have made the pilgrimage once in their lifetime are entitled to attach the suffix *hajji* to their name, a status symbol in Islamic culture.

THE SPREAD OF ISLAM
The Christian religion spread by ideology, whereas Islam spread by a combination of ideology, military conquest and trade. No other religion in recorded history spread as quickly as Islam. In AD 635, five years after its inception, the forces of Islam captured Damascus; in AD 636, Jerusalem and by AD 641, Alexandria (then the capital of Egypt). By AD 650, Islamic forces had reached Afghanistan and India in the east, and

Pilgrims gather around the Ka'abah during the annual *hajj*.

Tripoli in the west. The Arab-Islamic empire then stretched an east-west distance of about 5,000 km. By contrast, Christianity took hundreds of years to become a predominant religion. The first Roman emperor who converted to Christianity was Constantine in the year AD 321.

Over the next 100 years, the expansion continued to include southern Europe, sub-Saharan Africa and what is now Pakistan. While political boundaries have ebbed and flowed in the intervening centuries, the religious map remains much the same now as it was then, except that Arab traders later added Malaysia and Indonesia to the Islamic club.

Arab civilisation during the Middle Ages produced many innovations not the least of which was mathematics based on the decimal system and the concept of 'zero'. Arab numerology, now universally adopted, greatly simplified arithmetical operations compared to the system of Roman numerals that it replaced. (It is much easier to multiply 338 by 8 than to multiply CCCXXXVIII by VIII.) The Arabs also developed algebra and trigonometry and excelled in medicine, astronomy and the arts.

In the light of present-day tensions, it would now seem odd that the Jews of the time mostly welcomed the Muslim invaders (who were seen as liberators) into Europe. In the Middle Ages, Jews in Europe were mercilessly persecuted by Christians. After their liberation by Muslims, Jews of societies the Muslims conquered were treated on the same level as Christians in the new society—as second-class citizens. For Jews of the time, this was an improvement. Christians by contrast, dropped down a peg in the hierarchy.

TODAY'S ISLAM

Today, Islam is the second biggest religion in the world after Christianity. In 2002, 19.6 per cent of the world's population were Muslims against about 33 per cent for Christianity. Islam is also the world's fastest growing religion, principally because it flourishes in countries that experience high population growth. Few countries are expanding their populations faster than Saudi Arabia, which has an annual population growth rate of around 4 per cent.

As a religion, Islam makes great demands of its flock. Visitors to Saudi Arabia cannot help avoid being struck by the strength of the country's religious belief. Saudis expect their God to take a much more detailed and personal interest in every aspect of their life than do even the most dedicated Christians. By the same token, God imposes more stringent demands on his believers.

Whereas in Christian countries, Sunday is the day for religious activity, in Saudi Arabia, religion is scheduled for every day of the week. Saudis make official contact with their God five times a day through their *salat* prayers and many more times by references to God that pepper normal conversation. When Saudis greet each other, shake hands in greeting and saying farewell, they do not say 'hello' and 'goodbye, have a good day'. When they meet you, they will most likely say *Al-Hamdulilillah* ('Praise be to God'). On leaving you. they will most likely say *fee man Allah* ('May God go with you'). During a normal conversation, God may be called to account to bless you, your children, your parents, though normally not your wife. (In Saudi Arabia, discussion of people's wives is akin to prying, and out of bounds in polite conversation.) God may be asked to protect you (*Allah iyatech stir*) or leave you in peace (*allah ihennik*). God is continually praised (*Subhamdallah*) for whatever might or might not be happening. The Saudi Arabic equivalents for 'probably' and 'maybe' are *Inshallah*—'if God wills it'—defining the Saudi expectation that God regulates the minutiae of everyone's life.

Maybe atheists exist in Saudi Arabia, but almost all Saudis you will meet discharge their spiritual commitments whatever the state of their personal beliefs. Praying is politically and socially acceptable to a point where it is almost compulsory. At the personal level, relaxing the daily rigorous expressions of belief may be akin to a dangerous political statement in a land where religious police are constantly on patrol.

Daily prayers are conducted at a mosque if one is in the vicinity. If not, other arrangements are made. Most business offices and public buildings have a prayer room. In the absence of suitable facilities like mosques and prayer rooms, a prayer mat can be set down on any convenient level surface that points in the appropriate direction.

In days gone by, the call to prayer was uttered by a religious functionary, called a *muezzin*, who would lean out from the balcony of the citadel of the mosque and summon all believers within earshot to join him in prayer. Nowadays, there are too many mosques and too few *muezzins* to go round to continue this ancient practice. Instead of *muezzins*, the call to prayer is made through loudspeakers by whichever worshipper happens to reach the mosque first.

The call to prayer follows a set format that any visitor to the country will get to know since it is repeated 1,825 times in a normal year and 1,830 times in a leap year. The prayer call is repetitive. It has about eight words, the same words that are written on the Saudi flag. Freely translated, the message is 'God is great. There is no other God but God and Muhammad is his prophet'. In Arabic, the message has a mesmerising alliterative cadence that sounds to the non-Arabic ear something like 'allah Akbar... al ah, ill illah illah allah'.

A royal decree has proclaimed that no point in an urban area of Saudi Arabia can be more than 800 metres from a mosque. But Saudi Arabia is a large country, and not quite sufficient mosques have so far been provided to meet this requirement. The decree on mosque spacing has transformed mosque construction into a minor industry. There are over 38,000 mosques in the country and the number is increasing daily. Saudi Arabia has also financed the construction of about 2,000 mosques in other countries and has built a large number of colleges and schools to introduce the young to the faith.

For the sake of economics, some cuts have had to be made. Traditionalists amongst the country's lovers of mosque culture have grounds to be disappointed with the relaxation of architectural standards of contemporary mosques. Though many graceful buildings of the past decorated with minarets and Arabian arches can still be found, some modern-day mosques are merely Portacamp cabins that look like construction huts equipped with external loudspeakers.

One of the extreme effects of policy of the 800-metre mosque spacing rule is audio-overlap. In some areas where three different versions of the prayer are delivered by three different believers starting at three different times and singing in three different keys. Non-Muslims can find the frequent calls to prayer exasperating, particularly the first one for the day at between five and six in the morning. No one in Saudi Arabia really needs an alarm clock.

Ramadan

The most solemn event on the Islamic calendar is Ramadan—the ninth month of the Islamic year—the month that Muslims abstain from their earthly pleasures. Mandatory activities including fasting from dawn to dusk, giving up smoking and abstaining from sex. Ramadan is a period in which believers are expected to endure long periods of introspection and communication with their God.

The rules of fasting merit further elaboration. During Ramadan, Muhammad prescribed that nothing should be eaten between sunrise and sunset, but with exceptions that Muslims can use to their advantage if they feel so inclined. Exempt from fasting are children, the sick, the old, menstruating females and travellers. What constitutes a traveller is interpreted fairly generously. To some extent, just about everyone travels somewhere each day. Therefore most people can mount some sort of an argument that they can be spared the rigours of fasting if they feel so inclined. In fact, not many Saudis try to escape their fasting obligations. During Ramadan, most Saudis try to comply with the rules.

What Saudis give up during daylight hours in Ramadan, they may more than make up for at night. In recent times, the night hours of Ramadan have become a celebration of feasting and perhaps, overindulgence. During Ramadan, shops in places like Jeddah stay open all night. Supermarket complexes do a roaring trade. Packed restaurants serve food from dusk to dawn. According to apocryphal reports, many Saudis gain weight during Ramadan, their month of fasting.

That aside, guest workers dealing with their Arab hosts are advised to bear the rigours of Ramadan in mind. Muslims forgoing their oral and other pleasures may be more tense and irritable during Ramadan than they usually are. Tempers can fray. Less community services are available. Many shops will remain closed during daylight hours. Schools work on reduced hours. Some business people, Saudis and expats, schedule their breaks away from the country during Ramadan. Not only does business slow down, but tensions during the month tend to run higher than normal.

Ramadan and the Infidel

The strictures of Ramadan are not imposed on non-believers provided the forbidden pleasures are practised discreetly. You can do more or less as you like in your own home, but foreigners caught smoking, drinking or eating in public have been sent to prison until Ramadan ends. (Once you are in captivity, you will surely abstain from these bodily pleasures.)

Since the 354-day Islamic year is shorter than the Gregorian year, the months of the Arabic calendar regress through the solar years. Ramadan travels backwards through the seasons, from summer, through spring to winter and back to summer on an approximate 33-year cycle. When Ramadan falls in summer, things are particularly tough on believers. In summer, the fasting period from dawn to dusk is longer than in winter and the non-fasting period from dusk to dawn is shorter. In addition, the weather is hotter, making the obligation to refrain from drinking more trying.

As the days of Ramadan pass, everyone looks forward to the new month of Eid-el-Fitr. The first three days of Eid-el-Fitr, marking the end of Ramadan, are the biggest holidays on the Saudi calendar. During this period, all the activities that were given up during Ramadan are resumed in abundance. These three days are a period of feasting, gift-giving and general letting go; the rough equivalent of Christmas in the Christian calendar. This is the most likely time that you will receive a gift from your Saudi employer, if you have one. If offered, the gift should be accepted, but not with over-effusive thanks. Gifts tend to be accepted in Saudi without tremendous fanfare. Generally, you are not expected to return the favour. However, it's not a bad idea to present some sort of token of your esteem to your Saudi boss when returning to work from a major break, like an overseas trip.

PAN-ARAB BROTHERHOOD: IN FORMATION OR DISARRAY?

Arabs may feel a sense of nationhood less strongly than say Americans or Germans. The principal source of identity in Arab culture is the family. The extended version of the family is the tribe. Beyond tribal identity comes the notion of the wider tribe—the feelings of Arab brotherhood and of belonging to an even bigger group—the Islamic world. A further source of identity is the religious sect to which an individual belongs. Given this combination of allegiances, patriotism to a particular country may trail a long way from the top in the hierarchy of belongingness. Arab countries such as Iraq, split across tribal lines, have made somewhat incoherent nations. Similar tribal schisms, perhaps less pronounced, exist in Saudi Arabia.

Underlying many of the troubles of the Middle East have been disputes of boundaries decreed by foreigners in remote cities such as London, Paris or Washington. In the Middle East, the most obvious and vexing case of boundaries drawn with little regard to the indigenous population was Israel, which was partitioned from the Arab world by the West without the consent and/or the knowledge of its Palestinian inhabitants. Israel is a particularly poor example of the modern-day fashion in some countries for multiculturalism. Nearly a century after the Balfour Declaration of 1917, which later led to the creation of Israel, the consequences of this unilateral declaration of statehood live on, no closer to a resolution. The Israeli problem underlies much of the tension within Saudi Arabia itself and the Arab world in general.

Since the end of World War II, Israel has fought four wars with its neighbours. Egypt, Iran and Iraq have seen one revolution each. Lebanon, the meeting point of Christianity, Islam and Judaism was shattered by its own cultural conflicts and devastated by the US-supported Israeli invasion of 1982. Iraq and Iran staged a re-enactment of World War I trench warfare in which the atrocities of World War I were repeated down to the gassing of troops in trenches. Like in World War I, each side fought the other to a standstill with little territorial conquest and massive loss of life on both sides. Almost continuous civil wars have also been fought within and across countries created by lines drawn on a map with little regard to tribal boundaries on the ground.

It's handy to have a scapegoat for various causes and the Arabs have supplied plenty to the Western world. In 1982, Beirut was reduced to near rubble in Israeli air attacks. During the 1970s and 1980s, Libya, a desert country with a population then of about 3 million people, was accused of plotting against the West. In 1986, Tripoli was bombed into submission by the US with UK assistance for an incident in a Berlin nightclub which, it was later found, had been perpetrated by Syrians. Two *Intifadas* (uprisings)—the first between 1987 and 1993 and the second starting in 2000—saw Palestinian teenagers (described in the Western press as 'terrorists') throwing stones at Israeli battle tanks blasting away their rundown villages. Helpless to defend against the F-16-delivered missiles, helicopter gunships and tanks of the Israelis, the Palestinian teenage terrorists became their own weapons-delivery systems, detonating bombs strapped around their waists, thereby blowing themselves up along with their victims. Such is the hopelessness of life in the Palestinian territories.

At the turn of the century, scapegoat attention shifted from Iraq's Saddam Hussein to the terrorists of 11 September 2001, the Taliban in Afghanistan and Al Qaeda. After that we had the second Gulf War.

If the West has been hard on the Arab world, the Arab world has been equally hard on itself. In 1956, the Egyptian leader, Gamal Abdel Nasser, floated the notion of a Pan-Arab alliance to annex the Suez Canal. But these aspirations of Arab unity were never fulfilled. Arab countries split too easily along their traditional tribal lines. No recent event typifies this more than Iraq's 1990 invasion of Kuwait. At issue was an ancient territorial dispute that could never be resolved to the satisfaction of both parties. Two claimants wanted to own the same piece of land under which lay one of the Middle East's largest oilfields. Iraq exercised its historical claims to the country. The United States saw its oil interests threatened. A massive force was mobilised. Iraq was defeated but not conquered and remained a sore in the side of bellicose Western powers until the war of 2003, which saw Saddam Hussein deposed.

Pan-Arab Brotherhood:
A Good Idea Not Yet Achieved

In 1982, the Gulf Arabs set up the Arabian Gulf Cooperation Council (AGCC) as a union of Gulf States along the lines of the European Union. But the rival Arab states were unable to unify their objectives. At the 2002 AGCC summit, Saudi Arabia's Abdullah, then a Crown Prince, pondered the failure of 20 years of attempted Arab integration. Said Abdullah:

"...we have not yet created a united military force that deters enemies and supports friends. We have neither achieved a common market, nor formulated a unified position on political crises."

Compared to most countries in the region, Saudi Arabia has been relatively peaceful. Throughout the conflicts in the Middle East, self preservation has been Saudi Arabia's dominant motive. The Al Sauds perceive they have more to gain out of a divided Arab world than a united one. In 1952, Nasser toppled King Farouk from the Egyptian throne. The Pan-Arabian aspirations of Nasser were not well received by the Al Sauds. The last person the Saudi Royal Family wanted to lead the Arab world was a king-toppling Egyptian. They felt the same about Colonel Qaddafi who, in 1969, dispossessed Libya's King Idris in similar circumstances. The Saudis supported the Yemeni royalists in their fight with Nasser and supported the Christian Phalangists against their Muslim rivals in Lebanon. They provoked Iraq into action in the Iran-Iraq war, lending Iraq US$ 30 billion in military aid that was later used against the donors in the first Gulf War.

The policy has been successful enough. Saudi Arabia has never been attacked or occupied by a foreign power since the Turks departed its territories almost a century ago. All of Saudi Arabia's land boundaries pass through mostly uninhabited desert regions with mostly friendly countries. The other borders are its two coastlines. With the exception of the border with Kuwait, who are the Saudis' natural allies, the kingdom's boundary areas have little commercial value. Supported by the US, and with the nearby nations once more at peace, the country remains in a sound strategic position against outside invasion.

SUNNIS AND SHI'ITES

Like a number of Middle East countries, Saudi Arabia is far from unified. Wealth in Saudi Arabia is not evenly spread across the county. The Eastern Province, the location of the oil fields, is the country's wealth generator. However, the Eastern Province is noticeably poorer than the central and western half of Saudi Arabia where much the country's wealth is spent.

The mixture of Sunni and Shi'ite sects of the Islamic faith are divisive. The Eastern Province is Saudi Arabia's Northern Ireland, a centre of dissent within the Kingdom, with a Shia community that numbers up to 15 per cent of the local population. Like minority groups in many countries, Shi'ites in Saudi Arabia are discriminated against, economically and socially. Shi'ites cannot hold public positions. They cannot participate in the judiciary. They cannot join the army. They cannot join the public service.

Over 25,000 Saudis, mostly from the Eastern Province, have travelled overseas to fight for various Muslim causes, amongst them Bosnia, Chechnya, Palestine and Afghanistan. Upon returning home, these warriors were treated not as returning heroes, but as troublemakers. Many of them were arrested and detained as dissidents. Hundreds of suspects from Shi'ite ranks have been kept in jail for long periods without trial. Shi'ites are likely to feel far more affinity with their religious colleagues in Bahrain and Iran than they do with the power group in Riyadh.

Prisoners of Conscience

'There are currently hundreds of possible prisoners of conscience held mainly on political or religious grounds by al-Mabahith al-'Amma [General Intelligence Service] without trial and denied any opportunity to challenge the legal basis of their detention. They include Sheikh Salman bin Fahd al-'Awda, a religious scholar and critic of the government, who was arrested in September 1994. He was held incommunicado for months before he was allowed family visits. Now, three years later, he remains held in al-Ha'ir Prison still without trial and still without any opportunity to challenge his continued detention. Abdullah Abbas al-Ahmad, an employee of Aramco aged 40, and Kamil 'Abbas al-Ahmad, a student aged 25, were arrested in July 1996 and detained in the headquarters of al-Mabahith al-'Amma in al-Dammam. Both were held incommunicado for months and have to date only been allowed three short family visits. They remain held without trial and their family have not been informed of the reasons of their arrest or detention.'

—Amnesty International Annual Report, 1998

SAUDI ARABIA AND ISRAEL

The conflict between Arabs and Jews has an internecine quality. The eternal struggle for supremacy in the Middle East is between distant members of the same family. Arabs regard the Jewish race as their delinquent brothers. The Jews regard the Arabs likewise. Both tribes can be traced to Semitic antecedents who lived on the Arabian Peninsula at about the time that civilisation was first emerging in the region.

Jews and Arabs coexisted in the Middle East for centuries after the two races assumed their separate identities. Judaism was a strong force on the Arabian Peninsula until the rise of Islam. The advent of Muhammad was a watershed event in Jewish/Arab relations. In the first days that Muhammad was establishing Islam as a state religion, those who refused to convert from Judaism were either executed or banished from Mecca. Much of the present-day enmity between the Jews and the Arabs stems from that time.

On their maps of the world, Saudi Arabia does not recognise Israel at all. The land mass to the west of Jordan and to the east of Egypt is designated 'Palestine'. A particular problem from the Saudi point of view in the Palestine question was the backing of Israel by the United States—the trading and military partner the kingdom did not wish to offend. King Faisal supplied 20,000 troops to Jordan during the 1967 Six-Day War and was devastated when Israel triumphed. According to some accounts, after that King Faisal never smiled again for the rest of his life.

During the 1973 Yom Kippur War, the kingdom sent troops and weapons to aid the Arab states. In both the 1967 and 1973 wars, Saudi Arabia briefly cut off, then reinstated, oil supplies to the West. (Saudi Arabia also briefly cut off oil supplies to Britain and France for supporting Israel against Egypt during the Suez Canal crisis of 1956.)

For all that, Saudi Arabian support for the Palestinian cause has been ambivalent. The Saudis, who don't particularly mind seeing other Arab nations disunited, have provided support to extreme groups like Hamas

The Palestinian Problem

Saudi author Sulayman al-Hattlan analysed the Palestinian situation from a Saudi perspective in an interview on the Australian TV programme *Foreign Correspondent*, aired on 5 March 2003. The title of the programme was 'Saudi Arabia: Inside the Closed Kingdom'. Al-Hattlan commented: 'The more the Palestinians are oppressed and the more the Americans support Israel, the more popular Osama bin Laden and his like become. I think the core issue is Palestine. The trend of fanaticism or extremism cannot stop at any point until we really look seriously at the Palestinian issue.'

and Islamic Jihad as well as the Palestinian Liberation Organisation (PLO). During the first Gulf War, in response to the Palestinian support for Iraq, the Saudis expelled Palestinians guest workers and cut off financial aid to various Palestinian organisations, including the PLO.

OIL AND THE ECONOMY

Commercial oil production in Saudi Arabia commenced in 1938 at modest flows, and continued at about 300,000 barrels per day through World War II. After the war, serious oil revenues started to flow into the Royal treasury and additional oil wells on the eastern seaboard were drilled. In 1948, a pipeline—the TransArabian Pipeline, more commonly called the Tapline—was built to carry oil from the Arabian Gulf oilfields to the Mediterranean port of Sidon, in Lebanon. The Tapline passed through four politically volatile countries: Saudi Arabia, Jordan, Syria and Lebanon. The project was a technical success, but the Tapline crossed some of the most politically sensitive country in the world. In particular, the Golan Heights in Syria, became a regular battlefield between the Israelis and the Syrians. Over its working life, the Tapline was often out of action and sometimes sabotaged. In any case, after the development of supertankers, its use became

The Qatif oil producing plant in Damman which lies north-east of Riyadh.

Fumes emanating from the oil processing plants in Saudi Arabia can be seen from aeroplanes as they fly into the kingdom.

uneconomic. In the 1990s, after a tiff with Jordan, Saudi Arabia shut down the Tapline for good. These days, oil is shipped by tankers from the Gulf to its various destinations around the world.

Though the Saudi oilfields were originally developed by foreign oil companies, over the years Saudi Arabia bought back the rights to its own oil. In 1950, Saudi Arabia negotiated a 50-50 profit-sharing arrangement with the US oil companies in the Aramco consortium. In 1974, the Saudis increased their share of Aramco and in 1980, assumed full control of the company.

During the 1950s, oil was sold to a free market that established its own prices according to the laws of supply and demand. Saudi Arabian oil—abundant, near the surface, and close to the coast for loading into oil tankers—was cheaper to extract and ship to world markets than oil from most oilfields. Extraction costs of Saudi oil, according to one estimate, were US$ 0.25 cents per barrel.

Since oil was sold to the free market, regulating the oil price directly was impossible. Oil was cheap. The way to control the oil price, the Saudis realised, was to control production. Since about a dozen countries in the world were major oil exporters, production controls could work if a significant number of these exporters operated a cartel.

In September 1960, at a conference in Baghdad, Saudi Arabia, Venezuela, Iraq, Iran and Kuwait founded the Organisation of the Petroleum Exporting Countries (OPEC) where all member nations would agree on production targets for the various producing countries and thereby maintain oil prices. Despite occasional internal political tensions, OPEC has held together to the present day.

In 1973, using the latest iteration of the Arab-Israeli war as a pretext, OPEC shut down production, pushing up the price of oil by 400 per cent overnight, precipitating what in economic circles became known as the 'first oil shock'. Over the ensuing years, when production resumed, billions of dollars from oil revenues flowed into the treasury.

OPEC operations weren't always successful. In the 1980s and 1990s when members of OPEC exceeded their own

production quotas, the oil price dropped from a high of US$ 40 per barrel to a low point of around US$ 5. A further burden on the treasury was a US$ 51 billion debt to the US for the costs of protecting the country in the first Gulf War from a rumoured invasion by Iraq. Added to this was US$ 30 billion that the Saudis incurred bankrolling the military efforts of Saddam Hussein in its fight a few years earlier with Iran. The cost of maintaining the Royal Family—estimated by some at US$ 10 billion per year—was also burdensome.

Saudi Arabia does have resources other than oil. Its minerals include small amounts of gold, silver, iron copper, zinc, manganese, tungsten, lead, sulphur, phosphate, soapstone and feldspar. Saudi Arabia also has a small agricultural sector. The country's traditional crop is dates, of which Saudi Arabia is one of the world's largest producers. Elsewhere in the country, about two million tonnes of wheat are produced under irrigation by desalinated water and at a cost that is likely to be a great deal higher than global free market prices. The country even exports subsidised wheat to other countries.

For all its aridity, according to census information, Saudi Arabia sustains a population of 7.4 million sheep, 4.2 million goats, half a million camels and a quarter of a million cattle.

The south-west of the country, where the annual rainfall is around 400 mm (16 inches), is the main source of agricultural products. Coffee, fruit, vegetables and cereal crops are grown in these highland regions. But the aggregate economic results from these activities is modest. Oil, subject to its erratic highs and lows in price, is the main game and has been for many years.

Even as recently as 2002, the economy was sagging under the influence of low oil prices and accumulated debt. Economic salvation came courtesy of the dramatic oil price that started in 2002/2003 when, for the first time, a major global resource became in permanent short supply.

In 2005, in response to pressures from the US administration, Saudis from the government and Aramco announced plans to ramp up Saudi oil production from ten million barrels per day to 15 million phased over a number of years. A vigorous debate ensued on whether they could actually do it. Experts in the field of oil production, such as geologists C J Campbell and Jean Laherre, consider that oil production from Saudi oil fields is close to its physical limits. They think the new targets are unrealistic. Whoever is right on this question, output from Saudi oil fields seems likely to be maintained at least at current levels for quite a few years and should finance the kingdom's development activities, including a continued ability to afford a foreign workforce.

THE GOVERNMENT OF THE PRESENT DAY

Warlords have traditionally ruled Arab societies. The 20th century has brought little change to this practice. Of the modern day Arab nations, only Egypt is a democracy, and even Egyptian democratic claims are compromised by low election turnouts and allegations of unfair elections. In other countries in the region, a mixture of *emirs*, kings, dictators, presidents, *sheiks* and *mullahs* (none of whom are elected) rule most of the nations in the region.

Saudi Arabia remains an old-style kingdom still held together by a 250-year-old alliance between the Al Saud family and the reactionary Wahhabi scholars. The King is prime minister and appoints his own ministers, mostly senior members of his own family. Key government offices are all held by family members. Most of the cabinet are princes, brothers, half-brothers, sons and nephews from the House of Saud.

Ibn Saud's 30-year campaign to unite the country started a one-man population explosion. Two or three generations since Ibn Saud arrived on the scene, an extraordinary number of people can claim the royal bloodline. Two generations on, grandsons of Ibn Saud number around 1,400. All estimates of the size of the present-day Royal Family range from 5,000 to 25,000 depending on who's being counted. Of this impressive tally, one hundred or so are senior princes, a few thousand are second-ranking *emirs* and *sheiks* and the balance, lesser lights.

The institution of the monarchy, with its centralised power and long periods of reign, has stamped the kingdom with the personality of the current monarch. Under Saudi protocol, succession of the monarchy flows to the 'oldest and most upright' of princes. As a result, successive kings of Saudi Arabia have been increasingly old men. When he ascended the throne in 2005, King Adullah was 81 years old. Next in line is Crown Prince Sultan who claimed to be 75, though some authorities think he has exaggerated his youthfulness, and could be older. (No accurate records were kept in the 1920 and 1930s when Sultan was born.) After Prince Sultan, the line of succession will depend on which of Ibn Saud's sons are still alive. Under present arrangements, only after all of Ibn Saud's 44 sons have died is the crown likely to pass to one of his grandsons, the oldest of whom are presently in their sixties and seventies.

The sheer size of the Royal Family is one of the monarchy's strengths and at the same time a weakness as princes compete with each other for positions of power. Given its massive size, the Royal Family has closed ranks pretty well to hold out against such quaint Western notions as democracy and the right to vote. One of the family's techniques of reducing the power of their own dissidents has been to get rid of them. In the 70 years so far that the monarchy has stayed intact, it has publicly executed three of its own and privately disposed of a number of others.

The Wahhabi religious order also has a strong role in government. Although Saudi princes select the King, their choice must be approved by the Ulema, which also acts as an advisor to the government on a wide range of issues.

The Saudi answer to those who say that the kingdom is undemocratic is the complaints handling authority, the Majlis Al Shura, or Shura Council, appointed by the king in 1992. The Majlis, a committee of 150 delegates with no law-making power, serves as a forum to discuss the issues of the day. To underscore the alliance between the political and religious wings in the country, all appointments to the Majlis are ratified by the Ulema.

In theory, any Saudi citizens can take their grievance to the Majlis, and meet face-to-face with the king or other members of the Royal Family. In practice, the Majlis system is impractical in a nation with one king and 20 million citizens. Even though the king typically passes over matters to be settled to aides, in the time available, only a fraction of the issues that constituents wish to present are heard.

One of the agenda items of the Majlis committee, but yet to be implemented, is the establishment in Saudi Arabia of a bill of rights. Saudi Arabia remains a country where full and frank discussions with the authorities are not encouraged. The Board of Grievances (Diwan al-Mazalim) established under the Chief Judge, has the judicial power to investigate and resolve complaints between the people and the government. What hazards such a procedure might present to individuals is not known but it is widely believed that complainants assume a certain level of risk of being punished as dissidents.

There are 13 administrative centres in the kingdom each with a governor appointed by the King. All provincial governors so far appointed have been princes from the Royal Family. In addition, large cities appoint their own municipal governments. Local affairs in smaller settlements are governed by a council of elders.

The year 2005 saw a cautious experiment with democracy in Saudi Arabia. In Riyadh, representatives for half the seats on the town council were elected to office, with the other half appointed by the Royal Family. Despite recent enthusiasm in the West for introducing democracy into the Middle East, attitudes to democracy in Saudi Arabia are similar elsewhere in the Arab world. Only men were entitled to vote in the Riyadh council elections. Voter enthusiasm was muted. Only 30 per cent of the eligible voters bothered to register. Only about 150,000 votes were cast out of an eligible enrolment of over a million. On the other hand, the 700 candidates competing for seven council seats in Riyadh joined in the spirit of the occasion and campaigned vigorously. Campaign techniques ranged from traditional-style hospitality dispensed from Bedouin tents to websites and campaign promises transmitted as text messages to cellphones. While Saudi Arabia hasn't pretended yet to be a democracy, it has at least placed a tentative foot on the ladder of democratic rule. Whether this timid tilt at democracy will satisfy the sometimes disgruntled ideologically driven sections of the population remains to be seen.

WHO ARE THE SAUDIS?

CHAPTER 3

'I do not feel obliged to believe that the same
God who has endowed us with sense, reason,
and intellect has intended us to forgo their use.'
—Galileo Galilei

SEVENTY YEARS AGO, one might have imagined Saudi Arabia as a country of impoverished Bedouins enduring a life of extraordinary hardship in one of the most forbidding countries in the world. In a few short years after that, oil revenues created the more prevalent public image of the Saudi as a playboy jet-setting around the gambling joints of Europe, then returning home to his austere land to relax in his air-conditioned palace. Both stereotypes still exist. Small numbers of incredibly rich Saudis still travel the world spending money like water. Half a million or so Bedouins still roam the deserts. But between these two stereotypes lie the bulk of the people, the middle class, most of whom live urbanised lives.

THE POPULATION EXPLOSION

Saudi Arabia is widely regarded as a wealthy country. This is a misconception based on the well-publicised antics of the very rich. In fact, before the oil price spiked in 2003—in terms of GDP per capita—Saudi Arabia was well on its way to becoming a poor country. According to World Bank statistics, in the year 2001, Saudi Arabia lay in 62nd place in a list of wealthiest countries of the world, between Slovkia and the Seychelles. Through the 1980s and 1990s, the country had been caught in a debt trap, with export receipts falling and population rising. Since then, things have improved as rising oil prices eased the country's financial problems.

In terms of the sustainable carrying capacity of the country, Saudi Arabia is greatly overpopulated. Saudi Arabia's population tripled between 1980 to 2004. Its rate of population increase of about 4 per cent per year is one of the highest for any nation in the world. Saudi society's attitudes to family planning flow from cultural factors, not the least of which the cleric's interpretation of the Qur'an. Like Christianity, Islamic teachings on family planning—go forth and multiply!—were developed to suit the times. In the 7th century, large families were needed to replace people claimed by high infant mortality and to provide a steady supply of soldiers to be killed in battle. Over the years, the need for people diminished but the dogma stayed the same; hence the present population problem. The average size of the Saudi family, according to 2001 statistics, was 6.4 children with half the population under the age of 15. Millions of young Saudis will enter the job market in the next decade, to face one of the modern country's most insidious problems—unemployment of Saudi youth.

It is worth noting that birth control in neighbouring Iran, also as an Islamic country which also bases its legal system on the Qur'an, has got its net birth rate down to almost zero. In Iran, family planning advice, condoms, pills and sterilisation are supplied on request by the state. By contrast birth control is illegal in Saudi Arabia.

FAMILY VALUES

The family is the most important social group in Saudi Arabia. Saudi families are large with the oldest male being considered the head. Families tend to be more self-contained than Western families and more intergenerational. Three or four generations may live under one roof. The elderly are looked after by the younger generations and afforded respect. Saudi children tend to be indulged with not too much discipline within the home. Foreign labour is cheap in Saudi Arabia. Even not very wealthy families may have an Indonesian or a Filipina housemaid. In richer families, children may have their own allocated servants.

From a Saudi point of view, the ideal home is a self-contained villa away from the peering eyes of neighbours. Saudi houses are typically surrounded by high walls. Within the walled area, houses of extended families may be connected to each other in what resembles a walled estate. Not only do the walls keep out sandstorms prevalent in most areas of the country, in a figurative sense at least, they also protect the family inside from contact with the outside world. As a result, family members have closer relations with each other and probably less with outsiders than in other cultures. Family members get intimately involved in each other's affairs. Children are encouraged to stay in the home, and may well not leave it when they reach adulthood. Intergenerational Saudi families have a plentiful supply of babysitters, and generally a lesser need for them since so much social activity is conducted within the family and within the home.

Social rules between males and females are immensely complicated in Saudi Arabia by restrictions and rules flowing from religious beliefs. Social life, in particular for women, revolves around the extended family and close friends. Saudi women spend a lot of their waking hours inside

Chatting Over Coffee

In a *National Geographic* article, 'Women in Arabia', Marrianne Alireza noted: 'For city women like us the only activity besides living communally within the extended family was leaving our quarters to visit other women in their quarters.'

the home chatting with other women in what in the West might be termed 'coffee groups'. Some Saudi men even go so far as to lock their womenfolk inside the house from dawn to dusk

A male visiting a Saudi household is unlikely to meet a female resident of the house. Dining arrangements are similarly complicated. Women and girls eat separately from boys and men. One of the authors once received a lunch invitation to a Bedouin encampment—along with 20 or so other Westerners, both male and female. Arriving at the camp, men and women were separated and directed into different areas of a large tent that had been partitioned across its centre. Men dined on one side of the partition and women on the other.

A whole roasted sheep was the main item on the menu. The sheep was brought into the male dining area on an enormous plate and surrounded by rice. The plate was borne by the small boys of the tribe and placed on the floor of the tent. Squatting on rugs around the roasted sheep, the male diners used their hands to tear off whatever meat they wanted to eat. When the men had their fill, the boys returned and carried the plate to the women in the compartment next door. After the women had cleaned up the left-overs, the dogs were given the remains. The order of feeding reflected the pecking order of the tribe—men, women and dogs.

Saudi Children

In a land where religious instruction is the core curriculum, the grip of Islam on the young mind is every bit as strong as its hold on the older generation. With a heavy emphasis on religion in their education, Saudi youths generally respect their elders, undertake their religious duties, maintain strong family ties and do not openly engage in premarital sex. By the standards of the West, the majority of Saudi youth is unrebellious. Children tend to find their amusements inside the home rather than 'hanging out'. Though one place teenage Saudi boys like to gather with their friends is at the arcades in shopping malls, where behaviour codes are fairly relaxed.

Not Very Rebellious Youth

When the Saudi Arabian soccer team won the AGCC cup in January 2002, young Saudi men drove up and down Olaya Street in Riyadh with music blaring from their car stereos until the police appeared on the scene whereupon the youngsters sped off. This display of exuberant youth, that would have passed unnoticed in the West, was considered noteworthy enough in Saudi Arabia to have been reported as an important story in next day's newspapers.

On the other hand, religious fervour can inspire young Saudis to commit desperate acts. Dozens of disaffected Saudi youths have sacrificed themselves for causes that seem incomprehensible to most Westerners. Fifteen out of the nineteen 9-11 highjackers were young Saudis. According to *The Economist*, 'Hundreds of young Saudis are thought to have joined the *jihadists* in Iraq.'

NAMES AND LABELS

Though Saudis have a strong sense of family, they may not have a family name. In naming their children, Saudis string together a long series of first names, using the word *bin* to mean 'son of' (or *bint* meaning 'daughter of'), followed by their father's name. Depending on how many generations they care to go back in the family history, this can lead to some exceedingly long names. For example, one of the powerful princes in the Saudi dynasty is Faysal bin Turki bin Abdallah bin Mohhamad bin Saud—a name that extends as far back as the great-great-grandfather. Including the Saud name even as far back as five generations means the holder can claim to be Royalty and thereby enjoy some privileges. Given the reference to Royalty in the fifth link of the chain, the name is unlikely to be shortened by future generations.

An alternative to a naming convention that flows backwards in time is one that flows forwards. Saudis might like to be referred to as the father of their son's name. A Saudi man using this style of naming might be known as Abu Dhabi meaning the 'father of Dhabi'. For mothers, the equivalent nomenclature is Umm Said meaning 'mother of Said'.

INTERACTION BETWEEN THE SEXES

While the law allows a man to have up to four wives, the Qur'an states that rights to this privilege come with a condition that the man must look after his family members both properly and equally. In the modern world, this is a considerable restraint. As in the West, the average Saudi faces the same daily economic struggle that grinds down the rest of the world. Like kids from other cultures, the younger generation of Saudis demand their parents' full participation in the consumer economy. They need education, the latest in computers, music and whatever else is 'in'. In a country where women cannot work, most families have a single breadwinner. The customary complaint from polygamous husbands is the cost and time of attending to the needs of their multiple families. Four families expand the financial burden on the breadwinner by a factor of four.

Other than for the wealthy, multiple families are no longer commonplace. The major exception is the Royal Family which practices polygamy to excess. While the Saudi laws on marriage and divorce stipulates a man can have only four wives, there is a loophole. The law stipulates a man is restricted to four families *at any one time*. Over a lifetime, there is no limit to the number of wives a man may have. Taking advantage of this oversight by the Prophet, over the course of their lives, Saudi princes have taken an extraordinary number of wives. Following the example of their father, Ibn Saud, princes and kings of Saudi Arabia have spent much of their spare time marrying and divorcing women at will, and producing an immense number of royal children in the process. Marriage on this scale is expensive, but since the Royal Family is in personal charge of the country's treasury, money had proved no object in this pursuit of regal fecundity. The Royals can afford as many children as they like from as many wives they feel like taking. An extended Saudi Royal Family numbering thousands has been the consequence.

Although individuals are theoretically entitled to select their own marriage partners, most marriages are arranged between the respective families. Saudis don't marry their siblings, but marriage to a first cousin is considered desirable. Expatriates working in Saudi Arabia in the medical profession have reported frequent cases where intermarrying within extended families has lead to a deterioration in health of progeny through inbreeding.

Low Divorce Rates

The ease with which Arab men can divorce their wives has received wide publicity in the West. Much quoted are the divorce laws where all a man has to do is tell his wife 'I divorce you' three times and it's all over. This is not quite the way things are meant to work out in theory. The Qur'an allows divorce, but decrees that partners to a marriage are not divorced for frivolous reasons. Also, in theory at least, under Shariah Law, women can themselves initiate divorce proceedings. But in the real world, instances of women divorcing their husbands are rare. Despite the liberal divorce laws, outside the Royal Family where it is endemic, divorce isn't commonplace in Saudi Arabia. In fact, statistics show that divorce is less common in Saudi Arabia than in most Western countries.

As in many societies, attitudes to virtue are quite different for men and women. Saudis put a monetary value on the intact bridal state. Virginity amongst unmarried women is highly prized, some would say essential. Top bride prices are paid for virgins. Divorcees and widows attract smaller amounts. Unmarried non-virginity is in limited demand and can sometimes be life-threatening. By contrast, virginity amongst unmarried men isn't a consideration.

Attitudes of men to women are closely related to questions of honour and shame. To the great disadvantage of Saudi women, Saudi men see themselves as the fearless upholders of the female virtue. At issue here is the Arab question of honour, and its opposite number—shame. The concept of shame in Saudi Arabia differs from the equivalent idea in the West. In Saudi Arabia, shame describes the state of mind in a man whose 'honour' is besmirched not by his own behaviour but by the indiscretion (alleged or otherwise) of a close relative. A typical 'crime' committed by a woman bringing shame on the menfolk of her family is consorting with a man outside the family group.

Men who think nothing of taking concubines and wives a third of their age impose extraordinary punishment on women whose 'honour' has been 'besmirched' by men just like themselves. Women can have 'justice' exacted by male family members with little interference from the justice system. Killings of alleged female adulterers are rarely reported. Particularly in rural areas beyond the reach of the authorities, punishment for adultery becomes a private matter of family honour. The counterpart male adulterer is much more likely to get off than the female.

Associated with adultery is the thorny issue of rape. Rape victims are similarly shunned for the 'dishonour' that their unwilling participation in a crime brings to their families through their diminished status and compromised marital prospects. Though the kingdom provides the death penalty for rapists, to make her case, a raped woman has to present in court four upright Muslim men as witnesses to the crime. If she is unable to produce four honest voyeurs who happened to be in attendance when the crime was committed, she may be charged with slander and receive punishment additional to that which has already been received at the hands of the rapist. Since the level of proof is so onerous, rape cases brought by plaintiffs are exceedingly rare in Saudi Arabia.

In general, victims of crime are considered at fault to a much greater degree than in other cultures. In Saudi Arabia, perfectly innocent victims are held accountable for crimes they had no part in perpetrating. For example, blame is apportioned to innocent victims of road accidents on the grounds that if they hadn't been at the scene of the accident, nothing would have happened.

The status of women in Saudi society has earned widespread condemnation elsewhere in the world. The double standard so objectionable to women liberationists world-wide is alive and well in Saudi Arabia. Under strict interpretation of Shariah Law, a woman is meant to have the same legal rights as men. But in reality, women have difficulty obtaining their rights under a legal system run entirely by male clerics.

As the world moves into the 21st century, are there any signs of change of these 7th century attitudes? Possibly some. In recent times, young men and women have used modern technology in ingenious ways to circumvent Saudi Arabia's restriction on sexes. Pickup trucks of teenage boys and young men cruise the streets, pulling up beside chauffeur-driven cars full of girls covered from head to toe in *abayas*, their faces obscured by veils. Windows are wound down. Scraps of papers with cellphone numbers of the hopeful romantics are interchanged through the open windows. The cars drive off. The phones get busy. Text messages are sent and received. Contact has been made. The two parties speak to each other on their phones. But the next step, an actual meeting, is more hazardous.

SAUDI WOMEN

In most situations, Saudi women adopt a minimalist profile. Some people familiar with the workings of Saudi families claim that women may wield more influence than appears apparent from a Westerner's viewpoint. Strong-minded women may, for example, influence the behaviour of their

Saudi women in black *abayas* out on the street.

menfolk by determining the careers of their sons. But mostly, the role of women is subsidiary.

Women's behaviour is highly restricted, particularly outside the home. The street is the domain of men. Women in the street are usually on a mission—usually a shopping expedition. Otherwise, they are encouraged to stay indoors and avoid casual contact with strangers. Outside the house, women are not permitted to walk around alone. They must either be accompanied by other women or by a suitable male member of their family. Operating in pairs and threesomes and covered in *abayas*, women tread lightly through the outside world, flitting like wraiths amongst the shadows of the background.

The popular Western view that Muslim women hold diminished rights is quite at odds with official Muslim PR on this subject. The Muslim website, thetruereligion.org (http://thetruereligion.org), carries an article entitled 'Women's Liberation Through Islam' in which is described the Muslim take on gender equality in Saudi Arabia. According to this account, women are meant to enjoy equal status with men, the right to choose their own religion, the right to choose their own husband, and the right to vote. In the real world of Saudi Arabian street-life, these claims ring hollow. According to most other accounts, the reality for Saudi women is far more restricted. Most women marry partners selected by their families. The Muslim religion is compulsory. Women have no say in the affairs of state. In Saudi Arabia, few rights to vote exist for men, and none at all for women.

The stultifying boredom of women's earthly role in Saudi society was described in the biography *Princess* by Jean P Sassoon, a book claiming to describe the true-life story of a member of the House of Saud who told her tale under the pseudonym 'Princess Sultana'. The book describes how royal women lived in a closed society where they had absolutely nothing to do from one day to the next. A retinue of domestic help looked after the chores and the high-born women were not permitted to engage in any form of outside work, even voluntary work.

Princess Sultana and her female companions were encouraged to remain in their palaces. The law in Saudi Arabia applying to women, whether local or alien and of any rank, holds that to travel beyond their doorstep in Saudi Arabia, a woman needs the permission of a male guardian—called a *mahram*—generally the father or husband. Princess Sultana and her contemporaries felt like captives inside their opulent palaces—golden birds in gilded cages—from which they were rarely released by husbands they hardly knew. Husbands, by contrast, were out and about, doing business with each other and casually marrying and divorcing other women whose existence the principal wife might only suspect. Princes who married 50–100 wives in a lifetime are not uncommon in the House of Saud. Of all the kings who have so far sat on the Saudi throne, only King Faisal, had less than ten wives.

According to Sassoon's account, some cast-off wives turned to tranquillizers and drugs to alleviate their boredom. Others got into more serious trouble. Princess Sultana recounts how a group of such women arranged trysts with foreign men in one of the many houses owned by their husbands. They were caught. Charged with besmirching the honour of the family, one of the unfaithful wives was weighed down with chains and drowned in the family swimming pool after a 'trial' conducted by the male members of her family. Another was put into lifetime solitary confinement in a darkened room within a family house where, in short time, she went crazy and committed suicide.

Some Saudis have disputed the account of Princess Sultana. Defenders of the Saudi Arabian way of life, claim that 'Princess' is sensationalism, written by a woman's rights author for Western consumption with the express purpose of making money. There is no question that the book has made money. In fact, a sequel made even more money; then, for good measure, a third book was published.

As usual in this enigmatic country, the truth is hard to determine and the right balance is hard to strike. For those who want to hear the opposite viewpoint—that all is, in fact, well between womanhood and Saudi culture—an alternative is the book *At the Drop of a Veil* by Marianne Alireza. The book is a personalised description of an American women living in Saudi Arabia and married to a Saudi man—an arrangement that, according to the author, was generally satisfactory.

The most widely reported execution of a high ranking female for a sexual transgression was in 1978 when Princess Mishaal, grand niece of the then reigning monarch King Khaled, was put to death. Princess Mishaal, who had by the age of 17 already undergone an arranged marriage and had then been casually divorced, had fallen in love with a young man who requested her hand in marriage. But the House of Saud withheld its permission for this union. Princess Mishaal defied her family. She met her suitor, Khalid Mullalal in a Jeddah Hotel; but she was recognised and caught. Both were tried and privately executed in a car park in Jeddah. She was shot and he was beheaded. This was an 'honour killing' to avenge a perceived slight that had been perpetrated on the Royal Family. There was no trial, but there did happen to be a TV camera on location. The story made news in the BBC documentary *Death of a Princess* that the House of Saud subsequently spent about US$ 500 million unsuccessfully trying to suppress.

WOMEN AND RELIGION

The Muslim religion has had a tough time defining the precise status of women either on earth or in heaven. Women are expected to embrace the Muslim faith, but the Saudi clergy has not quite decided whether or not women should be admitted to mosques, or whether they should be restricted to pray at home. After 1,400 years of debate, this issue seems to be decided on an ad hoc basis. In some mosques, women are allowed to pray with men in a common area in which the two sexes are obliged to make minimum contact. In other mosques, women are allocated to a secondary area. For some other mosques, female participation is excluded completely. If they are allowed inside mosques at all, women are cautioned that wearing perfume is prohibited for fear that an alluring scent might distract men from their devotions.

Women and the Afterlife

Islam has been unable to resolve the role of women during their earthly existence. Defining the role of women in the afterlife has been just as difficult. Like Christianity, the reward in Islam for leading a good life on Earth is a place in heaven. Like Christianity, Islam believes heaven is its exclusive province. The details provided by the official Muslim website are sketchy on the question of what goes on in the Muslim afterlife, but a commonly quoted take on the Islam version of paradise for a man is a place of cool breezes, running water, and the companionship of a plentiful supply of beautiful females (72 virgins per man being a popular estimate for this service); in short, most of the things that are missing from life on earth for the average male in the deserts of Saudi Arabia. Over the ages, this vista of indolence and pleasure has been enough to tempt battalions of desert fighters to sacrifice themselves for some earthly cause in order to gain the keys to such a paradise while they are still young enough to enjoy it. Of course what attractions paradise might offer the female of the species—an eternity to service the bodily needs of designated men—is not really covered in this picture of the future.

ACQUIRING AN IDENTITY

The article 'Women's Liberation Through Islam' also claims that the Qur'an affords the right of women to conduct business and own property. Maybe so. The idea has tradition. The Prophet's first wife was a wealthy woman who ran a prosperous trading company. But this right has also not been well recognised by the Wahhabi version of Islam. Saudi women have had a tough time obtaining their rights in a legal system that imposes additional burdens on the fairer sex.

For most of its history, despite what the Qur'an has to say on the subject, Saudi Arabia has regarded a woman merely as an appendage of her family. In the physical world, Saudi women move through their community as anonymous black-clad objects who are indistinguishable one from another. The Saudi legal system treats women the same way. Women who raise legal issues in Saudi courts of law are such low profile creatures that their identity as unique individuals is typically at issue. In Saudi Arabia, establishing the identity of female claimants is an important part of the judicial process. Normal aids like passports, driver's licences and ID cards are not available to Saudi women. Since the *abaya* is such a ubiquitous coverall, photographs of Saudi women are rarely taken. Proving they actually are the people they claim to be proves a real burden to female claimants trying to obtain their rights through the court system. Is the person in the court the same person to whom the contested rights should have flowed?

Lacking an easy proof of identity, a woman trying to obtain legal rights, must produce two male relations to confirm who she is. Saudi women have had difficulty in Saudi courts fighting false claims to their property and obtaining their rights to inheritance. Imposters and false documentation have been used to swindle women who have fallen out of favour with their families. Should the man deny that the woman in the court is his mother or his sister, the man's word will normally be taken.

Some signs have emerged that Saudi women, hitherto their society's invisible people, are acquiring greater rights to their own identities. The main advance is in gaining restricted entitlement to the identity card itself. Saudi men are issued identity cards that are meant to be carried in public at all times. Hitherto, women have been named as dependants on their guardians' identity cards, meaning that, strictly speaking, women are not allowed in public without their guardian male on whose card they are included.

In 2001, a few chosen women were allowed their own identity card including their own photograph—unveiled but with the head covered and without make up. There are heavy restrictions on the practice. To qualify for an identity card, a woman must be a minimum of 22 years of age, must have written consent of her guardian, must be employed and must have a letter from her employer confirming her status as a payrolled employee. This is a highly restricted list of criteria, but at least it was a start towards greater equality for women. In 2002, about 3,000 of such identity cards were issued. Women who succeeded in getting identity cards also earned rights outside the court system. For the first time, card-carrying women could do manly things like open bank accounts without having to first rely on male relatives to confirm their identities.

Old Habits Die Hard

Commenting on the social advance of issuing ID cards to women on a restricted basis, the Minister of the Interior Prince Nayef bin Abdul-Aziz felt it necessary to state that the practice of recognising women as human beings with their own separate identity was no relaxation of Islamic rules but merely a pragmatic measure to fight fraud and forgery. Said the Prince, "The issuing of identity cards to women was dictated by the requirements of modern life."

Given this sentiment from on high, the intrinsic right of a woman to her own identity was not really conceded by the ruling elite. In granting this limited concession, old habits died hard. To make the point that a woman's right to a separate identity had been recognised with reluctance and only to convenience the commercial world, women's identity cards were issued to their guardians instead of to the card holders directly.

While a woman's right to an identity in Saudi Arabia is being conceded at glacial speed, in other areas too, are women in Saudi Arabia very gradually being afforded concessions. A handful of women in the country now own their own businesses, mostly dealing in specialist female products. Like the issue of ID cards, some degree of male influence over even that small incursion into male dominance has been maintained. Although women are allowed go into business in a few restricted areas, the enabling legislation stipulates that a man must look after most of the documentation.

Modern Saudi women with experience in the West sometimes express their frustration at the niggling rules of the male-dominated society. While in Saudi Arabia on business, one of the authors was invited to a dinner party where he met a single Saudi woman who had returned to Riyadh with a masters degree in psychology from Stanford University. During the meal, the conversation turned to the status of women in contemporary Saudi Arabia. After spending five years studying in the USA, how did an educated Saudi Arabian woman resolve the dichotomy of the two opposing cultures? In answer to the question of what restrictions really irked her about her return to Saudi Arabia she said, "I don't really mind having my husband chosen for me by my father. What I really resent is not being able to drive a car."

Though the Qur'an claims that men and women are equal in the eyes of God, there is still a long way to go in Saudi Arabia before the claim can be made that men and women are equal in the eyes of man.

QUR'AN AND THE LAW

The judicial system in Saudi Arabia is Shariah Law which combines the body of laws found in the Qur'an with the Sunnah—the collection of practices of the Prophet Muhammad—and the Hadith—the traditions and legends surrounding the Prophet. Like the Christian states of centuries past in Europe, religious beliefs and common law in Saudi Arabia are inextricably mixed. Saudi Arabia has adopted the Qur'an as its constitution. The Qur'an is not merely a religious text, it is also a lawbook.

Islam conducts far fewer debates than Christianity on how the rules written in its Holy Book should be interpreted. The Qur'an is far more straightforward and less ambiguous than the Bible. It is also much shorter. The English translation of the Qur'an runs to about 75,000 words—about the length of this book.

Unlike the Bible—which was periodically transcribed, written in three languages by many different authors in many different time periods—the Qur'an was written at one time, in one language recording the experiences of a single individual. While the Bible has been retranslated frequently, not one word of the Qur'an's 114 Chapters, known as Suras, has been changed since they were first written.

According to its adherents, Shariah Law was intended to be merciful. Compared to other systems of justice that prevailed at the time the Holy Book was written, it probably was. Elsewhere in the world in the 7th century AD, rough justice was widespread. In the throes of the Dark Ages, Europe, for example, was a lawless place. Such laws as existed were administered erratically by medieval courts at the whim of the Lord of the Manor.

The major problem with Shariah Law compared to the world's more modern legal systems is that it contains no provision for self-improvement. No doctrine of precedent exists. No body of case law can accumulate. No body of rulings accumulates to guide the next judge who hears a similar case. Each judge who hears a case decides the outcome based on his view of the Qur'an and that alone.

Judges rule the courts. No jury system exists in Saudi Arabia, though the hierarchy of appeal courts is similar to the West. Judges in the administration of Shariah Law are heavily provincial. The Judiciary is a kind of old boys club. More than three quarters of the 700-member Judiciary come from a region in the centre of the kingdom known as the Qasim, the home territory of Wahhabism. Nearly all the senior judges are from the Qasim region.

Decisions of the judges are known as *fatwas*. Their principal objective is to preserve Islamic purity. Shariah judges may issue *fatwas* on anyone, whether inside or outside their jurisdiction, and whether brought to trial or not. The most publicised *fatwa* of recent times has probably been that of author Salman Rushdie—a sentence of death, so far not carried out, which was imposed by the *mullahs* of Iran on Rushdie for his book *The Satanic Verses*, which was seen to parody Muslim beliefs.

The Qur'an is a key factor in a strange duality between the country's administration and its religious orders. Religion and civil administration overlap and merge imperceptibly. Saudi clerics paid by the government perform a simultaneous political and religious function. They are public servants, answerable to the rules of public service as well as to the Ulema. Clerics and government officials are mutually answerable to each other, and this is a source of tension for both parties. If clerics get out of step with the rulers, they may find that they are out of a job. If administrators and government officials stray too far from religious beliefs, they may find they have a palace revolt on their hands.

Religion permeates all Saudi institutions. Saudi Arabia not only has a civil police force, it has a parallel religious police force—the Mutawa'een—a shadowy organisation in charge of purifying thought and action in the community. The Mutawa'een is God's police force. Its full name is the 'Committee for the Preservation of Virtue and for the Prevention of Vice'. The Mutawa'een performs a similar role in modern-day Saudi Arabia to the Inquisitors of Christianity's most nefarious period. It seeks to impose its view of life on the population. It ferrets out the morally and religiously suspect, extracts confessions and brings the malefactors to court.

The civil and religious police forces answer to quite different organisations. Though the Mutawa'een are meant to be accompanied by the civil police when discharging its duties in the community, often this does not happen. The Mutawa'een can come and go as it pleases, entering private property without search warrants and detaining whoever it thinks fit. It patrols the streets, enters homes to ensure that people dress modestly and that the laws of Islam are practised, and checks that shops close their doors during prayer time. During Ramadan, the Mutawa'een is particularly active, entering businesses to ensure that employees are not eating, drinking or smoking cigarettes during daylight hours.

The Mutawa'een is strict and all-powerful. An extraordinary and widely reported event in Mecca in March 2002 illustrated the clergy's iron grip over common sense and humanity. A fire had broken out at a girl's school. Trying to escape the fire, the girls fled down a stairwell of the burning building to find the ground floor exit of the fire escape locked. Firemen managed to break down the door in time to let the girls out, but at that stage the Mutawa'een had arrived on the scene. The girls, the clerics determined, were unveiled and not wearing headscarves. The Mutawa'een cautioned firemen attending the scene that their morals would be compromised if the improperly-clad girls were released. Trapped in the stairwell of the burning building, on the wrong side of a door that the Mutawa'een refused to open, the doomed girls burned to death. Fifteen girls were killed and 52 others injured. The Saudis tried to censor the incident, but word leaked out to the wider world, alternatively bemused and incensed by the depth of the cultural divide.

SWAPPING CULTURES

A common Western view of Saudi Arabia is of people who are jealous of the West. According to this stereotype, Saudis strive to be more like the West, and would like to escape to the West and live a Western life. Many people who have lived in Saudi Arabia have recounted the following story, or one like it.

A Westerner is sitting in a plane, heading out of King Fahd International Airport in Damman or one of the other Saudi international airports. Next stop is London or perhaps New York. Seated nearby is a Saudi woman dressed in an *abaya*. She is encased from head to toe in a shimmering black sheath. Not far into the journey, the lady gets up from her seat, makes her way down the aisle and disappears into the aircraft toilet—never to be seen again. A little while later, a completely different individual emerges. She is elaborately made up, wears a dress with a revealing neckline, short skirt, nylon stockings and high heel shoes. She is clutching a Louis Vuitton bag out of which pokes the merest hint of black material. This stylish lady wiggles her way down the aisle, slides into the seat that was previously occupied by the Saudi Arabian woman. She shoves her bag under the seat and orders a cocktail.

A version of the story also exists for males of the species, who disappear into aircraft toilets dressed in traditional Arab clothes and emerge clad in smart business suits.

There are various theories why these mysterious and possibly mythical creatures are inclined to enter small enclosed spaces to change into the outfits of alternate tribal identities in the tradition of superwoman and superman. One view, favoured by some in the West, is that Saudis are uncomfortable with their own identity. Proponents of this view hold that Saudis share a desire with many other countries in Asia, to adopt the ubiquitous Western cultural identity.

The real reasons that Saudis slip easily between one culture and another may be far more pragmatic. For example, at least in the female version of the story, Saudis may wish to change their clothes merely because wearing an *abaya* is plain uncomfortable. Another explanation is the fear of mistreatment on arrival in the West, or the East. Since the 9-11 event in 2001, and the subsequent enduring terrorist scares, it may now be awkward, or even dangerous, to get around the streets of New York and other Western cities, dressed in a *thobe* and *gutra*—the apparel of a terrorist in a prevailing Western view.

Geographically, Saudi Arabia sits at the boundary of the West and the East. Culturally, its position is much the same. Arabs have fraternised with people from neighbouring countries for a long time and adopted many foreign ways. Many Arabs have already forsaken their traditional clothes in their domestic day-to-day lives. In places like Lebanon and Egypt, Western clothes are common. By contrast, most Saudis wear their traditional clothes inside their own country. Outside the country, as they see fit, some adopt the identity of the destination country while others stick with their own national dress.

SAUDI ARABIA'S BEDOUINS

Like other Bedouins, only two generations back, even the Al Saud Royal Family walked or caught a camel when they wanted to travel. Though the present generation of Saudi princes now live in palaces, members of the House of Saud have not strayed all that far from their Bedouin roots. King Abdullah, born in 1923, might just be old enough to remember a life of tents, camels and austere pleasures from the early days of his own life.

Since the House of Saud has been running the country, the policy of mutual support between Bedouins and the Royal family has worked well for both parties. The Ministry includes a specific office—the Minister of Bedouin Affairs—to represent Bedouin interests. For their part, the Bedouins have provided the bulk of the judiciary, most of the religious leaders and much of the Praetorian Guard that protects the King and his entourage from various potentially subversive forces (including elements of the Saudi military).

Despite the homogenising influence of globalism, much of Bedouin culture has survived intact, particularly in Saudi Arabia's more remote regions. Even in the 21st century, a significant nomadic population follows a close replica of the traditional Bedouin way of life. Modern-day Bedouins still pitch and strike tents, move their flocks about the countryside and generally behave in a Bedouin-like manner. On the fringes of the Empty Quarter—the desolate, waterless plains in the south of the Arabian Peninsula—the tribes of the Rub Al Khali (the Rashih, Saar, Manahil, Manhrah, Awamit, Bani Yas and Dawasir) still operate their traditional complex cultural mix of honour-based tribal lives of conflicts, raids and fragile alliances.

Land Compensation Claims, Bedouin-style

Bedouins have long lived by trading. Since they were traditionally on the move, Bedouins failed to develop a culture of property ownership common in societies which adopted permanent agriculture. However, when western influence arrived, some Bedouins cottoned onto the idea of land rights quickly enough and cashed in. Bedouin tribes, according to popular accounts, followed pipeline projects across the country, making financial demands on oil companies, claiming the companies were intruding on their traditional lands. The more audacious claimants, having learned of an intended pipeline route in advance, would set up an encampment ahead of construction and claim the pipe was infringing some ancient right. Appeals by oil companies to the king would normally be settled on the side of the Bedouins. Money would pass hands and the Bedouins would move their camps to establish their ancient civilisation somewhere else where a construction project was about to start.

According to some estimates, Saudi Arabia still has 600,000 full-time Bedouins and many more part-timers. In modern society, Bedouins may wear their tribal affiliations as a badge of honour. Bedouinism is like citizenship. It carries financial and social advantage. To some extent, modern-day Bedouins can have the best of both worlds. They can enjoy their Bedouinism without quite making the full commitment to the nomadic life style of their ancestors. Courtesy of its oil revenue, the government has created a fall-back position for Bedouins, the *markaz*—small towns of concrete block houses—to accommodate Bedouins wishing to adopt an urban lifestyle and in which they can receive health care and their children can receive education.

The success of the *markaz* programme has been mixed. Some Bedouins still prefer to stay in the desert to tend their camels in the traditional way. Others stay in town, perhaps reluctantly. Only a couple of generations away from life in the desert, urban Saudis with no obvious connection to the nomadic life may retain an affinity with their antecedents. According to one observer, "the first thing a Saudi does on building a house is erect a tent in the garden."

EDUCATION
Primary and Secondary Education
Education in the kingdom is universal and free for Saudis, but not compulsory. Most Saudis attend kindergarten followed by six years of primary school, three years of middle school and three years of high school. In a country where the sexes are kept separate, schools for Saudis are not co-educational. Teaching tends to be by rote learning of facts. Long passages from the Qur'an are memorised. Intellectual curiosity incompatible with religious dogma is discouraged. Aversion to other religious beliefs is instilled at an early age. Saudi children are encouraged to recite sayings such as 'I will purify the Arabian Peninsula of Jews and Christians' (attributed to Omar the second Caliph). The Wahhabi manifesto, the Tawhid, is compulsory study and it cites, amongst its teachings, that 'Allah has said never support the infidels'. The products of this educational system are

Students heading off to their classes at the King Saud University in Riyadh.

steeped in religious dogma that does not, in general, equip them to make their way in the modern world and hold down significant jobs.

Universities

In 2002, there were eight universities in the kingdom. Saudi universities include King Saud University in Riyadh, King Abdul Aziz University in Jeddah, and King Faisal University in Al Dammam. Other tertiary level institutions are the Technical Institute in Riyadh and the King Fahd University of Petroleum and Minerals in Dhahran. Various Western universities have campuses in Saudi Arabia. Segregation of the sexes is a complication in the educational system. Separate classes are provided for each gender.

According to *The Economist*, over the period 1995–1999, Saudi universities graduated 120,000 students but only 10,000 had technical qualifications such as engineering degrees, which is probably the skill the country most sorely needs. Approximately 40–45 per cent of young graduates thought to be unemployed—possibly unemployable—are themselves a significant source of discontent in the kingdom. The majority of the educated Saudi class who do find jobs find their way into the Saudi civil service rather than into their more traditional interests, the business world. The number of civil servants in Saudi Arabia increased tenfold between 1965–1985.

Prejudices in Education

Women, according to Saudi authorities, are entitled to an education. A hadith of the Prophet Muhammad states: 'seeking knowledge is a mandate for every Muslim (male and female)'. While statistics show that the female literacy rate is on the rise, it still lags behind that of its male counterparts. Women's colleges have been set up and more women are getting tertiary level education. But prejudice against Saudi females exists even among the educated, as evidenced by an editorial in the local Arab News. 'Is there any logical justification,' the editorial runs, 'for spending huge amounts of money on women's education when thousands of female graduates face the prospect of either remaining at home or entering a single profession?'

Expat Schools

International schools teaching an international syllabus are available at the major population centres to accommodate the needs of dependants of the expatriate workforce. International schools inside Saudi Arabia are co-educational as they are anywhere else. Further details are contained in the Resource Guide.

WOMEN IN THE WORKFORCE

Saudi Arabia imports an army of guest workers yet keeps half its potential workforce on the sidelines by denying women the right to work. In occupations where contact with women is inevitable, the provision that sexes must be segregated overrules the provision that women cannot work. With

Hanadi Hindi is the first woman pilot in Saudi Arabia.

Veiled Saudi women working in a hospital in Riyadh.

very few exceptions, only in specialist occupations, such as providing medical services that are specifically female, are women allowed to join the workforce.

Working Women and the Qur'an

The more general ruling by the clerics who write the law in Saudi Arabia is based on an interpretation of the Qur'an that seems to twist a man's obligation to look after his womenfolk into a restrictive covenant on a woman's right to work. This ruling that women are denied the right to work comes from the section of the Qur'an which was written to define rights of women to rely on their menfolk for support and sustenance. The clerics claim that the Qur'an states the husband's duty is to maintain his womenfolk and the woman's duty is to look after the house while the husband is away. The English translation of the appropriate section of the Qur'an reads:

'Men are the maintainers of women because Allah has given men more strength than women, and because men support women from their means. Therefore the righteous women are devoutly obedient and guard in the husband's absence what Allah would have them guard.'

— Qur'an, Surah 4:34

King Abdullah, when he was crown prince, hinted that restrictions on the employment of women might be relaxed. In all likelihood, further occupations will be opened to the participation of women in the future. Tentative steps have already been taken in the civil service where separate branches have been created that employ only women. This measure ensures that segregation between the sexes is maintained in the workplace—which can lead to interesting working conditions. For example, the Chief of Econometrics within the Ministry of Planning has a staff of 20 female statisticians. Modern technology comes to the rescue to preserve the rule that men and women cannot work in the same space. While the cleric's interpretation of the Qur'an prohibits face-to-face communication between men and women, nothing in the Qur'an bans video conferencing. Statisticians of opposite genders working in the same office talk to each other via closed circuit TV or through the intra-office Internet.

Saudi Arabia's rules restricting the activities of women contrast with most of its neighbouring Islamic Arab countries. Bahrain, UAE and Jordan all provide their women equal educational opportunities, and permit them to work and drive. In Bahrain, women even work as limousine drivers.

What a difference a border makes!

GETTING TO KNOW THE SAUDIS

CHAPTER 4

'A terrorist is someone who has a bomb
but doesn't have an air force.'
—William Blum, in his book *Rogue State*

THE CULTURAL DIVIDE

Rudyard Kipling, the great 19th century Anglo-Indian author once remarked 'west is west and east is east, and never the twain shall meet'. As many writers have observed, in no region of the world do Western and Eastern cultures clash so abruptly as in the great cultural melting pot of the Middle East.

On the surface, the culture of Western consumerism seems alive and well in Saudi Arabia as in most places. People strive to build enormous houses for themselves and their extended families. Young Saudi men drive souped-up cars, patronise fast food outlets and wear designer jeans. Shopping malls offer a global selection of merchandise and trade long into the night.

But at a deeper level, Saudi Arabia and the West are poles apart, divided by the fundamental source of Saudi Arabian inspiration and aspiration—Islam—the world's most dominant religious force. As a visitor, Islam is, to a degree, thrust upon you. Whatever you are doing in the kingdom, religion will affect some aspect of your day. Islamic beliefs underlie just about everything that happens in this country. Even though you may not be a member of the faith, its dictates will influence some aspects of your existence.

As a guest worker, how closely you align yourself with the culture of the host country is your own choice, though some aspects, such as participation in the Muslim religion, will remain off limits. Many Western expat guest workers, perhaps the majority, don't become deeply involved with the Saudi way of life. They arrive. They work. They get paid. They complete their contracts, then ship out to work somewhere else. Many expats work for years in Saudi Arabia without learning a word of Arabic and without significant contact with their Saudi hosts. Saudis have no problem with this attitude. A master/servant relationship has existed between the host country and its guest workforce for decades. To the Saudis, the guest workforce is paid good money to perform its task in their country. On the other hand, Arab nations have long traditions of hospitality. Saudis may well seek the company and friendship of their visitors. If so, your time in Saudi Arabia may be the richer for it.

THE WORKER BEES

Saudi Arabia's appeal as a country in which to work is only a recent phenomenon. One hundred years ago, Saudi Arabia was among the least visited countries on the planet. Apart from the Turkish conquerors in residence at the time, there was only one strong reason for anyone to visit this featureless piece of desert roamed by some of the world's poorest people. That was the annual pilgrimage to Islam's holy shrine of Mecca during the last month of the Muslim calendar, the month of Dhu al-Hijjah. One of the five pillars of Islam, the *hajj*, stipulated that believers, both local and from foreign lands should participate in this once in a lifetime voyage. Non-Muslims, by contrast, were banned from Mecca on pain of death.

The origins of the present expatriate workforce lay in the oil industry. The first oil industry workers, the geological survey crews, arrived in Saudi Arabia during the 1930s. By the early 1940s, after the first commercial oil wells were brought into production the first permanent expatriate workforce arrived to operate the country's oil industry. Saudis, at the time, were still nomadic people with no tradition of working in organisations, no skills and little education outside interpreting the Qur'an. Very few people were literate.

So far, the Saudis have been unable to kick the habit of importing their workforce. For two generations after its discovery, Saudi Arabia has lived almost solely off its oil revenue, reinvesting some of the proceeds in development projects. To staff their industrialisation programme, once more the Saudis turned to the wider world and the dependency on foreign workers continued unabated. In the 60-odd years after the first oil field came into commercial operation and the country started modernising, the guest workforce is still at work in Saudi Arabia—in greater numbers than ever before. The total population of Saudi Arabia in 2004 was 26.4 million of whom 5.6 million were expatriate workers. Two generations of Saudis have grown up in a country in which every fifth person is a foreigner—or in Saudi Arabian parlance, an *alien*.

The majority of these aliens may from Western eyes, be indistinguishable from the Saudis themselves. The largest single source of guest workers to Saudi Arabia is Yemen. Yemenis account for 10 per cent of the Saudi population, or about half the immigrant workforce. Other Arab people from Lebanon, Palestine and Egypt are also present in the kingdom in significant numbers. Arabic-speaking Muslim expatriates also come from Africa, in particular Somalia, which also provides a significant guest population.

These countries have long been a source of labour in Saudi Arabia. In the 1950s, Saudi Arabia largely filled positions like teachers and doctors from places like Egypt, Lebanon and Syria. From the point of view of a Saudi employer, non-Saudi Arabs had the advantages of speaking Arabic and being Muslims. But over the years, other expatriate groups from many corners of the world, and speaking many languages and practising different religions have also been imported to work in Saudi Arabia. Major source countries for the Saudi expatriate workforce include India, Pakistan, Bangladesh, the Philippines, Thailand, North America and Europe.

Such a large group of aliens from disparate backgrounds might have been expected to strain the social fabric of the guest nation more than it has. As things stand, relations between Saudi Arabia and its guest workers are reasonably harmonious.

Though the foreign workforce has exerted surprisingly little impact on Saudi society, once in a while, guest workers step out of line and suffer the displeasure of the authorities. From the point of view of the guest worker, this is an outcome to be avoided at all costs. In recent times, with the rise of terrorism worldwide, guest workers, in particular Westerners, have become targeted by disaffected religious groups objecting to the presence in the Holy Land of Islam of the immigrant workforce of infidels.

It is probably also worth noting in this context that having a foreign workforce in the country to perform both menial and professional tasks has a history that extends back before the discovery of oil. Saudi Arabia has had a long tradition of slavery. Slaves were taken (euphemistically termed 'harvested') from across North Africa in the days when slavery was considered an altogether normal activity. Slave traders tended to be Arabs; while slaves themselves were sourced from the northern African tribes in the same way the European traders took their slaves and sent them to the New World.

Slavery was only officially abolished in Saudi Arabia in 1961, under duress applied by President John F Kennedy. Modern day slavery in Saudi Arabia might sound worse than it really was. Slavery in Arabia was not quite the brutal racially segregated system of some other parts of the world. Slaves were probably treated about the same as their modern-day replacements, today's guest workers from the less privileged countries like India and the Philippines. Since slavery has existed within their lifetime, a semblance of the slave-owner mentality sometimes lingers on amongst some Saudis.

Unlike the floating population of guest workers, slaves were not returned to their countries of origin at the end of their assignments. They stayed on. Descendants of African tribes have integrated and intermarried with Arab society to gain the same acceptance as citizens. The merging between Arab and African genealogy is imperceptible. Little racial distinction is felt between Saudi Arabia of different ethnicities. As a testament to this history, you are likely to meet Saudi citizens with skin colours from very light to very dark and with features that range from Caucasian to African.

THE PECKING ORDER

The status of guest workers fits an established hierarchy of Saudi social order. Your tier in the pecking order depends on who you are, your country of origin and what you have arrived to do. If you are visiting Saudi Arabia to keep an appointment with the King, you will get the red carpet treatment afforded to VIPs anywhere. If you are a diplomat, you will be granted the normal perks and respect that the service attracts. If you are on a business trip, you have come to a place with long traditions in trading; most likely you will be treated well. As a salaried worker of some importance in a multinational company, you will be treated reasonably. If you have come to work for a Saudi company, your status may be somewhat more ambiguous.

An important factor determining your status is your country of origin. In Saudi Arabia, the hierarchy between guest workers from various countries and in various occupations is well established. At the top of the totem pole of privilege are the Saudis themselves. People from selected nearby Arab countries are next. High-ranking Arab countries in the eyes of Saudis are the oil producers—Bahrain, Kuwait, Oman, Qatar and the UAE. If you are a Westerner, depending on your job, you are likely to be afforded a status somewhere between the premier Arab states and the lesser Arab states. Arab countries not blessed with oil—Jordan, Egypt, Syria, Palestine and Yemen—rank further down the totem pole.

At the time of writing, the status of war-torn Iraq is ambivalent. Shi'ites in the south of Iraq are the natural enemies of the Saudis . The Sunnis, who were in power under Saddam Hussein, would, under more normal circumstances, be the natural allies.

Iran, a bastion of the Shi'ite faith in the Middle East, is also a traditional enemy. Saudis suspect the Iranians for fomenting discontent of their own population of Shi'ites mostly concentrated in the Eastern and adjoining Najarn Provinces, the closest part of Saudi Arabia to Iran. In Saudi Arabia, being a Shi'ite is almost akin to being a dissident.

Next level down are Third Country Nationals (TCNs), also known as Asian and Sub-Continent Nationals. Of this group, office workers—very often Filipino males, sometimes people from the Indian sub-continent—fare the best. These people tend to be professionals in their own country who work in Saudi Arabia in less intellectually demanding occupations at better pay than is available in higher status jobs in their home countries.

The bottom of the totem pole is a pretty crowded area of uneducated people from Third World countries—Pakistan, India, Bangladesh and Thailand—working in poorly-paid labouring assignments and service jobs or assigned to domestic duties in Arab homes in which Filipina maids tend to predominate. Eritrean and Yemeni street sweepers are other typical occupations and nationalities somewhere near the totem pole's bottom rung.

LONG-TERM IMMIGRANTS

An assumption that people tend to make on visiting a foreign country is that people you meet are likely to be locals unless they look like foreigners. Not everyone in the country wearing a *thobe* can be assumed to be a Saudi citizen. In fact, anyone working in a menial job in Saudi Arabia and wearing traditional Arab dress is almost certainly a non-Saudi Arab. At least half the non-Saudi workforce are migrants from surrounding Arab countries who speak Arabic and dress in a similar manner to the members of their host country. Though to the Western eye, Saudis and non-Saudi Arabs may look much the same, there are some traditional differences in the patterns and colours of the *gutra* that may provide a clue to the nationality of the wearer.

Non-Saudi Arabs tend to stay in Saudi Arabia for long periods and make a much larger commitment to their host country than First World expats who arrive on short-term assignments, bank their earnings in an offshore bank, then leave at the end of their contract period for another job somewhere else. Guest workers from nearby Arab countries—from places like Lebanon, Jordan, Palestine and Yemen—build their lives, businesses and families in Saudi

Arabia where opportunities are far greater than their home countries. These people have effectively emigrated to Saudi Arabia. Yemenis, in particularly, run some of the largest businesses in the country. The bin Laden family, owners of the country's largest construction company, originally came from Yemen.

SEPARATE SOCIETIES

In a melting pot society with many different cultures and languages, occasional conflicts are inevitable. Relations between the guest workforce and the Saudis may carry resentments on both sides. Ingoing perceptions are sometimes negative. Some Westerners disparage the Saudis as 'ragheads'—the not too respectful name for the characteristic apparel of Saudis and other Arabs. The Saudis, for their part, may regard their guest workforce as infidels.

With the objective of keeping their employees out of trouble, most large companies hiring expats to work in Saudi Arabia issue a set of guidelines with their employment packages recommending how their employees should interact with the local populations. For their part, to keep a lid on conflict between themselves and the guest workforce, the Saudis have physically separated the local people and the guest workers. On large construction projects, construction workers are typically housed in camps, which are themselves often internally segregated into racial groups. Large construction camps, housing say 2,000 workers, will have separate dormitories for different nationalities. They might have half a dozen mess-halls serving the main ethnic foods of those residing in the camps—for example, a choice of Western, Thai, Indian, Filipino and Middle Eastern food may be offered.

Some visitors like to adopt the culture of the country they are visiting. They like to learn the language, eat the local foods and generally 'go native'. The flowing robes and headgear of Saudi dress which have evolved to suit the climate of the desert might seem the logical apparel to wear in a country where most people are dressing that way. But guest workers are better to restrict the copying of the Saudi dress code to wearing loose-fitting clothes and wide brimmed hats, particularly in summer time. If you, as a Westerner, take to getting around in Arab gear, Saudis may consider that you are mocking their culture. You can certainly buy a *thobe* for yourself at the local shop but if so, it's best worn in the privacy of your house, perhaps in the street, but certainly not to work. While you are in their country, Saudis prefer you to act within the cultural norms of your country. In their eyes, your role is to be you, not them.

Politically Sensitive Dress Code

Expatriate English friends of one of the authors thought their work assignment would be a good opportunity to follow local fashions. They were working for a Saudi company alongside Saudis who sometimes showed up to work in Western dress, but generally wore their traditional thobes and gutras. The two English guest workers went downtown to get fitted up by the local tailor then one day, dressed for work in their newly acquired thobes and gutras. They were sent back home by their Saudi boss to change into their normal Western clothes. They did, but later persisted in violating this cultural norm. Next time they showed up at work attired as Arabs, they had their contracts terminated and were sent home.

EXPATRIATE WOMEN

Women in service occupations such as teaching or specialist female occupations such as female health care may succeed in getting a work visa for Saudi Arabia. Other than that, if you are a woman seeking work, Saudi Arabia may not be the place for you. Spouses of foreigners working in Saudi Arabia who are not themselves working are termed 'trailing spouses'. Trailing spouses are mostly women, though occasionally non-working foreign men live in Saudi Arabia with their working wives.

Occasionally, female dependents of male guest workers in Saudi Arabia may get work on a casual basis. But a certain level of risk, for both the employee and employer, is attached to the practice of working in Saudi Arabia without a work permit.

Removing Women From the Workforce

A multinational company in Saudi Arabia decided to employ some of its bored housewives as office workers. This was an unofficial arrangement and the women did not hold work permits. When the word got out to the wider community, a squad of Mutawa'een was despatched to investigate. As the Mutawa'een stormed through the front door of the office to determine if the laws relating to vice and virtue had been violated, the working women were bundled out the back, never to return to the workplace. The female secretarial staff were then replaced by men, mostly Filipinos.

Subject to the same irksome restrictions as their Saudi counterparts, foreign women living but not working in Saudi Arabia are likely to be prone to attacks of boredom. Saudis impose similar restrictions to foreign women in the kingdom as they do on their own women. The Mutawa'een are aware that foreign women hold liberated views on life by local standards and take steps to restrict such ideas flowing across the cultural divide into the heads of Saudi women.

One of the regulations in Saudi Arabia that most irritates expatriate women is the prohibition on driving. Though women are prohibited from driving in public streets, in some places, rules are bent sufficiently to allow foreign women to drive within compounds but not outside. In other places, rules are more strictly applied both within and without.

Most of the civil laws in Saudi Arabia have been taken from the Qur'an. But it is hard to believe that God's instructions delivered to the Prophet Muhammad by the Archangel Gabriel in the 7th century in some cave near Mecca intended that women in the 21st century should be prohibited from driving a car. But this is the interpretation the clerics have made.

One of the consequences of the restriction on women drivers is a work scheme for chauffeurs. A March 2002 issue of *The Economist* reported there were approximately half a million chauffeurs in the kingdom and payment of their salaries represented 1 per cent of the kingdom's income. A high proportion of these chauffeurs are employed driving women who would drive themselves if they were allowed to get a driver's licence.

Female Locomotion, Saudi Style

A particularly rebellious, bored and ingenious expatriate woman married to a male colleague of one of the authors tested the envelope of the rule book regarding the using of wheels in Saudi Arabia. Denied the use of a car, she bought a bicycle and proceeded to pedal it around her compound. When the Mutawa'een found out, they were not amused. They issued a directive—women on bikes were not allowed by the Qur'an. Unseated but undeterred, this stalwart for women's rights then bought a pair of roller skates and proceeded to skate around the compound. This time around, the Mutawa'een were even less amused. Any form of wheels at all were precluded by the Qur'an, they declared. There was talk of extreme punishment for breaking the laws of the land after getting a first warning. But all that happened was the woman and her skates were separated.

Wives or daughters of guest workers with entitlements to invite their dependents into Saudi Arabia may get frustrated to the point of exasperation by the niggling and seemingly pointless restrictions that the country imposes on its women. But even those inclined to rebel don't face much real danger. The same cannot be said for female guest workers further down the pecking order. Domestic staff from the Third World face a life of isolation from their own culture, and total dependency on the goodwill of their employers. For them, Saudi Arabia can truly be a hardship posting.

Whether or not employees so far down the pecking order notionally have any rights, exercising whatever rights they have is virtually impossible. If the employer decides to abuse, starve, sexually exploit and underpay his Third World employee, the employee has little option, other than suicide, than to put up with the maltreatment. The embassies of Third World countries like the Philippines, India and Pakistan are ineffective. In any case, the embassies may not learn of the abuses to their nationals since female servants are not allowed outside their house of employment without their employer's permission. In addition, abused employees cannot flee the country since they can't get hold of their own passports and if they could, they would be unable to get an exit visa without their employer's approval. Should the matter come to court, no Saudi court conducted by male religious appointees is likely to find in favour of a non-Muslim female guest worker from a Third World country.

Outside their place of employment, foreign domestic workers can also get rough treatment from any passer-by who happens to feel obliged to exercise social discipline. The authors once observed the Mutawa'een caning the legs of a pair of Filipino girls considered to be showing too much ankle. Similar scenes of public canings of females for no apparent reason were beamed in from Afghanistan during the reign of the Taliban.

Amnesty International and other human rights organisations relate tragic stories of Filipina domestic servants abused by their Saudi employers.

MALE BONDING

Acceptable body contact behaviour in Saudi Arabia is almost the opposite of its counterpart in Western countries. Only men frequent the crowded sidewalk cafes and coffee bars. You will often see men, young and old, walking down the street hand-in-hand or at coffee shops in deep conversations with other men serving coffee to them.

The fact that men are extraordinarily affectionate to one another may suggest to guest workers that they have arrived at the global centre of homosexuality. This is not so. Taking its cues from its founder, Islam is a strongly heterosexual religion. Homosexual activity is a criminal offence that can attract the death sentence or, at very least, a long stretch in prison, with the customary public flogging served as an additional punishment. Sex, both homosexual and heterosexual, is a taboo subject in Saudi Arabia more than in most places. The opportunities of young Saudi males to express their heterosexual desires are almost as limited as young Saudi females to express theirs. Wherever you go in the country, you are struck by the shortage of women in public places. What goes on between consenting unmarried people behind closed doors is the subject of much conjecture among the expat community.

Males do a great deal of touching in public whereas touching between males and females in Saudi Arabia is almost never seen. Anyone who works with Saudis will have experienced the capacity of Saudi males to show physical affection to even the remotest of chance acquaintances. Saudis tend to break off from whatever they are doing to engage in conversation with a passing friend. Until you get used to it, these sudden switches of focus can be disconcerting.

Reuniting with a Long Lost Brother?

On one occasion, one of the authors was deeply engrossed in a conference with his Saudi boss, Saleh, when another Saudi entered the office. When the Saudi visitor entered the office, Saleh leapt from his chair to embrace the man. They kissed. The visitor drew up a chair and they held hands while the coffee was brought. The subject of the conference was forgotten for 30 minutes while the two entered a deep conversation. The author sat silently watching all this, believing he was witnessing the return of a long lost brother. After the visitor departed, the author asked Saleh who the visitor might have been. Was that your brother? Was he some school friend who had gone missing for 20 years? Was he a favourite cousin? To the author's surprise, Saleh replied the man was a complete stranger. The two had never met before.

Such instant rapport and hospitality to strangers is thought to stem from the ways of the Bedouin a couple of generations before. For those who spent their time roaming the desert mounted on a camel and in the company of a flock of sheep, the sight of a stranger stumbling out of the desert was a welcome diversion! From the wanderer's point of view, equally welcome was sight of a tented encampment where water, food and shelter might be available. The tradition of the desert decreed that wandering strangers be offered the hospitality of the encampment in return for an account of the stranger's journey. In the offices of the modern world, the tradition lives on!

DRESS CODE FOR SAUDI MEN

The major item of apparel for Arab men is known as a *thobe*, an ankle-length coverall. Along with its accessory, the head scarf called the *gutra*, the *thobe* is the national dress of Saudi Arabia and surrounding Arab states.

Dress code in this area of the world varies little from one occupation to another. The *thobe* and *gutra* is ubiquitous apparel, worn across all socio-economic groups. There is no telling from his dress whether a man is an office worker, a shopkeeper, a construction worker or a taxi driver.

In summer, the *thobe* is a lightweight cotton garment, almost invariably coloured plain white. Wintertime *thobes* are a little more adventurous, made out of thicker material such as fine wool that may be patterned and are generally some pale colour such as ochre or grey. Men's headgear comprises a cap known as a *tagia* over which the *gutra* is secured by one or two cords known as an *egal*. In winter, men may also

Saudi men dressed in *thobes*, *bischts* and *gutras*.

wear something similar to an academic gown known as a *mishlah* or a *bischt*. Saudi men in high positions may dress up a bit more, sometimes in winter wearing a *bischt* edged in gold silk.

Saudis of whatever status like to wear gold—rings, watches, bracelets, necklaces and cigarette cases. The other accessory with which Saudis equip themselves—at least if they are office workers or important officials—is a set of prayer beads, colloquially known as 'worry beads'. The original purpose of the beads was to count the number of prayers during prayer calls. The beads come as a string like a small necklace, usually in a set of 33 or 99 beads. Outside their official function of counting prayers, the worry beads are habitually busy. Saudi men give their worry beads a good working over during most of their waking hours.

DRESS CODE FOR SAUDI WOMEN

Saudi women in black *abayas* dress even more uniformly than their men. As the national dress for women, the Judaic tradition of *abaya*-wearing stretches back to Biblical times.

According to Dr Zakir Naik, the President of the Islamic Research Foundation in Mumbai, India, the Qur'an stipulates the following as dress code for Muslims: 'The first criterion

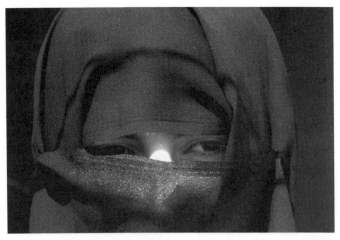

Viewing the world through the *hijab* (veil worn by Muslim women).

is the extent of the body which should be covered. This is different for men and women. The male should cover his body at least from the navel to the knees. Women are obliged to cover their entire bodies except the hands and feet.'

Additional rules prescribed for women's attire are the cut, closeness of fit, construction and style. To meet the approved dress code, clothes should be sufficiently loose-fitting to conceal the figure, should be of opaque material, should not be glamorous and should not be marked by symbols of unbelievers. Ultra-conservative Muslims believe for a women to reveal her face to anybody but her relatives is un-Islamic. Most women you see moving along the street are dressed in black *abayas* and have their faces covered; their sandaled feet, their hands and their eyes the only body parts on display. A minority cover only their heads leaving their faces uncovered.

While the style and cut of *abayas* is ubiquitous, the quality of the cloth may vary. As an indicator of social status, expensive *abayas* may have an upmarket brand label exposed for peer group approval. *Abayas* worn in public as black may be reversible, with blue on one side, black on the other. Within the home, *abayas* can be worn blue-side out.

Outsiders speculate how much Saudi women like or dislike wearing the *abaya*. Statements from Saudi women themselves regarding their society's insistence on wearing *abayas* are mixed. Some claim *abayas* are uncomfortable and that inside their own homes they discard the *abaya* for Western clothes. Others feel that the *abaya* affords the wearer valued anonymity and protection. The *abaya* also offers a convenience that no other garment can match. Saudi women can throw an *abaya* over any level of underclothing from pyjamas to a Dior outfit. An additional advantage for those who feel self-conscious about their figures: the *abaya* is an excellent cover against unfashionable bulges.

Female Liberationists Express Themselves

Neo-liberated young expat women have been seen registering their protests against abaya wearing 'punk' *abayas*—torn up in the manner of ancient jeans worn by young women of the wider world's grunge rock society.

Why the *abaya* should be coloured black is some sort of mystery that the authors have not solved. From a heat absorption point of view, black is the absolute worst colour to wear in the baking climate of Saudi Arabia. Reports are that life can get mighty hot inside an *abaya* and uncomfortable too since to keep the thing on, the wearer must incline her head forward in a way that she appears to be looking at the ground in an attitude of submission. Were these rules of apparel merely design flaws that happened by accident, or were they contrived to inconvenience the fairer sex? The Qur'an appears to the silent on this question. Dr Naik does not list the colour black as one of the Qur'an's dress code rules for *abayas*. But black they are.

In contrast with the *abaya*, we note as a sideline comment, the *thobe* worn by the Saudi male is white—the most heat-reflective colour of all, and therefore most climate-friendly. Saudi colour code is the opposite of Western colour code, where brides wear white (the traditional colour of purity) whereas bridegrooms (for reasons that can only be speculated) traditionally wear black. From a female perspective, this does seem a more realistic colour coding system than the Arabian alternative.

DRESS CODE FOR ALIENS: MEN

There is a story that when King Ibn Saud invited the oil company executives into Saudi Arabia in the 1930s, he insisted the Americans dressed as Arabs, which the American guests proceeded to do. But with the massive influx of guest workers into Saudi Arabia in recent years, sentiment in this area has changed. Saudis are touchy about sharing their culture with foreigners. Having foreigners getting around in their country dressed like Lawrence of Arabia has now fallen out of favour.

Office attire in Saudi Arabia is that appropriate to your country of origin. Businesspeople will be expected to wear suits—lightweight for most of the year and medium-weight for the few weeks of winter. For those further down the social order, shirt and slacks will suffice.

One exception to the advice of not adopting the local dress code is footwear. Almost all Arabs wear sandals, or at least opened-backed shoes that can be slipped on and off as necessary e.g. when entering places such as mosques where shoes are unacceptable. They rarely wear socks. This is sensible footwear for the locality. In most places, wearing sandals by Western expats is considered acceptable. But for most situations, sandals are about the limit of acceptable Arabisation in the apparel area.

Like many hot countries, Saudi Arabia has a parallel climate—the air-conditioning of offices, cars, restaurants and hotels. In a country of blistering heat, local fashion dictates that air-conditioning be turned down to a level that can chill the marrow in your bones. Saudi culture regarding air-conditioning seems to be based on some sort of macho idea that those with the lowest temperature settings are the highest in the social pecking order. Moving between

freezing air inside buildings to the desert heat outside can be discomforting and even health threatening. Those wearing glasses and exiting a building may be temporarily blinded by the mist of condensation when their cold lenses make contact with the hot moist outside air.

For those whose occupation requires them to move from office to office, carrying a coat is strongly recommended, if not for its formality then for its warmth. After a few near-death experiences from pneumonia occasioned by air conditioning, both the authors would carry coats with them whenever they were out visiting someone else's office, or were likely to hitch a ride in someone else's vehicle.

DRESS CODE FOR ALIENS: WOMEN

Dress code for alien women varies somewhat between regions of Saudi Arabia. Standards of modesty are more rigorous in Riyadh than in cities on either coastline. In most places, foreign women aren't expected to cover completely. Cool, loose-fitting clothes in light cotton fabrics are recommended. Exposing bare legs and arms is against the rules. Shorts and short-sleeved tops are unacceptable.

Slacks are also unacceptable because they are too revealing of the female form.

Some women find wearing a lightweight hooded coverall like an academic gown that can be slipped over normal clothes is the easiest way to comply with the dress code of the street. Some also carry a large black scarf that can be donned should the Mutawa'een suddenly appear on the scene.

Women have greater opportunities than men to pass themselves off as Arabs if they feel so inclined. A fully-covering Saudi ensemble of *abaya, hijab (*or *burka)* displays only the hands, the feet and the eyes. Foreign woman wishing to experience local cultural norms can dress Saudi style, find a friend and wander the streets. Since women do not normally interact with strangers, fluency in Arabic is not required to maintain the disguise. During the Taliban regime in Afghanistan, by dressing up as women, male reporters claimed they could walk around in areas restricted to Westerners. No one could tell that these creatures encased from head to toe in loose-fitting fabric, were in reality, cross-gender, cross-culture, cross-dressing reporters disguised to live long enough to file their stories.

Wings Clipped

The Saudi branch of the US military has, over recent years, maintained a delicate relationship with its Saudi hosts. After the first Gulf War, the US maintained a presence on Saudi soil with the objective of protecting the northern borders with Iraq and maintaining security inside Saudi Arabia. The presence of the US military personnel of infidels was opposed by clerics and religious fundamentalists. The US tried its best to fit in. Endeavouring to comply with local cultural norms, the military required the few female personnel based in Saudi Arabia to wear black, head-to-foot abayas. In 1995, Lieutenant Colonel Martha McSally, the highest-ranking female fighter pilot in the US Air Force, initiated an effort in court to end what she considered was discriminatory treatment. Lt Col McSally was licensed to fly supersonic fighters over Saudi Arabia and frequently did so. She objected not only to the dress code, but also to the prohibition preventing her from driving herself around the base. In her trips between the airstrip and her quarters, this supersonic pilot was relegated to the rear of a vehicle driven by a male officer who was subordinate to her rank, but held a valid driver's licence.

RELIGIOUS FREEDOMS

Despite sharing some common roots, prophets and angels, Islam and Christianity have historically been in competition for hearts and minds. Tensions between the two religions can present problems to devout Christians working in the kingdom. Some Muslims claim Islam is tolerant of other religions, but this tolerance is unlikely to be apparent to visitors to Saudi Arabia. The Saudi version of Islam is aggressive. As in the Catholic world of the late Middle Ages religion, law and the state merge imperceptibly. Like Medieval Europe, religious power is used to suppress political dissidents under the cloak of religious respectability.

Saudi Arabia has no Christian churches. Prayer meetings are held in private venues and may be banned at the whim of the Mutawa'een. Even wearing a crucifix can be illegal. The Mutawa'een exercises its power to haul those suspected of a religious crime into criminal courts. Though you might have entered 'Christian' on your immigration card and were allowed entry to the country, believers are advised to practise Christianity discreetly.

Of the individuals who might break the law, Saudis tend to come down hardest on those with least influence. Favoured victims of the Mutawa'een are people from the poorer Asian countries whose embassies are hard-pressed to maintain an effective presence in the kingdom. In professions of Christian religious belief, this usually boils down to Filipinos and Indians.

The Islamic calendar complicates the life of devout Christians. Thursday and Friday are the weekend in Saudi Arabia. Those who wish to attend Sunday service have difficulty doing so on the second day of the Saudi working week. Religiously-inspired Saudi employers may make a great show of checking whether Christians, and particularly Filipino expatriates, are in attendance at their Sunday workplaces.

For every service that is conducted, someone has to conduct it. Christian preachers in Saudi Arabia are taking a real risk. The Mutawa'een come down much harder on preachers of alternative religions than on the congregation. Amnesty International records many sad experiences of guest workers accused by the Mutawa'een of spreading a false faith.

The Risks of Preaching the False Faith

Amnesty International recounts the experience of Danato Lama, a Filipino national who had worked in Saudi Arabia for 15 years:

'Danato's ordeal began on 11 October 1995 in Riyadh when five plain clothes policemen came to his home, started to search his house without a warrant and found a photograph of him attending a Christian prayer meeting with others and a pamphlet about Islam. They then took him, without an arrest warrant, to al-Suleymania Police Station in Riyadh, where they held him incommunicado for two weeks. During this period, they interrogated him regularly, while shackled and handcuffed, and beat him into confessing to being a Christian preacher. He admitted being Christian but denied the preaching charge. They then asked him to sign a statement written in Arabic and said he would be released. But the statement he thought was a 'release clearance', was in fact a 'confession' to being a Christian preacher. He was transferred to Malaz Prison and left there waiting without explanation. Donato Lama's waiting came to an end over a year later, on 26 November 1996 when, suddenly, his jailers chained his legs, handcuffed him and took him to a court in Riyadh. His trial hearing lasted between 15 and 20 minutes, during which he stood shackled and handcuffed in front of the judge who questioned him about preaching Christianity. On 16 December 1996, he was returned to the court where he was told he was sentenced to one and a half year's imprisonment and 70 lashes. The judge told him he could appeal if he did not accept the sentence. Aware that he had only about four more months left to serve in addition to the time he had already spent in detention, and that other prisoners who had opposed court verdicts had ended up serving longer sentences, he accepted the sentence even though he did not accept the guilty verdict.'

In the scale of religious offences, worse than preaching in Saudi Arabia, is attempting to convert believers of other religions to Christianity. Saudi Arabia is not a fertile region for proselytisers. Young men from Salt Lake City and dressed in ties and shirts are not seen prowling the streets of Riyadh seeking converts. Christians thought to be promoting an anti-Muslim message face a possible death sentence on the grounds of heresy.

Saudis dance in celebration at a traditional wedding in Jeddah.

WEDDINGS AND FUNERALS

Weddings and funerals are strictly segregated affairs in accordance with the mores of Saudi culture. Weddings in particular are interesting in this regard, since in theory they celebrate a bonding between the sexes. But in Saudi Arabia, only one sex is present at wedding ceremonies which are held separately for men and women. Since no men are present at the bridal ceremony, women are allowed to discard their veils and let their hair down, at least with other women. (At some point during the wedding celebrations, or maybe after they have been concluded, it is believed the bride and groom do get together.)

Saudis pray at the simple unmarked grave of the late King Fahd.

Arrangements for funerals are even simpler. Though the Qur'an is not absolutely clear on the point, the clerics have ruled that women are not allowed to attend funerals (other than their own), probably on the grounds that doing so would involve women and men at social occasions mixing to an unacceptable degree. Funerals for deceased men and women are men-only occasions.

FALLING FOUL OF THE LAW

Saudi Arabia is not a country in which to step out of line. You'll get a feel for what you can and can't do after you have been there for a while. Those who are in daily contact with Saudis are at the most risk from the Saudi legal system. For dealings with Saudis which turn out badly, guest workers are handy scapegoats.

Finding a Scapegoat

After being charged with bribery in his dealings with a Saudi contractor, a colleague of one of the authors was put under house arrest whereby he was compelled to stay inside a house in Saudi Arabia for many years after his contract was meant to have expired. Even the world's largest construction company, of whom he was an employee, couldn't save him. Other guest workers implicated in building collapses on other projects elsewhere in the kingdom have faced manslaughter charges. The Saudi authorities alleged poor design, though the more likely cause was poor construction by Saudi contractors. The accused were detained in the country at the leisure of the authorities while none too accurate enquiries by authorities qualified in Shariah Law as distinct from engineering, determined why structures failed.

The various macabre forms of punishment, some for seemingly trivial crimes, are well publicised. Saudi Arabia has an unsavory reputation with humanitarian groups like Amnesty International. Political prisoners are detained for years without trial. Torture is commonplace. Public whippings are often part of the sentence. Amputation of the right hand is the prescribed punishment for theft. Highway robbery is punished by amputating the right hand and the left foot.

Brutal punishment is regularly perpetrated on the local population and the guest workforce alike. Often, the victims of the judicial system are convicted on the skimpiest of evidence. Even if you are not a suspect, you need to be careful in your dealings with the authorities, or better yet, avoid them entirely. The Saudi Judiciary is unpredictable. Punishment can be random and casually applied.

A Case of Wrongful Arrest

In a well-reported case, a Westerner thought he had lost his watch in a hotel room. In the intervening period between last noticing the watch and losing it, his room had been made up. Foolishly, as it turned out, the guest reported the loss of his watch to the hotel management who, after a search, reported it to the police. Suspicion fell on the maid who had tidied the room. The maid was a Filipina. Here was a small target that the Saudis could punish without undue fuss to tidy up the case. The maid was picked up, interrogated, found guilty and punished. Her right hand was amputated. Only later, after the hotel guest found his watch in his luggage, did the complainant learn of the maid's fate.

SECURITY AND SAFETY

Guest workers in Saudi Arabia are subject to an additional level of risk from the 'war on terror' waged by the US and its allies after 9-11 against real and perceived Islamic terrorists. The mastermind behind the 9-11 attack is widely thought to be Osama bin Laden, who had once been a Saudi citizen. Bin Laden, whose views were well known to the Saudi Royal family, has been persona non grata in Saudi Arabia for a number of years and had his citizenship revoked in 1994. On the other hand, the bin Laden family has been enormously enriched by its close association with the Saudi Royal Family as well as the Bush family in the US. The bin Ladens also have substantial construction interests on the east coast of the US and may have even received contracts to repair some of the 9-11 damage.

The US insists that the Saudis spare no effort apprehending terrorists for their crimes. Anxious to keep the alliance intact, the Saudis have co-operated vigorously and, at times, randomly. Risks to guest workers are not only from the terrorists themselves, but from Saudi authorities seeking innocent foreign scapegoats to blame for terror attacks.

In the Wrong Place at the Wrong Time

To avoid inciting their own militants to action and to avoid increasing the influence the hawkish wing of the US administration criticising Saudi Arabia for its tolerance of terrorists, Saudi authorities would far rather pin the blame for bombings on anyone other than their own citizens. In his book *Saudi Babylon: Torture, Corruption and Cover-up inside the House of Saud*, British anaesthetist Sandy Mitchell explains how he was framed by the Saudi authorities for two bombings that occurred in Saudi Arabia in 2000. When he was first picked up, Mitchell thought his was a case of mistaken identity. He expected to be released as soon as the small problem of establishing his identity was cleared up. He was quickly disillusioned. He was refused rights to a lawyer and spent two and a half years inside a Saudi jail where he was tortured into signing a confession and forced to admit his guilt for the bombings on Saudi TV. He was sentenced to death, but released before the sentence was carried out.

Outside the court system, at a personal level, disputes between fundamentalists and the US in particular have increased the risks of working in Saudi Arabia. The kingdom has suffered a number of bombings directed at foreigners. In 1995, a bomb exploded at a US-operated Saudi National Guard training centre in Riyadh, killing five Americans. Four Saudi men were charged with the bombing and confessions were extracted. The accused were beheaded in Riyadh's main square. An oil-tanker explosion in June 1996 was in retaliation for this execution and in the same year, a truck bomb blew the façade off the Khobar Towers, a multi-storey US residential tower block, killing 19 US servicemen. Thirteen Saudis and one Lebanese were indicted for the attack. In May 2003, car bombs exploded in a Riyadh residential compound killing a targeted group of expatriate workers plus the car bombers themselves.

Advice from the US Embassy (2001)

The US embassy in Saudi Arabia has urged its citizens in the country to adopt extreme care. Advised the embassy:

'We strongly encourage all American citizens visiting or resident in Saudi Arabia to maintain a high level of vigilance and take appropriate steps to increase their security awareness and reduce their vulnerability. Americans should maintain a low profile, vary routes and times for all required travel, and treat mail and packages from unfamiliar sources with suspicion. In addition, American citizens are urged to avoid contact with any suspicious, unfamiliar objects, and to report the presence of such objects to local authorities. Vehicles should not be left unattended, if at all possible, and should be kept locked at all times. American citizens are urged to park their motor vehicles in protected areas with restricted access and to inspect the vehicles before using them, looking underneath, inside the engine compartment, and inside the trunk. The use of a flashlight for vehicle inspections at night is recommended. Suspicious activities, individuals, or vehicles should be reported to the US Embassy or nearest Consulate General. Licence numbers of vehicles and descriptions of individuals are extremely helpful. Saudi officials continue to co-operate closely with the Embassy to ensure the safety of all Americans.'

THE ULTIMATE PENALTY

The method of legal executions in Saudi Arabia is beheading with a sword. Saudi Arabia employs as its executioner a full-time swordsman who travels to the various execution sites

around the country. From reports published in the media and other sources within the country, estimates of the number of executions range from 100 to 200 per year. Most human rights organisations believe the actual figure is much higher. For the year 2000, Amnesty International estimated that Saudi Arabia had the second highest rate of legal executions per capita of population after Singapore, followed next in order by China, Egypt and the United States (statistics for African nations were not included). Drug dealing, heresy, adultery and assault are some of the crimes that can attract the death sentence in Saudi Arabia.

Erratic Sentencing

According to Amnesty International, two Filipinos—Arnel Beltran and Roel Janda—suffered the ultimate penalty for what in other societies might pass as a minor crime. In addition, claimed Amnesty International, the charges against the two accused were unproved. 'Arnel Beltran and Roel Janda, Filipino nationals, were executed on 4 May 1997. The two were charged with assaulting a shopkeeper and attempted theft. According to the witness, during their detention, they were taken to court twice but each time the alleged victim of assault failed to appear in court. They apparently were under the impression that their trial was pending until the other party appeared in court. They had no idea that they had been sentenced to death.'

As a guest worker, you may well abhor the idea of executions. But capital punishment is practised in Saudi Arabia on a regular basis. Saudis are not the least bit ashamed of these practices. Quite the reverse. Executions are ceremonial events held in public and conducted on Fridays, the holy day in the Islamic week. The populace—local and alien—is encouraged, or at the very least not discouraged, from attending. If you happen to stray too close to 'Chop Square' in your local town (as the execution sites are nicknamed), you may find yourself pushed to the front of the crowd. Saudi Arabia believes in the deterrent power of executions. It likes its guest workers to witness punishment for crimes committed and thereby encourages them to keep their minds focused on their work and not on side issues.

At a local execution, after being pushed to the front of the crowd in this way, a British reporter once asked a bystander the reason why people wanted him to stand in the front of the crowd. "To add to the sinner's punishment," a Saudi witness to the execution explained, "So the last thing the sinner sees as he leaves this world is your face: the face of the infidel."

PAYING BLOOD MONEY

The case of the two British nurses, Lucille McLaughlin and Deborah Parry was well publicised. These two were accused of murdering a fellow worker, an Australian nurse, and faced punishment of 500 lashes and eight years jail for McLaughlin and execution by beheading for Parry. But there was an out. The principle of Shariah Law known as *diya* allows the victim or the victim's family to accept blood money in exchange for clemency. The victim's brother, Frank Gilford, was the accepted spokesperson for the family of the victim. The case made worldwide news and the British government got deeply involved in the affair. After a long period of negotiation and refusal, Gilford finally agree to accept blood money for his sister's death. Subsequently McLaughlin and Parry were pardoned by the king and were repatriated to Britain. No doubt if a couple of Filipino nurses had been found guilty of the same crime, the punishments prescribed by the courts would have been exacted. Like most places in the world, under the *diya* system, justice flows to those who can best afford it!

SECURITY OF SAUDI ARABIA: THE COUNTRY

Since the 1940s, when the commercial oil industry first got underway, oil for protection has been the essence of the contract between the US and Saudi Arabia. This arrangement has endured. As the leader of OPEC, Saudi Arabia keeps the Western world supplied with oil and influences fellow members of OPEC to do likewise. In return, the US provides the promise of military backing to keep the Al Saud regime in power.

This is a marriage of mutual convenience in which, not too far beneath the surface, the partners are deeply incompatible. Though the incompatibilities are papered over, occasionally they come to the surface. Many Americans believe that Saudi Arabia is a hot-bed of terrorism. Fifteen of the 19 hijackers involved in the 9-11 attack were Saudi nationals, mostly from the strongly anti-US Asir region near Yemen.

A Pentagon paper in 2002 was one of many statements that questioned Saudi Arabia's devotion to America's cause of waging a war on terror. It stated that '...the Saudis are active at every level of the terror chain, from planners to financiers, from cadre to foot soldier, from ideologist to cheerleader'. The Pentagon paper went on to recommend that the US issue an ultimatum to Saudi Arabia to stop sponsoring terrorism or face the seizure of its oilfields and financial assets. Other hawkish comments from the Pentagon and in conservative US newspapers described Saudi citizens as 'terrorists' and recommend Saudi Arabia be bombed 'back to the stone age'.

For their part, the clerics and many Saudi citizens, maybe the majority, sympathise with the Al-Qaeda cause of Osama bin Laden. Islamic fundamentalists regard both parties as the partners to an unholy alliance. Members of the Saudi leadership are considered godless despots who prefer to party in the West rather than make a pilgrimage to Mecca. The US is considered the axis of evil. In addition, particular tribal groups within Saudi Arabia grind various axes against the Saudi monarchy more deeply rooted than the US-Saudi detente. Hijazis from areas around the holy cities of Mecca and Medina, pursue a grudge against the Wahhabi religious leadership that goes back 250 years.

The dissident movement inside Saudi Arabia is an embarrassment to the Saudi government and an ongoing sore point for the US administration. If the regime is too soft on terrorists, the conservative lobby in the US issues hawkish threats. If it comes down too hard on terrorists, pressure rises from its own citizens. The Saudi administration attempts to plot a middle path.

Finding the Middle Path

In 1992, over 100 Wahhabi clerics sent a 'Memorandum of Advice' to King Fahd, criticising the monarchy for corruption and allowing US troops to remain in the country after the first Gulf War. King Fahd responded by dismissing seven of the 17 members of the country's highest clerical body, the Supreme Authority of Senior Clerics, for not denouncing the memorandum. Two dissident clerics were jailed for precipitating public protests. The monarchy was later forced to cede more power to the clerics when these prisoners were released. After this, the uneasy alliance between clerics and royalty continued.

Outside government, citizens in the US took things into their own hands. In the US civil courts, in mid-2002, a trillion-dollar class action was launched on behalf of the victims of 9-11. The action originally named, among the defendants, three Al Saud princes, including the former intelligence chief Prince Turki Al Faisal and the defence minister Prince Sultan bin Abdul Aziz Al Saud. The lawsuit was expanded later that year to involve other parties including three more princes and the Saudi-American Bank (SAMBA), the second largest bank in the country and partly owned by Citibank. No sooner was the lawsuit underway when stories circulated that the wife of the long-serving Saudi ambassador in Washington, Prince Bandar bin Sultan, had been accused of making donations to Al Qaeda. She has since claimed her innocence.

For its part, Saudi Arabia countered US claims that it was soft on terrorism by suggesting that the US could do more to remove the triggers for terrorists, specifically US support for Israel's suppression of the Palestinians.

Memo from One Head of State to Another

'Crown Prince Abdullah sent President George W Bush an angry letter on 29 August 2001. He warned that Saudi Arabia was being put in an untenable position and reportedly wrote: 'A time comes when peoples and nations part. We are at a crossroad. It is time for the United States and Saudi Arabia to look at their separate interests. Those governments that don't feel the pulse of their people and respond to it will suffer the fate of the Shah of Iran.'
—Source: October 2001 report in *The Wall Street Journal*

In May 2003, after the car-bomb attacks on expatriate compounds in Saudi Arabia, the monarchy once again tried to shift the balance of power in its favour while placating the demands of the United States to crack down on terrorist sympathisers. According to reports on BBC, 'more than 1,700 clerics' had been relieved of their duties or forced to undergo 're-education'. In addition, three clerics were arrested over alleged links to terrorists. Political commentators interpreted this move as a purge of militants within the kingdom who might have posed a threat to the existing political order.

A new generation of almost unemployable Saudi youth poised to enter the labour market poses an additional potential terrorist threat for which there is no obvious solution in the short term. To some, this pool of bored and unhappy young people on the loose appears to be a pool of ready-made recruits for the next generation of terrorists.

Under tensions such as these, from time to time, commentators speculate whether a revolution could occur in Saudi Arabia similar to the Iranian revolution of 1979 to unseat the Saudi monarchy and rid the country not only of Western influence, but also its Western workforce.

It seems unlikely.

So far, Saudi Arabia has held together politically, despite the tensions and occasional outbreaks of violence. The Royal Family in Saudi Arabia seems far more secure than was the Shah in Iran. The sheer size of the Royal Family—thousands of major and minor Royals spread all over the country and among all levels of society—is, at the same time, a strength and a weakness. At least five different power groups have been identified as operating within the family. Though its size, numbering thousands, makes the family difficult to act cohesively, these thousands of family members do share a common interest in staying in power. The interdependency of the Royal Family and the Ulema is another important factor. In Iran, the religious movement was the natural enemy of the political leadership. In Saudi Arabia, the Ulema and the Royal Family share an alliance going back over at least three centuries.

Since the loyalty of armies can never be guaranteed, the Saudi Royal Family has tried to protect its power base by establishing an administrative structure to minimise the chances of a coup d'état. Protecting the Royal family are the National Guard composed of Bedouins thought to be the strongest supporters of Saudi royalty. In addition, reporting to the Interior Ministry are the Public Security Police (which includes the *mubahith* or secret police and the regular police) and the Special Security force (the equivalent of the US SWAT team).

In any case, most analysts believe if a revolution were to break out in Saudi Arabia, the US would be unlikely to stay out of the contest and allow Saudi oil to fall into uncertain hands. The alliance between the US and the House of Saud not only protects the Saudi regime against external threats, but also against its own dissidents.

SETTLING IN

'I do not want my house to be walled in on all sides and my windows to be stuffed. I want the cultures of all the lands to be blown about my house as freely as possible. But I refuse to be blown off my feet by any.'
—Mahatma Gandhi (1869–1948)

EXPECTATIONS

For some, flying to the Middle East for the first time, the standard two-year contract duration may seem like a long time to spend in what is generally portrayed as a tough assignment in a tough location. For others, the prospect of life in Saudi Arabia, with no income tax, few financial responsibilities, a house provided and lots of paid holidays, may lessen the perception of Saudi Arabia as a hardship posting. For most guest workers, the assignment works out. Many find, after their arrival, that the advertised hardships of Saudi Arabia have been greatly exaggerated—that Saudi Arabia is, in fact, an easy number. In actuality for some, particularly those with high status jobs, working in Saudi Arabia is a career highlight, with luxurious living and working conditions. But for the few whose assignment, for some reason, goes off the rails, Saudi Arabia can make life tough for its guest workers.

En route to Saudi Arabia, you will probably have formed some mental image of what lies ahead. Maybe friends, who have worked in Saudi Arabia, will have recounted many a lurid tale, suitably embellished to increase your anxieties. Your mind may be gripped with ill-defined fears, particularly if you are a woman. In women's circles, this place has definitely acquired a reputation as a male-dominated society where women are afforded little respect and few privileges. To the guest worker visiting the kingdom for the first time, Saudi

Arabia may be just a little bit scary. But the chances are, your fears will prove unfounded.

VISAS AND DOCUMENTATION

The only tourist visas issued into Saudi Arabia are for approved tour groups following organised itineraries and for Muslim pilgrims intending to discharge their *hajj* obligations. Other than that, unless they are diplomats, travellers to Saudi Arabia are workers or dependants of workers who must be sponsored by a company or a Saudi citizen living inside the country. Providing that passports are valid for at least six months, visitors will then be issued visas after presentation of the correct paperwork prepared by their employers. Family members are entitled to visit Saudi Arabia under similar arrangements. Their visa applications will also be processed by the sponsoring company. Visas are obtained through Saudi embassies or consulates in the passport holder's country of origin.

Getting a Visa

In the experience of the two authors, a working visa from the Saudi embassy in London takes about a week to issue and a business visa from the embassy in Canberra takes about two or three days. The only exceptions to these arrangements are 24- or 48-hour transit visa, which are hard to get and rarely issued.

On departing the country, say for R&R or a business trip, visitors must obtain an exit permit arranged by their employer prior to leaving and an exit/re-entry permit if they are returning to the kingdom after their sojourn away. Employees are not normally obliged to attend immigration offices either within or outside Saudi Arabia for this process. As each entry and re-entry visa requires an entire page, people making trips in and out of the kingdom will consume their passport pages at an impressive rate. Those who expect to travel frequently in and out of the kingdom should consider acquiring passports with more than the standard number of pages (most countries offer this option).

Visits to Saudi Arabia by women are subject to additional rules. To comply with local requirements that women be accompanied wherever they go in Saudi Arabia, sponsors must meet females of dependants on entry into the country otherwise they may be held at airports for long periods, possibly indefinitely. On the return journey, married women and children need their husband's permission to leave the country.

The Paper Mill

Saudi Arabia has a large bureaucracy that has a commensurate appetite for paperwork. Once inside Saudi Arabia, you cannot be sure what documents will be needed, only that you're likely to need plenty of them! Experienced Saudi hands assemble document packs, including many passport size photographs of each member of the family, photocopies of ID, copies of most other important documents in your CV—birth certificate, marriage certificate, 'no objection' letters and employment contracts—health cards, certificates of academic qualifications preferably all attested to by your country's own embassy in Saudi Arabia.

Under Saudi law, the employer is obliged to hold its employees' passports while employees are in the kingdom. This rule can have a real downside if you are unfortunate enough to work for an unscrupulous employer. Without a passport, in the event of a dispute between employer and employee, there is no way for a disgruntled employee to get out of the country. Situations in which the employee is completely at the mercy of the employer have led to occasional sad stories of employee abuse.

No one who has an Israeli visa stamp in their passport can get a visa for Saudi Arabia. Anyone who wants to visit both Israel and Saudi Arabia needs to get two passports, or make an arrangement with the Israelis for a removable visa. An extreme case of anti-Jewish sentiment in the authors' experience was the censoring, by an over zealous censor, of the word 'juice' from cans of fruit juice in the local commissary. Presumably this word was too close, phonetically, to the collective noun for the Jewish race. On each can, this word was blacked out by the Saudi censor's ubiquitous accessory—the black marker pen.

In a parallel story, a past Australian ambassador to Saudi Arabia related the story of an Australian businessman who did a little jail time on his first visit to the country after a misunderstanding with an immigration official. The Australian businessman, it seems, had a slight speech impediment. When the immigration official asked what was the businessman's country of origin, he evidently thought he heard the reply 'Israel' instead of 'Australia'. Handcuffs were duly installed and the offender was whisked off to jail without so much as an opportunity provided for the offender to present his passport.

PRE-ARRIVAL CHECKS

The climate of Saudi Arabia, being hot and dry, is intrinsically bug-resistant. No injections are stipulated by the government as a condition for entry. Some visitors obtain a meningitis vaccination. Hepatitis A shots are recommended by many doctors. Those visiting the coastal plains of south-west Saudi Arabia—well away from most normal tour of duty areas—might be advised to take anti-malaria precautions. Those travelling near Mecca in the pilgrim season may consider taking precautions against Meningicoccal disease or meningitis that may be brought into the country by pilgrims from nearby more tropical Muslim countries.

Health

Saudi Arabia spends about 5 per cent of its gross domestic product (GDP) on health care—about one-third the rate of the United States and half that of the OECD (Organisation for Economic Co-operation and Development) countries. Medical care is provided to Saudi citizens free of charge. Western health care workers report that Saudis tend to be on the opposite end of the health care scale to hypochondriacs. Saudis don't visit doctors unless they feel seriously unwell, thus reducing the strain on the health care system. Given the strength of their religious beliefs, Saudis probably aren't quite as obsessed as the typical Westerner with an ambition to prolong life as long as possible. The average lifespan of men is a modest 66 years and of women, 69 years.

Health care in Saudi Arabia is a curious mixture of rudimentary primary medical care and a few lavishly equipped Western-style hospitals staffed by a combination of expatriates and Saudis. Gradually, the Saudis are training up to contribute more staff to their health care system but the system is still predominately run by expatriates. By 2001, Saudi employment in the health system had risen to 18 per cent.

Guest workers may or may not have to pay for health costs depending on their employment conditions. Many large projects employ their own doctors, with health care included in employment packages. Despite the high standard of their hospitals, primary medical care is still fairly basic. If health care is not provided in the employment package, selection of one's health care provider is important. From an expatriate point of view, some excellent hospitals are available—along with some that are not so good.

ACCOMMODATION

As a guest worker in the country, how you live will depend on who you are, what you have come to do and the organisation you are working for. If you are a Western businessperson heading a major corporation, you will enjoy the same luxury appointments in Saudi Arabia that you have come to expect wherever you travel. If you are working for a branch of a large company, you will probably be given comfortable accommodation, not quite up to luxury class. If you have come to work for a Saudi company, the likely standard of your accommodation is harder to predict. Large Saudi companies house their employees in all standards of accommodation, from the opulent to the very ordinary. At the other end of the employment scale, if you are an Indian houseboy in a luxury house, you would normally have a small room, though accommodation in stairwells, cupboards and shipping containers in the back garden have also been reported. Four or five labourers from Pakistan and Yemen might typically share a room someplace and sleep on the floor.

As a Western expat worker, the most common style of accommodation in Saudi Arabia is the 'compound', which is essentially an expatriate enclave kept fairly separate from the Saudi Arabian mainstream community. The model for this society evolved in the first days of Saudi Arabia's now well-established imported labour programme. Aramco was established in 1948 to develop Saudi Arabia's first major oil strike at a favourable geological formation called the Dhahran Dome near the eastern seaboard. The area was arid and featureless. One small trading post, the now bustling town of Al Khobar, nestled nearby on the shores of the Persian Gulf. The nearest inland settlement was an oasis at Hofuf, about 150 km (90 miles) to the south. The site of the future oil wells and extraction facilities was a wide expanse of empty land. Ready-made accommodation for Western visitors was non-existent.

To develop this great new oilfield, specialist expatriate workers to the Middle East, mainly US citizens, were imported to drill the wells, lay pipelines and build facilities needed to pump the oil into tankers pulling into Persian Gulf ports. To meet the need of this imported workforce for Western-style

Children hitch a ride on a donkey cart in an Al Khobar street.

accommodation, the oil company created a typical American suburb amongst the wastes of the Dhahran desert, importing everything they required from kit homes to the grass for their sidewalks. They set up shopping facilities, banking, schools, hospitals, sports facilities and a radio station. The suburb, somewhat unimaginatively christened 'The Aramco Compound', was built and peopled by Americans who acted American, spoke American and might have been living in downtown Burbank.

As the nation's oil revenues rolled in and were expended on development projects, replicas of this kit-form city were built elsewhere. At various large projects around the country, a number of Western-style towns have been constructed, initially inhabited by construction personnel, and later by Saudis. If you have come to Saudi Arabia to work on a construction site or to work in an existing industrial city, you have an excellent chance of living in a 'compound' that resembles the suburb of a dusty desert town, perhaps with neat streets, gardens and lawns irrigated by desalinated seawater. With increased security concerns in recent times, some compounds are now fortified settlements and are surrounded by walls and a cleared security area with high razor-wire fences patrolled by the Saudi Military. Within the compound, you can probably live a pretty similar life in Saudi Arabia to the one you left in your country of origin. Residents of compounds tend to conduct most of their activities inside the compound's boundaries. Likewise, indigenous Arabs tend to stay outside.

The standard of accommodation offered in compounds could be a single room 'dog-box', a trailer home imported fully assembled or a luxury permanent home in an established suburb. Suburbs and compounds of large cities are generally well-equipped with sporting facilities, community centres, movie theatres and shops. Some visitors may feel right at home in these facilities. Others may find that living in the company-provided accommodation of Saudi Arabia superior to anything they have experienced back home in their countries of origin! A few might feel that compound life is artificial and yearn to pitch a tent in the desert.

If you are working in a city, instead of a compound you may live in an apartment or perhaps in a hotel. Apartments and hotels in Saudi Arabia are much the same as Western-style apartments and hotels anywhere else. This is no run-down country where you have to visit the well to pump water. Saudi Arabia has a developed infrastructure. Almost everywhere you will find the full suite of services—electricity, running water, sewerage and motor car access.

For those not living in company-supplied accommodation, large towns and cities have real estate agents. Real estate ads are also carried in newspapers. Rental leases can run either for an indefinite period or a specified period. Short-term and long-term leases are available. Rental accommodation is customarily provided with basic furnishings. The cost of rental accommodation, if required, varies greatly with location. The most expensive real estate in Saudi Arabia is in Mecca during the pilgrim season. As an expat, you are unlikely to live in Mecca unless you work for a large building contracting company with a contract to construct a high-rise building to service Mecca's construction boom. Jeddah, Riyadh and Al Khobar are more likely destinations. A website for those who wish to enquire about rental apartments and homes is:

http://www.real-estate-immobilien.com/travel-guides/
saudiarabia.html

You may also wish to contact them for more information at email: info@asinah.org.

FACILITIES FOR THE HANDICAPPED

By the standards of Asia, Saudi Arabia is reasonably user-friendly for the handicapped. Good hotels and public buildings tend to have reasonable access to ramps. Outside, the infrastructure may be difficult to negotiate, depending on where you are in the country. In the smaller towns, surface conditions of streets and sidewalks may be hazardous. In the large cities, facilities are generally reasonable.

MONEY AND BANKING

The monetary unit of Saudi Arabia is the Saudi Riyal (SAR), which since 1986 has been pegged to the US dollar at the rate of SAR 3.745 to the dollar. The highest denomination note is SAR 500 and the smallest SAR 1. Other notes of various denominations are in circulation down to the smallest value note of one riyal. The minor unit is the *halalah* which, at 100 to the riyal, is of nuisance value only.

Changing travellers cheques is generally more difficult in Saudi Arabia than most places. Many banks and money changers simply won't accept travellers cheques. Others will exchange only the particular issue of travellers cheques they deal in themselves. Also, unlike most places, you will need to present your original purchase receipt when cashing your travellers cheques.

US dollar bank notes, everyone's favourite currency, are easy to exchange. Whatever you are changing, you are likely to get a better rate of exchange from money changers than from banks.

Cash withdrawn at the local Automatic Teller Machine (ATM) linked to a home-based bank account is probably the easiest way to generate cash in the kingdom. Two advantages of ATMs, apart from convenience, is that they don't discriminate against females or close down for prayer calls. Credit cards are also widely accepted. Whatever method you select to meet your day-to-day expenses, people working in Saudi Arabia, living in free company housing, sending their kids to free school generally enjoy a highly subsidised lifestyle and don't need much more than petty cash when in Saudi Arabia.

Except for restrictions on females, guest workers can open accounts with Saudi banks. But generally there is no need to do so. One of the authors did open a cheque account with a local bank while in Saudi Arabia, and closed it shortly afterwards. The hassles of operating the bank account were hardly worth the effort for little advantage. Most expatriate workers get their pay cheques credited directly into the banks in their own countries or elsewhere. There are no restrictions about sending currency out of Saudi Arabia. If you do want to enquire about Saudi banks, there are many available that may or may not have links to your offshore bank. A complete list of all the banks in the country, along with contact details, is available from the website:

http://www.aiwagulf.com/directory/sa/sp.asp?pc = 56

Local Banking Ethics

The Saudi Arabian banking system isn't comfortable with some of the ethics of modern commerce. The Qur'an contains provisions precluding money usury, which is alternatively defined as 'interest' or 'exorbitant interest'. Whether exorbitant or not, Wahhabis aren't keen on the notion of interest at all. By the same token, the realities of the commercial world are recognised. Since interest is the keystone of the banking system, this ideological difficulty has rather limited the opportunities for Saudi banks.

To overcome the problem, Saudi Arabia, in line with other Middle East countries, has two banking systems—Islamic and Western. Islamic banking invests only in companies that provide acceptable goods and services, develop Islamic products and conform to Shariah Law. Companies that provide social welfare services are favoured. Companies that deal in tobacco and alcohol are precluded. Some major international banks such as Cititbank and Hongkong Shanghai Banking Corporation have Islamic banking divisions operating in Saudi Arabia.

Trading Hours

Traditionally Saudi Arabia has worked siesta hours. Commercial hours for retailing are customarily from 8:00 am–1:00 pm, then 4:00 pm–8:00 pm (some variations may occur). Government offices may skip the afternoon shift and may only be open from 7:00 am–1:00 pm. Some may stay open till 2:30 pm. These trading hours were established to suit the rigorous climate of the country. With the advent of air-conditioning, the climate is less relevant than it once was—at least inside the offices and malls. Many offices now work more normal business hours—9:00 am–5:00 pm, or something similar. These hours apply most of the year except Ramadan, when retail businesses are extensively shut during daylight hours, but are normally open in the evening.

Since Friday is the religious day, the working week is from Saturday to Wednesday. Weekends are on Thursday and Friday. Businesses and government offices are normally closed and most shops are normally opened during weekend trading hours.

As well as their regular opening and closing times, shops will also close three or four times a day for prayers. The practice of closing down for prayers can seem remarkably inconvenient to the Western shopper. Experienced shoppers time their shopping expeditions to fit in with prayer timetables. The most efficient shopping expedition is one in which prayer time is spent travelling either to or from shops. Prayer times vary according to a sliding scale depending on the times for dawn, dusk and the phases of the moon. Lists of prayer times obtainable from places like bookstores are worth getting as an aid to scheduling appoints and shopping expeditions. Prayer times are also provided in daily newspapers.

APPLIANCES

Electricity supply is reliable and power cuts are uncommon. Electric power is supplied principally at North American voltage and frequency—110 volts and 60 Hertz. But in many offices and hotels and some residential homes, a 220v/50Hz outlet is available. Voltage regulators are recommended to protect appliances from supply fluctuations. Sockets and plugs are not standardised and vary between the British, US and European types. Those travelling in Saudi Arabia are advised to take a transformer to obtain the correct voltage for their appliances, and to carry a plentiful supply of adaptors to fit the various plug types.

HELP AROUND THE HOME

Saudis of quite modest means engage domestic servants from East Asian and sub-continent countries. Guest workers in upper socio-economic groups may wish to do the same. Unless it is provided in the employment package, expatriates who wish to employ domestic help will probably enter into an informal arrangement with someone already in the kingdom working for someone else. Plenty of Third Country employees are on the lookout for moonlighting jobs to supplement their incomes. More permanent arrangements are unlikely to be convenient since the visas for domestic employees bind employees to specific employers and no one else. Saudi Arabia expects its guest workforce to visit the kingdom for the specific purpose of undertaking an employment contract for a specific employer for a specific contract period at the end of which they are expected to leave.

TRAVEL BY CAR

Visitors with a valid driver's licence from most countries, or an international driver's licenses, are allowed to drive in the kingdom. In addition to holding a valid licence, you may also be required to donate a pint of your blood to the Saudi licence testing authority (blood for road accident victims is always in short supply in this country).

Good quality highways connect major cities. Travelling long distances in quick time is comfortable provided your car has a good air-conditioner. Petrol is cheap. Inside towns and cities, the customary traffic snarls may sometimes occur as they do anywhere. But between cities, traffic flows freely. Compared to most countries, the traffic on roads is light. Car ownership statistics are about one third the rate in the West. In 1996, there were 1.67 million passenger cars, with a ratio of about 6 people per car. One factor in this low rate of car ownership is that women—over half the indigenous adult population—are not permitted to drive.

That's the good news about driving. The bad news is that the nation's highways and byways are downright dangerous places to be. Those who hold that the female of the species is the more dangerous one on the roads than the male will find little support for their case from the road accident statistics of Saudi Arabia. That Saudi roads are perilous places is evident merely by driving through the countryside. The nation's highways are littered with wrecked cars that are merely dragged to the side of the road and abandoned as a silent testimony to the hazards of driving on the nation's roads.

The Perils of Motoring

According to a year 2000 report by the Department of Neurosciences, Riyadh Armed Forces Hospital, Saudi Arabia, between 1971 and 1997, 564,762 people died or were injured in road traffic accidents, a figure equivalent to 3.5 per cent of the Saudi population. A World Bank report of about the same time found that Saudi Arabia, along with Malaysia, Thailand and South Africa, were the most dangerous countries in which to drive, based on fatalities per head of population. Saudi Arabia fared even worse in comparison when this was measured in fatalities per vehicle. In studies conducted to determine the cause of Saudi Arabia's high accident rate, very high speed has been pinpointed as a major cause of road accidents. This is certainly the experience of the authors. Many Saudis seem to adopt a carefree disregard for human life when behind the wheel, both their own and other people's.

Driving standards in Saudi Arabia are on a par with the worst anywhere. In the opinion of the authors and absolutely unsupported by any research that we know of, there is one particular element of Arab culture that seems to us to make

driving hazardous. Science has shown that about 40 per cent of the evaporative losses from a human body labouring under a hot sun are through the top of the head. Arabs developed the appropriate headgear to deal with this problem. For camel driving across the sunny deserts of Saudi Arabia, the *gutra* is no doubt ideally suited to the job of providing shade and preserving bodily fluids. But this item of national apparel is not equally suited to all forms of locomotion. One aspect of *gutra*-wearing renders it particularly unsuited for driving cars. The fall of the material on both sides of the face obscures peripheral vision. Saudi drivers seem particularly bad at seeing other cars coming at them from the side.

In addition, a popular view among expats is that Saudi drivers bring to the roads their carefree fatalistic attitude that events on the road, and in life in general, are in the hands of a higher authority than themselves. This being the case, they might argue, what difference does it make to speed around blind corners and over crests on the wrong side of the road? What is going to happen is going to happen.

Whatever the cause of their bad driving, Saudi Arabia is a country where you should, above all things, drive defensively. When you are at the wheel, assume that the nation's roads are likely to be peopled by semi-blind maniacs travelling towards you at high speed and not necessarily on their side of the road. Never suppose that people will stop at intersections or stop at red lights. In cities, always expect that cars may pop out in front of you from streetside parking spots. And remember that whatever the circumstances of an accident, under Shariah Law, if you hit a car driven by a Saudi, you will most likely be blamed, however blameless you consider yourself to be.

Handling Road Accidents

Assuming you are tolerant of religion, not mounting a crusade to topple the government and refraining from selling alcoholic drinks to the local population, the most common legal problem you are likely to encounter in Saudi Arabia is a road accident. That said, many expats do drive in Saudi Arabia and emerge from the experience unscathed. But if an accident occurs and you are involved, the Saudi authorities will dispense blame for the accident in a fairly ad hoc manner across whoever happens to be at the scene of the crime. Rough justice can be administered, with the risk that the innocent may be enmeshed in the outcome along with the guilty.

Underlying Saudi law is the concept of *qisas*, or retribution. Under this code, when a crime occurs, a similar level of suffering is meant to be inflicted on the perpetrator of the crime as has been inflicted on the victim. Saudi law may take the Biblical maxim of 'an eye for an eye and a tooth for a tooth' quite literally. For example, in 2000, an Egyptian expatriate worker had his eye surgically removed after he threw acid in the face of another man, causing his victim to lose an eye.

As an alternative or an addition to punishment, the Shariah Law of *diya* also allows the concept of blood money. The perpetrator of a road accident, as well as being punished by the state, is expected to compensate the victim, or if the victim has been killed in the accident, the victim's family. Saudi courts will prescribe the payment of blood money based not so much on the injuries inflicted but on the status of the victim and the ability of the perpetrator to pay. (The West, which has a very poor record for compensating victims of crime, might take note of this!)

Getting Third Party Insurance
(And Staying Out of Jail)

In recent years, compulsory third-party insurance has been introduced in line with what is practiced in most countries. Since 2002, both resident and non-resident drivers in transit are required to apply for *rukhsa* (driving licence insurance) at the National Commercial Bank, Al-Rajhi Banking and Investment Corporation or at driving schools. The rate is SAR 350 for those over 21 and SAR 700 for those below. The cover provides up to SAR 500,000 in damages and also covers third-party rights to blood money (*diya*). A statement from Allied Company for Co-operative Insurance and Reinsurance provided these words by way of explanation:

'*Rukhsa* covers the blood money of a person killed. In the absence of this cover, the erring driver would remain in police custody until the blood money, a bond or a guarantee from his sponsor was furnished.'

The Saudi government has acknowledged that the road toll in the kingdom is high and that Shariah court rulings have been arbitrary and harsh. Talk of setting up special courts to handle traffic offences has been ongoing from 2001, but nothing has happened yet.

There are a couple of common sense rules about road accidents. In the first place, if this is someone else's road accident—stay out of it. Saudi Arabia is not the place to discharge the role of good and dutiful citizen. If you come across a road accident, and feel a compulsion to become involved, bear in mind that when the authorities arrive, the first thing they are likely to do is throw a cordon around the scene of the crime. Anyone inside the cordon will be considered involved. The damaged cars will be dragged to the side of the road, where they may stay for a very long time and perpetrators, victims and bystanders at the scene of the accident are all likely to be taken away by the authorities for processing. Justice can operate very rapidly and inaccurately. Or the enquiry may be prolonged. Perfectly innocent bystanders might have to spend weeks in jail while enquiries are conducted regarding their degree of involvement. Once released, if the case is not concluded, witnesses might have to stay in the kingdom for months, denied exit permits while cases drag on. Only those with a hyper-acute sense of public duty are going to get involved in someone else's road accident in this country.

If this is your own accident, things are decidedly trickier. It is easy enough to state that you should avoid an accident. But the nature of accidents is that they happen. One of the risks of driving in Saudi Arabia is to be involved in an accident in which, in your own country, you would have been considered entirely blameless. Various judges have enunciated to guest worker defendants of traffic charges the principle of Saudi law on this matter— the accident must be your fault, since if you had not been there, the accident would not have happened. One of the authors has personal experience witnessing an accident at an intersection where the Saudi driver went through a red light and collided with a car—driven by an expat—executing a left-hand turn. The expat was held guilty on the grounds that the light showing on the street he was turning into was red at the time of the accident. Besides, if he hadn't been there, he wouldn't have been hit. That sort of logic is hard to beat in court.

As a last word on this subject, if you do happen to end up in jail for some reason, make sure someone knows you are there. Saudi Arabia is a free enterprise economy. Jails in Saudi Arabia provide only the minimum of accommodation services. Luxury items like food, water and toilet paper are meant to be provided by friends or family of the detained.

TAXIS

There are two types of taxis in Saudi Arabia—coded by colour—white taxis (limousines) and yellow taxis (ordinary taxis). In most cases, limousines, which also co-ordinate with hotels, are to be preferred should the choice be available. Fares are generally reasonable. As an additional caution, unaccompanied women are advised against taking a yellow taxi due to the problems that might ensue from being caught by the religious police with a strange man in an enclosed space.

The habits of Saudi taxi drivers are similar to the habits of taxi drivers worldwide. They drive fast and they have a reputation, whether earned or not, for sharp practice. The standard of taxi-driving in Saudi Arabia is probably no better or no worse than anywhere else. A fair statement about the taxi drivers in most countries is that they drive more aggressively but with a higher level of skill than the average of other drivers. Saudi Arabia is probably no exception. In a country where the accident rate is amongst the highest in the world, you are probably safer in a taxi than with most Saudi drivers.

In taking a taxi, as in all aspects of life in Saudi Arabia, religion may influence the experience. Taxi drivers are theoretically supposed to stop whatever they are doing when prayer time is announced. (Airline pilots seem to be exempt from this requirement.) In practice, many taxi drivers may pull over during the journey and conduct their prayers at the side of a road or even in a mosque. The polite thing for you to do in this situation is to wait. Another option is to catch a bus, should you be able to find one heading in your intended direction. Clerics appear to have granted bus drivers a general exemption from the obligation to pray—at least while in the act of driving the bus.

POSTAL

Saudi Arabia runs a privatised postal system that has been greatly expanded in recent years. In 2001, the system included 477 main post offices and 185 branch offices. The three main postal complexes are in Riyadh, Jeddah and Dammam. Saudi Arabia is widely bilingual in Arabic and English. Much of the commerce is conducted in English. Addressing of mail in English is widely practised and not a great deal different from anywhere else in the world. Most places don't have street delivery and the normal practice is to use a post office box number.

TELEVISION

The Saudi Arabian Ministry of Information extensively scrutinises media entering the country for religious purity and political correctness. Detailed interpretation of the Qur'an during the 1970s determined that screening a film for public viewing in a cinema was against the rules, but broadcasting the same films into people's homes on TV was permissible. In reaching this ruling, the Saudis may have objected less to the content of the films than to the cinema itself. Neither the clerics nor the authorities liked the idea of a crowd of strangers gathering in a dark place where conspiracies could be hatched, lewd acts could be performed and bombs could be exploded. This rule was cautiously relaxed in 2005. The cinema is located at Riyadh Hotel and shows foreign cartoons dubbed in Arabic. The audience is excluively women and children and sidesteps religious demands for gender segregation.

Though cinemas are restricted, most popular films, Western and other films are screened on TV. Government censors hack and slash content at will. Politically offensive material, such as content interpreted as pro-Israel or anti-Muslim, may be taken out. Large gaps in films when the screen goes blank (as distinct from cutting and splicing) may appear without notice, indicating that material showing physical contact between male and female has been removed. Since the dialogue also goes missing in the sequences, this can render the story line hard to follow.

A Word from the Chief Censor

The level of censorship can be quite informal and unpredictable and can be subject to decisions at the highest level. In one incident, at 10:00 pm one night, King Fahd telephoned the Saudi Minister of Information, Mr Ali Al Shaer, to complain about an Indian film that was being screened. The call came through on a party line and was heard by a Lebanese newspaper editor, who reported it to the wider community. "I don't care if you are halfway through the film," the King is alleged to have said, "stop it and put on an American film instead."

If you are curious to find out what Saudi television is about and you are a non-Arabic speaker, Channel 2 broadcasts exclusively in English, except for a French-language newscast every night at 8:00 pm. Those in the Eastern Province can also receive Aramco's TV station, Channel 3. It tends to be more up-to-date than Channel 2.

State-owned and censored Saudi TV has come under intense competition in recent times from TV broadcasts by more liberal neighbours. Arab TV newscasting really made a hit with the world during the second Gulf War. Likewise, Al Jazeera, the Qatar-based news channel, presented a much more balanced view of the war than the likes of CNN. Al Jazeera had more correspondents on the ground in Iraq during the conflict and presented a ground-based view of the fighting. During this time, Al Jazeera claimed 35 million viewers and its reports made from within Iraq were carried by TV stations around the world. (According to documents subsequently released, George Bush proposed to bomb Al Jazeera in Qatar for presenting what he considered an 'anti-American' view of his war in Iraq. Allegedly, he was talked out of taking this action by British Prime Minister Tony Blair.)

A new station, Dubai-based Al-Arabiya, is broadcast on Jordan and Saudi state-owned TV and reaches a potential audience of 13 million, in addition to its satellite audience. Abu Dhabi TV is also well established and is second to Al Jazeera in popularity. Satellite TV is now widely available, allowing guest workers to stay in touch with developments back home and elsewhere. Theoretically, satellite TV is illegal in Saudi Arabia. The profusion of satellite dishes on roof tops and the walls of buildings bears testament that this provision is not widely enforced. The website AiwaGulf.com at http://www.aiwagulf.com/ent/tv/, lists 16 channels that are favourites around the world like American sports, CNN, BBC and Discovery.

For those seeking local flavour, Saudi TV soap operas and political entertainment are also available. The two state-owned TV channels in the country are likely to appeal only to those with a keen interest in Saudi culture. The standard programme is of two Saudi men having a long conversation with each other over numerous cups of coffee on a single indoor set. This curiously static performance probably quite accurately portrays the social activities of the male, unemployed coffee-house set. But it doesn't make for riveting TV, whatever the intellectual standard of the dialogue being exchanged.

In addition to TV, various radio stations broadcast a wide content in various languages. Radio AFRD, the US military station, *The Voice of the Desert*—in 1950 one of the first radio stations in the world to broadcast in FM—pioneered the idea of completely ignoring the culture of the host nation. To sooth its troops, AFRD played only a format of Western music. Radio Aramco, specialising in American country and western music like a broadcaster in backwoods Virginia, did likewise.

SHOPPING
Shopping is a major social activity for Saudis, particularly women, who otherwise tend to be housebound. Shopping

A Saudi waits for customers in his well-stocked shop.

in Saudi Arabia can be like shopping anywhere, or it can have its own distinctive flavour. Like the rest of the world, Saudi Arabia offers a choice of shopping malls, shopping plazas with Western-style supermarkets filled with familiar brand names.

In Jeddah, the Jamjoom Commercial Centre, just off the corniche, is a distinctive blue glass and chrome complex. In Riyadh, the Al-Akariyya Mall is well known for its high fashion and wide range of European merchandise. Shopping centre prices are mostly fixed, though a spot of bargaining can sometimes yield surprising results. Merchandise on sale is not quite unlimited. The normal Saudi standards of modesty apply in malls as elsewhere. Shops in the kingdom do not stock the chic merchandise that can be seen in the neighbouring countries like the UAE or Qatar.

The country has also retained its *souqs*—markets of street stalls found in every large town where gold, fabrics, wall hangings, jewellery, brass coffee pots and bric-a-brac are on sale, and the aroma of incense and spices hangs in the air.

An expatriate man accompanies his wife and mother as they go shopping in the *souq*.

Riyadh's camel market is one of the largest in the world and is said to sell about 100 camels every day.

Gold in the form of coins, small bullion bars, jewellery and ornaments is widely traded in the country.

At the *souq*, the price of almost anything is negotiable to a point known only to the vendor. If you have the patience, you can haggle down to rock bottom prices, but the process takes time and can be hard work under the pitiless Arabian sun. Serious bargaining requires certain rituals to be conducted, including walking out on your vendor's 'last price' at least a couple of times.

Feminine hygiene products do not sell well in supermarkets. Saudi women are likely to be too embarrassed to take such items to the (male) checkout 'chick'. Instead, Saudi women source their personal hygiene needs at the *souqs* specialising in these products and staffed by other women. In the Kingdom Shopping Centre in Riyadh, an exclusive floor into which men may not venture is provided for 'Ladies Only'.

If you happen to be in the market to buy a camel, the world's largest (and allegedly smelliest) camel market is situated on the outskirts of Riyadh, about 30 km (18.6 miles) from the city centre.

FOOD AND ENTERTAINING

CHAPTER 6

'Saudi Arabia's food is a reflection of the country's history
and its people's customs, religion and ways of life.'
—Ni'Mah Isma'il Nawwab, *The Culinary Kingdom*

TRADITIONAL FARE

Traditional Saudi food derives from ingredients that were available in historical times. Milk products, including yoghurt and cheese from goats, sheep and camels were animal-based staples. Dates, rice and millet were vegetable-based staples. Meat was scarce, but appreciated. Sources of meat for the Bedouin were their own animals and the occasional wild game that once lived on the Arabian Peninsula (and has since been hunted nearly to extinction). Fresh fruits and vegetables were available at oases and in the high country in the south-west.

Nowadays, diet tends to feature meat, mostly imported, as the main ingredient. Cooking methods derive from the open fires of the Bedouin. Meat is generally flame-cooked, roasted on spits, either vertical or horizontal. Dishes are often served with a rice base and served with various spiced and spicy vegetables and sauces. Most main dishes are accompanied by a great variety of *pita* or *khboz* (flat) breads that are cooked to order and eaten fresh from the baker's oven. The most common ingredient in sweets is dates, which is really Saudi Arabia's traditional foodstuff.

Saudi Arabia's water supply is a mixture of ground water (rapidly depleting) and desalinated water. Depending on the area, you may be advised to use bottled water for both drinking and cooking. Bottled water is widely available across the kingdom.

Dates are one of Saudi Arabia's traditional foodstuffs.

Stuffed Camel and Other Favourites

To amuse themselves during their not so busy hours, a group of expat women on a construction site in Saudi Arabia wrote and published a cookbook, *Stuffed Camel and Other Favourites*. The book is not currently in print, but one of the authors has a rare copy, thought to be priceless due to its scarcity value. This sample of dishes from the book is a representative sample of a few Saudi favourites:

- *Capsa* — boiled flavoured rice with chicken or mutton (probably Saudi's number one dish)
- *Shawerma* — thinly sliced lamb or chicken rolled with pickles.
- *Falafels* — deep fried balls of ground chickpeas, flavoured with garlic and herbs
- *Muhammara* — hot pepper dip
- *Salatat Bathinjan* — aubergine appetiser
- *Al-Motubug* — stuffed pastry squares
- *Adas Bil Hamod* — lentils with lemon juice
- *Hummus bi Tahina* — chickpea and sesame dip

You can get most foodstuffs in Saudi Arabia, but the one item definitely off the menu is pork. For those who must eat bacon or pork, the nearest source, at least for those on the east coast, is across the causeway in Bahrain.

RESTAURANTS

As a country that caters for its international workforce from most parts of the world, you can probably find a restaurant to enjoy your own cuisine—or anyone else's—in Saudi Arabia. Western, other Middle Eastern (e.g. Lebanese) and Asian (Indian, Thai, Filipino) food of various styles—even fish and chip shops—are all readily available. Most globalised fast food outlets are also represented in the kingdom; McDonald's, Burger King, Pizza Hut and Wendy's are just some who have operations in Saudi Arabia. In recent years, Saudis have adopted McDonald's strategy and created fast food outlets of their own, thereby undercutting the US fast food chains.

Food is inexpensive in Saudi Arabia, bearing in mind that it is mostly imported. Restaurant prices are generally reasonable. Budget meals can still be obtained for about US$ 4–5. Prices in classier establishments go up from there. Tips are not generally expected by table staff. Most restaurants levy a service charge, generally thought to be appropriated by restaurant owners instead of waiters, who tend to be underpaid.

As in most things, dining out imposes restrictions on women. The general rule is that women who are out and about should be accompanied by a male who is a close family member. Women not accompanied by an appropriate male may not be served. Arrests of women dining in restaurants unaccompanied by males, or accompanied by the incorrect male, have been reported. Many restaurants will not admit a group of women without a male guardian in attendance. Fast food outlets like McDonald's have separate sections for men and women.

The act of eating poses problems with the female dress code requiring that the only parts of a woman's face the outside world allowed on display are the eyes. Lifting the corner of the veil to allow passage of food to the mouth violates strict rules on covering. To overcome this difficulty, when dining at restaurants, Saudi women are customarily positioned at tables so they are facing the wall, whereas the men of the family will sit with their backs to the wall facing outwards. This, in theory, avoids the problem that a stranger might catch a glimpse of prohibited flesh when a female lifts her veil to allow the passage of food to the mouth. Alternatively, to ensure seclusion, individual tables in restaurants may be curtained off from other tables.

DOMESTIC HOSPITALITY

Like people elsewhere in the world, a Saudi may derive much pleasure and pride from his house. Once a Saudi gets to know you, an invitation to his home is likely to follow. Such an invitation may not merely be to enjoy the pleasure of your company. Like people elsewhere, Saudis may also be displaying to their visitors and new friends a statement of their assets, their skills at interior decorating and their status in life generally. Appreciative comments you make about the quality of the structure and the standard of the appointments will be highly valued. But be cautious with your remarks. Arab culture errs on the side of generosity. After effusive praise of some item that's not bolted to the floor, the next thing you know your Saudi host may try to give it to you! It is better to restrict your compliments to immovable objects like architecture, dining tables and carpets.

Saudis, it is probably fair to say, have a different idea of interior decorating to much of the rest of the world. Value of the artefact rather than consistency of style is the major criterion. Saudis enjoy decorating each room in all the colours of the spectrum and displaying objets d'art of many different styles. Clashes of colour and culture are the norm, not the exception. You are likely to find a valuable vase bought in Florence, coloured blue, next to an antique bronze Persian coffee set displayed on an ultra-modern anodised bronze setting in a room painted in four different colours with a patterned carpet that includes all the colours of the rainbow. Needless to say, the hospitable thing to do is to praise the display lavishly, as Saudis would of the contents of your home, whatever they really thought of them.

Central to the entertainment area of some Saudi Arabian homes is a bar. A fair number of, though not all, Saudis take an impish delight in flouting their country's prohibition laws. If a bar has been installed, it is likely to be incredibly well stocked. In a country where the street value of spirits is over US$ 100 from a black market supplier, your host will probably offer you anything that an upmarket hotel would supply.

The finishing (or lack of it) is another cultural aspect that is likely to catch the eye of those who are being invited to comment on the splendours of a Saudi house. Saudi building contractors are remarkably slack about finishing their jobs. The million-dollar display of family possessions is as likely as not to be illuminated by a naked 100-watt globe hanging from the ceiling by a frayed electrical wire. Electrical switches may protrude from the wall supported only by their wiring. On the porch of the house may lie a pile of masonry waiting collection by a civic authority that may have disbanded some years before.

Saudis seem oblivious to such incongruities. The country has not adopted a culture of tidiness. Litter abounds. Piles of masonry are likely to lie scattered beside and on the streets of expensive suburbs. Exteriors of buildings tend to have panels missing. Saudis are not maintenance conscious. If bits fall off their buildings, they are unlikely to be replaced in a hurry, if at all. Saudis are notorious in failing to service their cars, then abandoning them by the roadside when they break down.

Perhaps the attitude stems from the country's appearance as one huge building project: a nation that seems perpetually unfinished. The population of the country is growing at nearly 4 per cent per annum, which means that it's doubling every 18 years or so. City construction is proceeding at a prodigious rate to accommodate this burgeoning urban population. One of the most common vehicles on the road is the ubiquitous Mercedes truck, usually coloured grey, carrying loads of fill material to reshape the Saudi landscape in accordance with the requirements of man.

ENTERTAINING, BEDOUIN STYLE

Arabs are traditionally hospitable, outgoing people. Some of this tradition stems from the Bedouin days when custom required that any visitor who might stumble onto the campsite be offered a meal. In the days when water and food were scarce, nomads relied on mutual support for survival.

Some Bedouins adopt their nomadic ways only on a part-time basis, spending the rest of their time living a life indistinguishable from the rest of the population. A Bedouin may be a geologist, a doctor or a bell hop. Or he may be the Saudi working at the desk next to yours who will one day surprise you with his Bedouinism when he invites you out to meet his extended family camping out in the desert nearby. If you accept his invitation, your colleague may arrange a lunch in your honour. He may take you to the family tent pitched somewhere in the desert. When you arrive at the destination, having probably travelled by minibus rather than by the more traditional camel, you may observe that many of the traditions of the tribe are still in place—the tents, the goats, the sheep, and camels. Blended with traditional items are the inevitable accoutrements of the modern age—motor vehicles, portable TVs and today's most ubiquitous mandatory accessory, the cellphone. Most likely you will then spend an hour or two sitting around an enormous tray bearing a spit-roasted sheep resting on a bed of rice flavoured with raisins, nuts and spices. The meal will be washed down with cardamom-flavoured coffee served in tiny cups.

Dining practice Bedouin-style is an area where things are pretty liberal. The custom is to take food with the right hand, tearing and rolling them up in bread, rice or whatever other absorbent foods might be available, before transporting them to your mouth.

Saudis are not sticklers about their table manners. Since they use their fingers as cutlery, they are not too fussy about licking their fingers clean, though finger bowls are often provided. Eating heartily when invited to dine is considered good manners. Over indulgence isn't one of the seven deadly sins of Islamic culture. Burping appreciatively after an expansive meal verges on being considered good form. Take your cues from the other diners in this area.

Meals and coffee drinking are central to traditional Arab hospitality. Most people visiting Saudi Arabia have heard the story, thought to be factual, of the sheep's eye. According to this account, the eye of the animal being eaten is offered to the most honoured guest. The guest accepts this delicacy since refusing would create offence. (Western visitors knowledgeable on this point of etiquette will most likely endeavour not to be the honoured guest.)

On the other hand, if you charge unannounced and uninvited into a Bedouin camp (according to an Australian senior diplomat), don't be surprised if your initial greeting is a bullet, a warning shot whistling past the windscreen of your pickup. Gun culture ranks Bedouins as one of the world's most heavily armed societies. Most guns and explosives that enter the country for illicit purposes such as trading to Saudi Arabia's *jihadi* are smuggled across the 1,300 km border from Yemen. More traditionally, the smuggled commodity has been *qat*, a leafy stimulant grown in Yemen and, like the guns, also illegal in Saudi Arabia.

After the sound of the shot across the bows of the pickup dies down, the recommended procedure to demonstrate, for Arabic speakers is to announce your peaceful intentions by shouting, "*Salaam Alaikum!*" ('Peace be with you'). One word of caution though. Protocol regarding the use of the phrase *Salaam Aliakum* is rather controversial since the greeting was prescribed as a declaration of peace between believers, rather than between believers and non-believers. To avoid such cross cultural complications, it may be safer to say "Hi" or "Hello" when trying to make friends with a Bedouin pointing a smoking AK47 in your direction.

After such an intimidating introduction, the situation will most likely improve. Survival in the desert has long been precarious. The code of the desert was, and still is, to lend a helping hand to other nomads, knowing that one day you might need the favour returned. After the exchange of greetings is completed, you will most likely be invited inside the tent to drink tea or maybe partake of a feast if one is available.

COFFEE SHOPS

Streets scenes in Saudi Arabia have a European flavour, though perhaps not everyone would agree that downtown Al Khobar resembles the left bank of the Seine. But Saudi Arabian towns do share with the streetscapes of Paris the penchant for coffee shops. The sidewalk tables of coffee shops seem to spill out carelessly in all directions.

Saudis camp at these tables for what seems like an entire day sipping coffee out of tiny cups and perhaps smoking with their companions through a common rosewater filled *hookah*. Coffee shops are one of the major social outlets for the not-very-well-off of Saudi male society. These shops are the Saudi equivalent of a bar or pub in the West. A recent variant has been 'parlours', separated into booths containing a *hookah* that can be shared between its guests.

Coffee is a central feature of Saudi life. Arabian coffee is thick and sludgy, and taken in tiny cups. Other types of coffee—Turkish, American or French—are generally available if preferred. Traditionally, coffee is served in decorated brass coffee jugs with long slender spouts and delicate metal handles. The modern version of this item is a thermos flask that replicates the traditional shape. When you are offered Arab coffee, your cup will continually be refilled unless you make the appropriate gesture of refusal—shaking your cup to show you have had enough. The custom is to drink two or three cups. If you drink only one cup, you may send an unintended signal that the quality of the coffee is not quite up to scratch.

The Arab world has some claims to the invention of coffee as a beverage, although its origins are uncertain. Arabian legends of antiquity mention a 'black and bitter beverage with the powers of stimulation'. The Ethiopian region of Kaffa, according to most historians, originated coffee and supplied the basis for its name. According to this account, Arab traders brought the beans across the Red Sea into present day Yemen, to the port of Mocca (Mocha), which also became a word synonymous with coffee.

Arabs call coffee *gahwa*, a word that later became Arabic for 'that which prevents sleep'. The first coffee shops in the world were probably those which opened in Mecca around the mid-15th to 16th century. This is, in itself, curious. Under strict interpretation of the rules of Islam, consumption of coffee is prohibited since it is a stimulant. Saudis of rigid orthodoxy will not take coffee. However, the bulk of the population maintains a steady intake of the black and bitter beverage, and may, as an additional vice, even chew coffee beans while at prayer in the mosque.

ALCOHOL

In its first days as a multiracial society, prohibition against drinking alcohol in Saudi Arabia applied only to Muslims. In 1930, after a passing drunk assassinated the British Vice Consul in Riyadh, prohibition was extended to the general community, including guest workers.

Like other countries that have practised prohibition, the consumption of alcohol has not ceased but merely gone underground, in Saudi Arabia's case, not far underground. Though Saudi Arabia is a prohibition state, the authorities tolerate discreet consumption of the evil fluid of the infidel provided its production and consumption does not become too obvious. Saudis don't really care all that much whether alcohol addles the brains of its guest population. Everyone, including the Ulema, knows that violation of prohibition measures is common among the expat population and even Saudis themselves.

Amateur beer and winemaking in Saudi Arabia is a minor industry and a major interest in the lives of many expats. Supermarkets in the kingdom sell vast amounts of the four principal ingredients for home brewing—sugar, hop-flavoured malt, alcohol-free beer and grape juice. Hop-flavoured malt, ostensibly for making bread, is the key ingredient in locally brewed beer. Grape juice, sold in resealable bottles to store the final product, is the key ingredient for locally brewed wines, and provides the container for both home-brewed beer and wine. Expats organise competitions and award each other accolades for the best in home-made wine and beer. The increased security levels has made it more difficult for people living in different compounds to visit each other and a consequence of this is that illicit activities like the brewing of alcoholic beverages has been driven further underground.

In addition to home brew, a full range of spirits are available in the kingdom to all and sundry through an extensive black market. Wine is not quite so easy to get. Black market booze is a highly profitable business for the whole supply chain from the importer to the final distributor. The operation to flout the government's laws, a multi-million dollar import business that has been running for decades, could hardly be conducted without the knowledge of the consent and involvement of the highest authorities in the Department of Customs.

The Case of the Tipsy Piano

On one occasion, the story goes, a shipping container, ostensibly containing pianos, was inadvertently dropped on the wharf at a Saudi port, with remarkable side effects. The pianos appeared to be leaking. A strange liquid that smelled remarkably like Scotch whisky dripped from the base of the container—one of thousands of cargoes that have entered the country under false documentation.

Commercial spirits of every conceivable kind—whisky, gin, bourbon, whatever the market demands—enter the country by the container load and are distributed through an extensive network of dealers to consumers paying US$ 100-plus a bottle. Various stills in the country produce large quantities of hooch called *sidiqui*, which in Arabic means 'my friend'. T-shirts proclaiming, 'Sid Diqui is my friend' are popular apparel amongst Western expatriates working in the kingdom.

Discreet drinking of alcohol in the privacy of your home or someone else's home in a compound is fairly risk-free. Authorities are prepared to tolerate the home brew alcohol industry provided activities remain within expat communities. Even so, it's not a good idea to indulge in selling home-made booze, even to other expatriates. It's a much worse idea to sell booze to the Saudis. Expat 'bootleg bandits' who sell alcohol to Saudis take a big risk and, at the same time, may jeopardise the entire home brew subculture by attracting the attention of the authorities. Driving while under the influence is also a very serious offence and a very bad idea. Penalties for drugs offences are more serious again —the penalty for drug trafficking is death, and there are no exceptions.

Home Brewing and Poisoned Microbes

Though the authorities have reached a tacit agreement amongst themselves to leave the home-brewing industry alone, the Mutawa'een can be unpredictable. Occasionally people get caught and are charged. One acquaintance tells of living in a compound of expat Westerners in which wine- and beer-brewing was an established subculture. Wine and beer tastings were an accepted form of entertainment, as was an annual competition for the best wine. People had hundreds of bottles of wine and beer in cupboards around their houses, fermenting and reaching a drinkable condition. One day, a rumour circulated that the Mutawa'een were intending to raid the compound looking for alcohol. Residents were advised to unload their stocks—which they all promptly did by draining their bottles down the sink—with little thought for where the product might end up after it had been discharged into the drainage system. Shortly after a slug of alcohol arrived at the sewage treatment plant, it killed those bacteria whose role in the grand scheme of life is to eat waste products that humans must produce to stay alive, and thereby convert active sewage into harmless constituents. As a result, the sewage plant was knocked out of action for a month.

SIGHTS AND SOUNDS OF SAUDI ARABIA

CHAPTER 7

'Travel expands the behind.'
—Sir David Frost, BBC commentator,
Surviving the Climate

To a potential visitor, the image of Saudi Arabia is a country of endless desert and blistering heat. Perhaps this is an exaggeration. The daytime temperature over most of the country is ferocious in summer and most of the country is desert. But from about November to February, the weather in the area is really quite pleasant. In fact, in parts of the country, nights and early mornings can even become quite cold. Inland, in winter, the minimum temperature can drop below 0°C.

Come Spend Your Next Holiday in Saudi Arabia

An imaginary tourist brochure might advertise the charms of the Persian Gulf and Red Sea settlements in words such as these:

'... spend winter in the country where the sun shines all day long. You can book a pleasant room in a seaside hotel, take a stroll along the esplanade in the warm winter sunshine, and breathe in the exciting flavours of the east. The sea is warm, calm, clear and inviting. The beaches are sandy. The temperature outside is just right. The fresh northern breezes blowing down the Gulf cool your skin. Shopping in the *souqs* of the crowded market place is exotic and tantalising. Gold is cheap. Myrrh and frankincense are available in gallon jars. You can buy shimmering fabrics, elaborate coffee pots and the most fantastic range of jewellery. Down the road, the minarets glint in the early morning sunshine. Out on the peaceful waters of the Arabian Gulf, you can take a trip on an authentic Arabian *dhow*, just the way it was when these ships used to sail to the East to return with the fabled products of the Indies...

What a place for a holiday!'

It has to be said, few tourists are tempted by this splendid vista of mild winter weather and sparkling blue waters for the very good reason that visas are not offered to tourists except under most exceptional circumstances. Other than for pilgrims and the most intrepid adventurers, Saudi Arabia has yet to make a significant impact on the tourist map. But for guest workers, the pleasant winter conditions are there to be enjoyed, hot weather and aridity notwithstanding.

While the country is generally arid, it does rain occasionally. Riyadh, the capital, averages 81 mm (about 3 inches) annual rainfall. Jeddah, on the Red Sea coast averages 50 mm (about 2 inches). What rain there is falls as brief winter downpours that disappear rapidly into the thirsty sands which, a few days later, may display a tinge of green. Life in the desert is nothing if not tenacious.

In paved areas, storm drainage systems range from inadequate to non-existent. Many buildings have been built below street level. For a day or so, passing clouds that stray from their normal flight paths can turn arid Arabian towns into quagmires. After a cloudburst, traders patiently bail out their stores and wait for normal weather conditions to return. So before setting off for Saudi Arabia, don't forget to pack your umbrella! This item is not readily available within the kingdom for the few days when it is needed.

For visitors from more temperate climes, the sight of rain may be a reminder of an event they never thought they'd miss. The noonday sun is not the only climatic phenomenon into which mad dogs and Englishmen venture. English expats working in Saudi Arabia to escape from the weather back home have been known to immerse themselves into these brief and occasional storms, to perform a dance of gratitude to the rain god.

The other distinctive climate feature in Saudi Arabia is wind. The prevailing wind, the north-westerly *shammal*, rises in the mountains of Turkey and blows down the axis of the Arabian Peninsula. A less frequent wind, the *qaw*, sometimes blows with equal force from the opposite direction. When winds blowing across deserts reach a certain strength, they start to pick up sand. *Shammal* has become Saudi Arabia's

Shammals are north-westerly winds that can pick up force and cause sandstorms.

generic term for a full on sandstorm, from whichever direction it blows.

Walking around in a *shammal* in daylight hours is an eerie experience. Your world is suddenly reduced to monochromatic orange. No features are visible. The sun is blotted out and complete disorientation is but a step away but for one thing—you can navigate by the direction of the wind. *Shammals* can last for periods ranging from a few hours to days. Millions of tonnes of desert migrate this way and that in a swirling sand curtain that may extend one hundred feet into the air. Sand settles everywhere and anywhere. It gets into your house through the smallest crack. Possessions inside and outside buildings get covered with a fine grit. If the winds are high, painted objects like cars may be sandblasted back to bare metal. In coping with *shammals*, the ancient rule of the Bedouins still applies: during a *shammal*, rug up and stay inside.

WHAT DAY IS IT?

At certain times of the year, figuring out the date may be a little more difficult in Saudi Arabia than in other places. The basic units of time—the second, the hour, the day and the seven-day week—originated thousands of years ago by the early Sumerians, are the same in the kingdom as they are elsewhere. To measure the span of its years, Saudi Arabia has adopted the Islamic lunar calendar with a starting date in AD 622, the year the Prophet Muhammad fled Mecca for Medina, an event known as the Hejira. Islamic years are denoted as 'AH' or Anno Hejira, just as 'AD' means 'Anno Domino', the Latin phrase meaning years since the birth of Christ.

Based on the lunar cycle of the moon's orbit of 29.53 days, the Islamic calendar alternates 29- and 30-day months. The Islamic year has 354.36 days—the time taken by the moon to make 12 earthly revolutions. The fractional day is accommodated with a leap year of 355 days at three-year intervals to synchronise the orbital period of the moon with the rotational period of the earth. Further, finer adjustments to align the third and fourth decimal points of the lunar and solar orbits are made at longer periods. This is similar to the one-day adjustment made to the Gregorian calendar every 400 years.

Because the Islamic year is shorter than the Gregorian year, Islamic months occur either ten or 11 days earlier in the solar year than they were the year before. The entire cycle of days between the two calendars takes about 32.5 solar years (33.5 lunar years) to complete.

Another effect of the shorter lunar year is that the gap between the two calendars is narrowing. The year 2003 on the Gregorian calendar was the year 1424 on the Muslim calendar (or most of it was!). The original difference between the two calendar years has narrowed from 622 at the start to 579 at present. The gap will continue to close. Years showing on the two calendars will momentarily coincide on the first day of May in the year AD 20,874 which will also be the first day of the fifth month (Jumada al-awwal) of the year 20,874 AH on the Islamic calendar. After that, the Islamic calendar will show more years than the Gregorian. Or perhaps by then, both calendars will have ceased to exist.

For those who need to know what day it is, Saudi Arabian timekeeping has an additional complication. In line with ancient practices, the official start of the new month is not determined by the number of days that have elapsed since the month started, but by the sighting of the new moon. For a new month to start, the crescent sliver has to be observed not merely by some ordinary mortal but the particular *mullah* in a particular observatory.

Sighting the New Moon

Until the official eye has observed the new moon and broadcast this news to the community, no new month can start. Words from the website of Dr Monzur describe the drawbacks of this method:

'Islamic months begin at sunset on the day of visual sighting of the lunar crescent. Even though visual sighting is necessary to determine the start of a month, it is useful to accurately predict when a crescent is likely to be visible in order to produce lunar calendars in advance. Although it is possible to calculate the position of the moon in the sky with high precision, it is often difficult to predict if a crescent will be visible from a particular location. Visibility depends on a large number of factors including weather conditions, the altitude of the moon at sunset, the closeness of the moon to the sun at sunset, the interval between sunset and moonset, atmospheric pollution, the quality of the eyesight of the observer, use of optical aids etc. Since ancient times, many civilisations and astronomers have tried to predict the likelihood of visualising the new moon using different 'minimum visibility criteria'. However, all these criteria are subject to varying degrees of uncertainty.'

As official literature on the subject describes, the new month may not begin on time for a hundred different reasons: the skies above the official astronomer may be cloudy, the telescope could be out of action, the official astronomer may have mislaid his glasses, and so on. Months may start a day or two behind schedule, which can play havoc with schedules of all sorts.

The problem is felt most acutely during Ramadan, the month everyone wants to end at the earliest possible moment. Without the official observation from the official observer, Ramadan continues, and Eid-el-Fitr—the holidays of feasting– cannot begin. This unpredictability of the religious culture plays its minor havoc in the modern world, particularly at airports. Though airports operate on the Gregorian calendar, support services may not. Day one of Eid-el-Fitr is not a good date to plan your exit from the country.

The Islamic Calendar

The 12 lunar month Muslim calendar runs as follows.

First Month	Muharram
Second Month	Safar
Third Month	Rabi'al-awwal (Rabi' I)
Fourth Month	Rabi'al thani (Rabi'II)
Fifth Month	Jumada al-awwal (Jumada I)
Sixth Month	Jumada al-thani (Jumada II)
Seventh Month	Rajab
Eighth Month	Sha'aban
Ninth Month	Ramadam
Tenth Month	Shawwal
Eleventh Month	Dhu al-Qi'dah
Twelfth Month	Dhu al-Hijjah

PUBLIC HOLIDAYS

All but one of the holidays in Saudi Arabia are observed on specific days of the Muslim calendar. The exception is Saudi National Day which is observed on a specific day of the Gregorian calendar (23 September).

Public Holidays in Saudi Arabia

1 Muharran	Islamic New Year (First day of Muslim Calendar)
12 Rab'al-awal	Birthday of Prophet Muhammad
1 Shawwal	Eid-el Fitr (Feasting at end of Ramadan)
Variable date	Jenadriyah National Festival (Festival lasts about ten days and celebrates the founding of Saudi Arabia by King Ibn Saud)
23 September	Saudi National Day
19 Dhu Al'Hijjah	Eid al-Adah (Feasting day celebrating the pilgrimage to Mecca and the sacrifice by Abraham of his son)

Since the Islamic calendar is based on the 354/355-day year, from one year to the next, on the Gregorian calendar each of these holidays (except Saudi National Day) is either ten or 11 days earlier than the year before on the Gregorian calendar.

ARCHITECTURE

The austerity of the Arabian Peninsula contrasts with the splendours that history supplied on the other side of the Red Sea. Despite Egypt's proximity, no one built pyramids in Arabia. Nothing was built to compare with the Hanging Gardens of Babylon just over the northern border. With no administrative focal point in the region and little permanent agriculture, the nomads of Arabia lived on the move, leaving only limited physical evidence on the landscape to mark their passage. Nevertheless, with the antiquity of its civilisation and the incessant travelling of the Bedouin, pottery remnants are commonplace across the desert sands. A fossicking trip into the desert often yields something of historical interest.

Likewise the conquerors of the Arabian Peninsula who came and went left behind them only a few physical structures. Of the foreign invaders, the Turks established permanent footholds that have lasted through to the present day. The low forts and houses they built had thick walls and slits for windows to deal with the heat. On both coastlines, coral was the principal building material and usually coated with a hard lime plaster. Further inland, mud brick buildings are found in the central Nejd Plateau. Buildings up in the mountainous regions, where rainfall is higher, are built with stone plastered over with mud or lime. Only a few major stone buildings, of which the Grand Mosque of Mecca and the Prophet's Mosque in Medina are the standout examples, bear testament to the splendours of Arabia's finest hour—the Islamic empire of the Middle Ages.

At the beginning of the 20th century, only a few trading posts dotted the gulf coastline. Jeddah, Mecca and Medina were the settlements of the west. Riyadh was an oasis township surrounded by low mud brick walls.

Most of the infrastructure of Saudi Arabia has been built in the last 50 years. With the globalisation of architectural standards, the downtown parts of Saudi cities—made up of high-rise buildings—may remind you of any place you have

The past and the present. The remnant mud-dwellings (left) in the city of Di'iyyah, the first Saudi capital is a far cry from the modern architecture (right) that can now be seen in the kingdom's current capital of Riyadh.

ever been. Yet, architectural design elements that are distinctly eastern convey an Arabic flavour that reminds you where you really are. Saudi Arabia has some spectacularly graceful buildings combining spires, minarets, domes, and highly decorated arches that are all unmistakeably Arabic. Stylised arabesque calligraphy and intricate geometric carvings are worked onto external surfaces. Domes in striking blue, green, yellow or gold make interesting features. Ochre renderings in red mixed with brown and white complement the austere desert surroundings and soften the harsh desert light.

Amongst buildings worth seeing in Saudi Arabia are the King Khaled International Airport and the Ministry of the Interior building in Riyadh, and the Humane Heritage Museum in Jeddah. Various mosques built along traditional lines, with minarets and slender towers, are also lovely buildings. The finest mosque of all—the Grand Mosque of Mecca—is unfortunately off limits to all but card-carrying Muslims.

MUSEUMS
The country is not known for its antiquities since so few permanent structures were built. The largely nomadic

ancestors didn't leave a lot of physical remains behind to mark their passage through life. Nevertheless, Saudi Arabia does have a few museums of good standard. Principal among them is the Riyadh Museum in the Department of Antiquities office. Displays at the Riyadh Museum are the history and archaeology of the Arabian Peninsula from the beginnings of settlement through to the golden age of Islam. Jeddah also has a couple of museums worth visiting if you are in the area—the Municipality Museum and the Museum of Abdul Raouf Hasan Khalil. The former is in a restored traditional house and is the only surviving building of the early 20th century British Legation in Jeddah. (In 1917, T E Lawrence, aka Lawrence of Arabia stayed at the Legation.) The Museum of Abdul Raouf Hassan Khalil is a private museum and has over 10,000 items displayed in four houses.

LITERARY AND VISUAL ARTS

Sometime in the 8th century, paper made its way from China to Baghdad and from there to the rest of Arabia. A paper mill was built in Baghdad around this time. Later, the Arabs introduced paper to Europe, trading it for scarce metals. In the holy cities of Mecca and Medina, the printing and publishing of the Qur'an and other religious and philosophical books were important industries that serviced the period when the Arab dominions led the world in science, mathematics, astronomy and medicine.

The Mongol conquest in the 13th century started the decline of Arab literature. Later during the Ottoman conquest, Arab literature took flight in Egypt and Lebanon. Reverting to its Bedouin ways, Saudi Arabia lost its culture of literacy. Nomadic Bedouins travelled light, relying on oral traditions of storytellers reciting tales. Paper did not return into Saudi Arabia in significant quantities until the 20th century. Though the kingdom is not noted for an enormous volume of literature, arguably its best known pulication, the Qur'an, is the most influential book of all time. Outside Medina, the government runs a giant press printing around 10 million Qur'ans each year in 40 languages. The books are distributed free throughout the world.

In recent times, novelists writing about life inside contemporary Saudi Arabia are bound by the same strictures as the rest of society. Saudi Arabia is not a country where critics of the system fare well. In the case of popular Saudi novelist Abdelrahman Munif, not only was his *Cities of Salt* trilogy banned for being critical of the House of Saud, but the author was stripped of his Saudi nationality as well!

Like literature, other outlets for artistic expression are also controlled. In a country run by clerics, it probably comes as no surprise that the clergy determines the rules of painting. Once more the Qur'an has something to say on this subject. Images of real objects are not favoured. You will see no pictures of sweeping desert scenes hanging in Saudi houses. Saudi custom prohibits the painting of what are loosely described as naturally occurring objects—people, animals, or scenery in general. Saudi art is restricted to calligraphy and its extensions, of which there are some fine examples. In Arabic, letters and geometrical shapes that look like letters weave intricate patterns that are unmistakably Middle Eastern. Saudi art with its geometrical patterns tends to resemble Eastern carpets and vice versa. Such art is liberally applied to many surfaces—plates, canvases, plaques, tiles, textiles, sculptures and wall hangings.

The rules of the clerics also fashion the performing arts. It hardly needs to be said that female dance is prohibited in Saudi Arabia. The Royal Ballet never books Riyadh on its tours of the world. No performance of *Hair* is ever likely to be staged in the kingdom. However, performance of Saudi Arabia's traditional dance, the *ardha*, is allowed. This dance has military origins and features barefooted males clad in their normal street clothes of *thobe* and *gutra* jumping up and down mostly in one spot while wielding swords. Parents be warned! This is not a dance that should be performed by your own children in your own home.

Music is not banned in the kingdom. On the other hand, no visiting rock band has been known to perform in Saudi Arabia. But the dictates of the Qur'an do allow some forms of traditional music to be performed. Arabian music is probably an acquired taste. The traditional musical

Saudis making music with traditional instruments.

instruments of Saudi Arabia are those of the Bedouin—the tambourine (*rigg*), drum and stringed instruments—the *oud* and the *rebaba*, which muster four strings between them. Another interesting traditional song and dance known as the *al-mizmar* is performed in Mecca, Medina and Jeddah. The dance features the music of the *al-mizmar*, a woodwind instrument bearing the same name as the dance and similar to the oboe.

FINDING YOUR WAY AROUND

Since tourist facilities in Saudi Arabia are underdeveloped in most Saudi cities, finding your way to a building you have not visited before is not easy. Streets are poorly sign-posted if at all, and addresses are not well numbered. Street directories are non-existent for most places, though street maps may be available for the larger cities. Even if street maps are available, many of the minor streets and alleys will not be marked. Since street names are poorly marked and difficult to read with poor language skills, a common sort of direction from the person you are visiting is likely to be: "I live in such and such street opposite such and such a landmark." Before setting out on a journey you haven't made before, it's a good idea to make your own map if you can, including marking on it some prominent landmarks by which to navigate.

THE SAUDI ARABIAN COUNTRYSIDE

Not all that many guest workers bother to go sightseeing when in Saudi Arabia. Many never journey further astray than the road between their compounds and the nearest airport. If they travel within the country at all, they usually do so by air.

However, driving over the nation's highways is an entirely practical adventure. Saudi Arabia is a large country and sparsely populated between its major cities. Travel by car is swift. Motel-style accommodation is reasonably available. Failing that, more adventurous spirits can camp under the stars, which are spectacular away from the towns.

The countryside has its own austere charm, but the normal precautions of desert travel apply. Don't stray far off major roads. Preferably, travel in convoys of at least two vehicles in case of accidents. Take spare parts such as fan belts, engine oil, petrol and water. In case you get stranded, take food rations plus plenty of drinking water. Take some warm clothes too—the desert airs can get chilly at night. And take plenty of documentation that will testify who you are.

Except for off-limit religious areas like Mecca, you are free to travel wherever you wish, though you are meant to carry appropriate documentation. In this regard, bureaucratic obstacles are steep and numerous. Since while in the kingdom the employer holds the passport of the employee, the fundamental document of ID is not available to the traveller. As a substitute (and many people don't bother), non-Saudis travelling within the kingdom are meant to carry letters from employers authorising their travel and authenticated by an immigration official or a Chamber of Commerce office.

Rules are always changing (and may do so while you are in transit!). People who want to travel should ascertain the appropriate travel documentation before commencing their journey. In theory at least, those who get caught without the appropriate paperwork and can't convince the arresting officer to take a lenient view, are liable to Saudi Arabia's customary punishment—imprisonment for an unspecified period.

Once en route to your destination, you pass through countryside that holds few surprises. You are picked up from, say, King Fahd Airport in Dhahran in the Eastern Province. In the town itself, a few eucalypts—now the world's most ubiquitous tree—line the sidewalks. (Eucalypts seem to be the tree in general global use for areas in which no other tree will grow.)

If you happen to be driving through the heat of the day, the light is intense. Passing out of town, you drive past rock formations that may well remind you of pictures beamed from the Sea of Tranquillity by Apollo astronauts: interesting rock formations, quite appropriate as a moonscape; but for earthbound mortals, starkly austere. Further out of town, bare rock gives way to deserts of small dunes. The eastern side of the country is flat and monotonous.

From Dhahran, you can head up the eastern highway north towards Kuwait, through Jubail and Ras'al Khafji. The other choices of highways from Dhahran are south through the oasis town of Al Hufuf towards the UAE, or west through Riyadh to the Red Sea coast. Roads in Saudi Arabia are elevated to prevent sand building up on the bitumen surface. The surface is high enough that the sand is blown across the road instead of being deposited. Incidentally, driving through a sandstorm is not advised. Not only is visibility reduced to near zero, but the wind-driven sand can eat up your paintwork very rapidly.

Whichever way you are travelling, the initial scenery is similar. In the first part of the journey, the road passes through the coastal plain, low dunes that are flat and featureless. The black road snakes ahead over a pale orange landscape. Perhaps you will see an occasional palm tree or perhaps the low dunes may sport sparse tufts of marram grass. Here and there amongst dunes, the flared gas of an oil well shoots a tongue of red flame and a contrail of dirty gas into the sky. But mostly the vista is endless sand in various shades of yellow, orange and red.

The most interesting landscapes as well as the major historical icons are to be found in the western half of the country, in particular the south-west. As you head west, the country the landscape crinkles into the ranges that run along the western seaboard. Towards the Yemen border, the road winds through high hills and relatively fertile valleys atypical of the rest of the country. To the north, the highway heads up to the Jordan border, sometimes through rolling arid countryside, sometimes along the coastal plain.

Places of Interest
Riyadh

Riyadh is the capital of Saudi Arabia with a population of nearly 5 million. Riyadh took over from Jeddah as Saudi Arabia's most important and largest city in the 1970s. The city is a stronghold of religious zeal. Wahhabism had its origins in this area. The Committee for the Preservation of Virtue and for the Prevention of Vice, The Ministry of Religious Affairs and the Mutawa'een have their headquarters here.

The city sits in a basin surrounded by barren mountain ranges. It is sited on one of Saudi Arabia's largest oases formed at the confluence of three underground rivers, called *wadis*. In past eras, desert travellers sought Riyadh as a welcome staging post of trees, gardens and parks in the centre of a vast desert. Desert travellers could trade their wares for dates and other fruit from Riyadh's ample gardens. Today, the city is still known for its greenery, though not enough underground water is now available to sustain either its population or its vegetation. Riyadh is supplied by desalinated water piped from Jubail, 400 km (290 miles) to the east, through one of the world's largest water pipeline systems.

One hundred years ago, Riyadh—surrounded by low sandstone walls—was a city small enough to be conquered by King Ibn Saud and his 40 stalwarts armed with the best in breech-loading rifles that the British arsenal could supply. Today, remnants of the old city walls remain as a tourist attraction. But the modern city has sprawled well beyond its original boundaries. It is a modern city, having been substantially built from the 1960s. From an oasis in the more traditional sense, Riyadh has become an oasis of high-rise. The infrastructure and standard of accommodation and facilities is good. Being near the centre of the Arabian Desert, the city is hot in summer and subject to a wide temperature range between day and night.

Jeddah

Jeddah (alternatively spelt as Jiddah) is the commercial capital of Saudi Arabia and the country's second largest city with a population of over 2.5 million. Jeddah is the kingdom's major seaport and dates from pre-Islamic times as a fishing settlement which later became a transit point for the spice trade and a gateway to Mecca. During the centuries of occupation by the Ottoman Turks, Jeddah became a fortified walled town. Fragments of the original city remain, though 20th century developers have demolished most of the historical structures as a source of building materials.

Jeddah's most famous landmark is the floodlit corniche that separates the main commercial area from the Red Sea coast. The city also features what is claimed to be the world's tallest fountain and some bizarre sculptures that are worth seeing including a giant steel fist mounted on a granite block, a penny farthing bicycle as high as a four-storey building and crashed Cadillacs sticking out of a three-storey high building and featuring tail lights that illuminate at night.

As Saudi Arabia's most cosmopolitan city, trade through Jeddah has, to a degree, eroded the religious strictures of Saudi Arabian theocracy. Jeddah is about as free and easy as it gets in Saudi Arabia.

Taif

Taif, Saudi Arabia's 'summer capital' is located in the Hijaz Mountains, a spectacular two-hour drive from Jeddah. Standing at about 2,000 metres (6,000 ft) elevation, Taif has a pleasant year-round climate with mild summers (25–30°C / 64–90°F) and cool winters that sometimes get below freezing. The normal population of Taif is around 400,000. Population doubles during summer with an influx of vacationers escaping the heat elsewhere in the country. Taif is a typical Saudi Arabian city of contrasting old and new. Glass-clad modern buildings, several stories high, rise cheek by jowl with the old mud plastered stone structures with wooden louvred windows and carved wooden doors. The city is located in the high rainfall area of Saudi Arabia (around 400 mm or 16 inches annual precipitation). As a result, the surrounding countryside is less barren and supports agriculture. in particular vegetable gardens. The traditional Bedouin *souqs* are well known amongst collectors of Bedouin wares such as pottery, jewellery and carpets.

Mecca

Mecca, Islam's holy city with a population of 1.5 million, is a jumble of high-rise buildings. Fast growth in religious tourism from overseas pilgrims who can afford airfares into Saudi Arabia has propelled land prices in Mecca to amongst the highest in the world.

> *The Economist* comments on land prices in Mecca: 'Mecca is getting ready for another boom. Land prices of $60,000 per square metre are many times more than in other expensive places such as Hong Kong.'

For all that, Mecca is a major tourist attraction to the Muslims allowed to go there. In developing Mecca, the Saudi municipal authorities have not been particularly fussy about preserving their antiquities. On the hill of Ajyad district, an 18th century Ottoman Fort—built as a defence against Wahab maurauders—has been demolished to make way for seven apartment towers, six huge hotels and a four-storey shopping centre. In the Mount of Omar District, developers plan to clear many of the old buildings and build 120 residential towers, each 20 stories high and able to accommodate a total of 100,000 people. A further five massive development projects, due for completion in 2008, will add 50 per cent capacity to Mecca's housing market. Facing the gate of the main mosque, Saudi bin Laden is building a mammoth complex of skyscrapers for the Al Saud family.

Medina

Medina, with a population of around 800,000, is Saudi Arabia's other holy city. Situated about 400 km (250 miles) north of Mecca, Medina is the city to which the Prophet Muhammad retreated after he was persecuted by the establishment at Mecca, and which later became his burial place. For that reason, it is an important destination for religious tourists. The city is situated on a plateau, about 700 metres (2,300 feet) in elevation, in the low mountain range that runs along the western seaboard of the country. Medina's most important building is the Prophet's Mosque. South of Medina and worth a visit for historical interest are the plains of Badr, the battlefield where Muhammad fought his most successful campaign against the army of his Meccan enemies.

Dammam

Dammam and Al Khobar are separate townships that have joined at the edges. The third adjacent town, Dhahran—the site of the first of the country's oilfields—was built mostly by Aramco as accommodation for the oil workers who developed the oil installations on the country's Eastern Province. Dammam, Al Khobar and, to a lesser extent, Dhahran can be regarded as a single settlement. The cities, built on the Persian Gulf shore, have a long history as trading posts. They are an interesting mixture of the old and the new, with *souqs* and crumbling mud-brick structures giving way to shopping malls and high-rise.

HOTELS

Most hotels in Saudi Arabia are in the mid to expensive range. Hotels in Riyadh are usually slightly less expensive than those found in many major European cities. Budget hotels can also be found in Saudi Arabia but, generally speaking, the bottom end of the hotel market is not well served. This is not a country to which backpackers flock in droves. The best information to be had for the low end of the market is to be found in publications like the *Lonely Planet* series. Hotel information for those making *hajj* and *umrah* pilgrimages may be obtained from tour operators specialising in this business or at websites such as http://www.islamic-travel.ch/. For more general information on all classes of hotel accommodation, try:

- http://asiatravel.com/saudi/index.html
- http://www.hotelstravel.com/saudi.html

TRAVEL BY TRAIN

By the time Saudi Arabia got around to developing its infrastructure, air travel was well established over most of the planet. Having made the great leap forward from the 10th century to the 20th century in a single bound, and jumping right over the 19th century in the process, Saudi Arabia never got around to developing a rail system of any consequence. Instead, they built roads and airports.

The total length of rail in the country is less than 2,000 km. The major railway line is that between Riyadh and Dammam which is used almost exclusively for freight. But that could change in years to come if the government carries through its rail development plan by building new lines. On the drawing board is a cross-country rail network with links between Riyadh and Jeddah (945 km or 587 miles); Dammam and Jubail (115 km or 71 miles); Riyadh and the Hudaitha border post with Jordan (610 km or 379 miles); and Mecca and Medina (425 km or 264 miles).

A site of interest for *Lawrence of Arabia* enthusiasts is the Hijaz railway built by the Ottomans that connected Damascus in Syria to Medina. Lawrence and his troop of Bedouins blew it up during World War I on the Jordanian side of the border. The event was famously depicted in the 1962 movie, *Lawrence of Arabia*. Remnants of the railway are still visible on the Saudi side.

TRAVEL BY AIR

According the CIA website (which provides the most easily accessible statistical thumbnail sketches of the countries of the world), in the year 2004, Saudi Arabia had 201 airports, including military airports. Of these, four are international airports, located at Riyadh, Dhahran, Jeddah and Jubail.

The national airline of Saudi Arabia is Saudi Arabian Airlines (Saudia), operates both domestic and international services. In its earlier days, Saudia earned a reputation for eccentricity within the industry. In the 1960s and 1970s, it suffered a rash of minor but newsworthy accidents. Stories, possibly apocryphal, circulated of travelling Bedouins attempting to barbecue their own meals in the aisles while the planes were airborne and pilots taking their hands off the controls during electrical storms and leaving things to fate. Since those days, the safety statistics of Saudia have been excellent. The airline has earned itself a Rating 1 on the US Federal Airports Authority's safety assessment programme.

Local Rules on Flying

Saudia still maintains its reputation as an anachronistic airline. No alcohol is served on Saudia flights, either within Saudi Arabian airspace or internationally. During the daylight hours of Ramadan, packaged food is handed out, but cannot be eaten. The cabin crew advises passengers to take the food off the plane and eat it after dark. In addition to the normal pre-take off safety features announcements, after the safety features are identified and prior to take-off, a video is screened offering prayers for a safe trip. The policy seems to be working. No planes have crashed in recent times.

Air travel within the country on Saudia is configured for business passengers rather than the economy class tourist industry that is more common in other parts of the world. Other than for conveying Muslims to their religious destinations, demand for tourism class airflight within Saudi Arabia is limited. Flying around Saudi Arabia by Saudia is considered expensive by international standards. According to one account, one reason for this is that minor Saudi princes have developed a practice of flying liberally within the kingdom, displaying their Royal credentials to booking staff, rather than buying a ticket. The revenue shortfall from this act of royal self-indulgence is recovered as a 'royalty' levy from less distinguished passengers. Hence the higher ticket prices.

THE NUMBER ONE ATTRACTION

The principal industry in Saudi Arabia is oil. A trivial pursuit question guaranteed to stump all but the most inveterate Middle Eastern buffs is the identity of the country's second biggest industry.

The answer is—tourism.

At first glance, tourism might seem a small scale industry in Saudi Arabia. With one exception, the only visas available

to Saudi Arabia are those associated with work permits and business visas. Nevertheless, a significant number of Saudis make their living from this one exception. Tourism, Saudi Arabia's fastest growing industry with annual revenues to the order of US$ 3 billion with over 3 million tourists a year, is based on the pilgrimage to Mecca that Muslims are encouraged to make once in their lifetime.

The Hajj Business

In recent years, businesses associated with the *hajj* pilgrimage have become the fastest growing sector of the economy, employing four times as many employees as the oil industry. Since Islam is now a global phenomenon, and with the easy availability of air travel, the yearly influx of pilgrims has expanded past anything that could have been envisaged by Islam's founder. In December 2002, Hajj Deputy Minister Hatim bin Hassan Gadi noted that 'the *hajj* season creates about 40,000 temporary jobs for Saudis. Positions include butchers, barbers and coach drivers.'

Pilgrimage to Mecca is an ancient rite that extends well into pre-Islam days. The star attraction then (as it is today) was Islam's most sacred icon, the Hajar ul Aswad, the black stone of Mecca. The *hajj* was an idea adopted from older religions.

A *hajj* pilgrimage is quite unlike most people's idea of a holiday. It is hot, tiring and hazardous work. Mandatory pilgrim activities include hours of walking, a great deal of praying, much queuing and incessant crowds. Each pilgrim must perform a series of intricate rituals in strict chronological order, and at certain days of the holy month of Dhu al-Hijjah.

Pilgrims are required to perform a number of rituals during the *hajj*, many of which are symbolic of Abraham's journey in the desert. Pilgrims must cut their hair at the appropriate time and to the appropriate length. They must throw pebbles at the Jamrah—three stone pillars in Mina, the nearest monument to Mecca—a certain number in the correct order and at particular times during the *hajj*. (The stone pillars are meant to be symbols of evil. Bombarding them with pebbles is thought to purge the stone thrower of whatever evil resides in the pilgrim's soul). Pilgrims must also touch the sacred Hajar ul Aswad and walk around its containing structure, the Ka'bah, a prescribed number of times in certain directions. Live animals must be sacrificed according to methods specified by the Prophet. (Saudi Arabia imports six million live sheep each year to be slaughtered at Mecca for this purpose.) Between these activities is interposed a great deal of praying. The entire process takes up to two weeks, with the result that Mecca gets pretty crowded during the pilgrim season.

Throughout history, merchants around Mecca have made a living from the once-yearly influx of tourists. Local commercial tradition seems to demand that pilgrims are fleeced in one way or another while on their pilgrimages. Non-Arab pilgrims from countries like Pakistan, Malaysia or Indonesia— foreigners who are unfamiliar with local customs and prices—are particularly targeted since they can be overcharged with little resistance. More indirect means are

Pilgrims flock to the Al-Masjid Al-Haram (Grand Mosque) in Mecca each year.

also applied to relieving pilgrims of their money and their possessions. One of the requirements of the pilgrimage is that pilgrims must leave their possessions behind in a camp somewhere on making the final leg into the Grand Mosque. This is an opportunity for pilfering (though the more savvy pilgrims discretely wear money belts around their bodies).

During his pilgrimage, the pilgrim faces a number of physical hazards to life and limb. For example, the pillars of evil, the Jamrah, are contained in a pit surrounded by a low stone wall that can be approached, and stoned, from all points of compass. On occasions, poor aim and over-enthusiastic throwing have taken out a number of fellow pilgrims standing on the opposite side of the pit. Another risk is being crushed by crowds of excited individuals pressing forward against the circular wall in which the Jamrah resides. Over the years, large numbers of pilgrims have been crushed or stoned at this site with fatal results.

The gathering of tribes with historical enmities also raises tensions. Pilgrims from within Arabia itself may come from other tribes with whom the natives of Hijaz are traditionally not on speaking terms. Shi'ite pilgrims from countries like Iran are denounced as heretics by the extreme elements of Saudi clergy. Many Shi'ites have been officially executed over the years as a result of their pilgrimages, and others have been killed more casually. In 1991, the Saudi papers quoted Abdallah bin Jibreen, King Fahd's appointment in clerical ideology, describing Shia believers as 'idolaters who deserve to be killed'. In making their pilgrimages, Shi'ites are venturing into enemy territory.

Open warfare had broken out on occasions. In November 1979, after the Shia inspired revolution in Iran, a force of about 300 Wahhabi fanatics led by religious activist, Juhayman Otteibi stormed the Grand Mosque of Mecca in a bid to overthrow the Saudi Royal Family and start an Islamic revolution. The dissidents charged that corruption and close ties to the West had cost the Al Saud regime its legitimacy to govern. The fanatics held the mosque for ten days despite attempts by the Saudi military to recapture it. The situation was becoming internationally embarrassing and the Saudis called in overseas support. French paratroopers regained control, first by flooding the Grand Mosque, then by electrifying the water. More than 100 fanatics and 127 Saudi police died in a shoot-out. Surviving dissidents and suspected dissidents were later publicly beheaded throughout the cities and towns of Saudi Arabia. For the benefit of those unable to attend these beheadings in person, executions were broadcast live on Saudi TV.

In July 1987, another fight broke out between pilgrims and the Saudi authorities. Iranian Shi'ite pilgrims to Mecca clashed with Saudi police and the casualty list from the engagement numbered 400 killed with many more injured. After another major riot of Shia pilgrims in 1989, Saudi Arabia cut off diplomatic relations with Iran.

Some pilgrims to Mecca escaped death at the hand of man only to succumb to the hand of God. In 1990, a tunnel packed with pilgrims collapsed resulting in a total death toll of around 1,400. A further 270 pilgrims died in 1994, crushed in an accidental stampede. In 1997, about 340 Muslim pilgrims were burned to death when their campsite near Mecca caught fire. Two more stampedes during the stoning ritual in 1998 and 2001 saw a further 150 pilgrims killed.

In view of the recurring high casualty rate, Muslims from countries outside Saudi Arabia have queried whether Saudi Arabia has the infrastructure and organisational skills to host the annual influx of pilgrims. But the pilgrimages continue. Despite the hazards, the number of pilgrims increases each year. Some travel agents in Islamic countries outside the kingdom specialise in *hajj* tourism. Kuala Lumpur, for example, has a multi-storey building dedicated to arranging *hajj* tours for its pilgrims. Travel agents offer their Muslim clients a full 14-day Mecca/Medina experience, including detailed guides on how to discharge their *hajj* obligations. Package tours offer the obligatory rituals at Mecca along with side trips, such as visiting Muhammad's tomb at Medina. Guided tours take the pilgrims to the various religious sites at the appropriate times.

With the *hajj* now a major industry involving millions of customers, far more people arrive to perform their *hajj* obligations than the holy icons at Mecca can easily accommodate. Given the overwhelming demand for the *hajj* from rapidly expanding Muslim populations across the globe, the intricate rituals that pilgrims undertake at various sacred icons have become bottlenecks. Management studies have been conducted to investigate ways of speeding up pilgrim throughput. Saudi authorities encouraged religious scholars to be more flexible in interpreting pilgrims' religious obligations.

One obvious measure that could be taken is to extend the pilgrim season. The basis for this idea is the *umrah*, which is a simplified version of the *hajj*. While the *umrah* incorporates many of the elements of the *hajj*, it is not accepted as the full substitute. But the *umrah* has great advantage over the *hajj* that it can be performed during the entire year. According to *The Economist*, *umrah* travel is now growing at 10 per cent annually with three-quarters of a million *umrah* pilgrims coming from Egypt to visit the holy cities of Mecca and Medina.

To expand facilities for pilgrims and ease the burdens of pilgrimage, the Saudi government has spent more than US$ 35 billion since the mid-1960s in improving infrastructure at Mecca. Despite these improvements the government has been forced to restrict the number of tourist visas it issues. Each Muslim nation has a quota of about one *hajj* visa for every 1,000 Muslim citizens, meaning that during the course of their lives, Muslims have only a 4 per cent chance of fulfilling one of the pillars of their faith. Despite the difficulties, the risks and the costs, the demand for pilgrimages exceeds the availability of visas. Not only is the *hajj* one of the five pillars of faith, becoming a *hajji*, the term for a pilgrim who has successfully performed the *hajj* obligation, is also a badge of honour.

Non-pilgrim Travel

Saudis recognise that the leisure tourism industry outside the *hajj* pilgrimage is heavily net cash negative. Cashed-up Saudis travel overseas to spend the country's money and not too much is coming the other way. One objective in promoting

Saudi tourism had been to make travel within the country more attractive to the Saudis themselves. Another has been a tentative attempt to attract non-*hajj* tourists.

While demand for Muslim pilgrimage has reached saturation point, the same cannot be said for inward tourism more generally. In fact, by making things difficult for its visitors, Saudi Arabia has ensured only the most dedicated non-Muslim tourists are likely to visit the kingdom. Entry qualifications are stringent. You need to find someone inside the kingdom to sponsor you. Your travel plans must be 'approved'. Only approved destinations can be visited. Your travel will be chaperoned to some degree. The paper chase of visas and permissions prior to your trip will be exacting and laborious. But assuming success, you may then make an officially sanctioned trip to the kingdom, to be taken on an (expensive), controlled, but nonetheless interesting, 'approved' tour.

TOURING OUTSIDE THE KINGDOM

One of the great cultural contributions the USA has made to the world has been the invention of R&R (Rest and Recreation) leave. For Western expatriates, most employment contracts in Saudi Arabia will have an R&R component. Typically, two R&R leave entitlements of about 10–14 days are allowed each year, in addition to annual leave. Under most employment contracts, R&R must be taken outside Saudi Arabia. Within reasonable limits, the company gives you an air ticket to the destination of your choice. This is a terrific opportunity to see some interesting parts of the world at someone else's expense.

Saudi Arabia happens to be very centrally situated to many attractive and interesting R&R destinations. It is also within range of places that make an intriguing weekend away. Cairo, Beirut, Damascus, the history-packed islands of the Mediterranean, Cyprus, Crete and Rhodes are all within easy reach. Within a chronological diameter of nine hours flying time is most of South-east Asia, most of Africa, all of Europe, the other countries of the Middle East and Russia. In terms of travelling to somewhere else, Saudi Arabia is central.

Though North America is a little out of reach, non-stop flights are available to east coast cities.

The easiest country of all to get to from Saudi Arabia is Bahrain, which is now connected to the kingdom at Dammam by a 25-km causeway. Taking a holiday in Bahrain may not sound all that exciting to some, but attractions are relative. Many on the east coast make the journey to partake of two of Saudi Arabia's forbidden fruits—pork and alcohol.

But the Saudi immigration authorities have also heard of the availability of pork and alcohol in Bahrain. They are diligent in ensuring these prohibited items do not make the return journey across the causeway. At the checkpoint between Saudi Arabia and Bahrain on the causeway connecting the two, immigration authorities customarily perform rigorous checks of all vehicles inbound into Saudi Arabia. Standard procedure is to use mirrors to check the underside of the car for packages bolted to the underside of the body pan.

Such has been the influx of Saudis into Bahrain after the causeway was completed, and such has been the attendant collateral damage by single alcohol-impaired Saudi men, that for a while five-star hotels in Bahrain restricted its bookings to Saudi families only. The worst time to travel to Bahrain via the causeway is Thursday morning when long delays at the border crossing points can be expected from Saudi weekenders heading for their rest and relaxation activities in Bahrain. For the same reason, the return trip on Friday evening also tends to be congested.

Paying Attention at the Border

As in all things in the kingdom, a greater than normal level of care can keep you out of trouble. But lapses of concentration are human nature. A British sales executive of 'African and Eastern' (one of the three authorised distributors of alcoholic beverages in Bahrain) had a sideline business in soft drinks inside Saudi Arabia. To service this business, he would drive his own car across the causeway into Saudi Arabia. While in Bahrain, he customarily carried a sample of his company's products—a case of beer—in the boot of the car. One day, he travelled to the kingdom at short notice and forgot about his samples. At the border, Saudi immigration officials found the beer. The sales executive was first jailed, then fired from his job, and finally deported.

Further down the coast from Bahrain, is the United Arab Emirates (UAE), a coalition of seven emirates, the main three of which are Abu Dhabi, Dubai and Sharjah. By car or by taxi, any of the emirates is accessible from any of the others. Modern and progressive, the UAE, about a two-hour flight from east coast airports, is well worth a visit. As a base for a tour into the area, Sharjah or Dubai are probably the best places to stay. Both are very modern, attractive Arab-style city-states.

For the guest worker and dependents, air travel around the Middle East on regional airlines may involve an extra degree of uncertainty. The fact that you hold a confirmed booking may not guarantee you a seat on the flight. If an Arab passenger decides at the last minute that he wants your seat on one of the Middle East airlines like Gulf Air or Saudia, the chances are he will get it. You may be 'bumped' off the flight, a practice that is not entirely unknown in other parts of the world, but particularly prevalent in the Middle East.

One of the authors has had a personal experience at being bumped off a flight from Bahrain to Cyprus and, as a result, enduring a near-death experience from freezing in Bahrain's extravagantly air-conditioned airport during a 24-hour wait for a ticket out on the next available flight. Expatriates tend to be bumped off flights in the reverse order of the Middle East racial hierarchy. Those with the least status, Asian and sub-continent nationals from Third World countries, will find themselves 'bumped' ahead of Westerners. On one Kuwait Air flight taken by one of the authors, the flight crew read out the names of four Filipinos who were asked to identify themselves as the flight, which had already been loaded, awaited to take off. Everyone knew what was going on. Not a soul admitted to their identities, but the individuals were identified from the passenger manifest, extracted from their seats and bundled off the plane to be replaced by four Arabs. Filipinos stick together. After the extraction was completed, the atmosphere in the plane crackled with resentment. A near riot broke out when the plane landed in Dubai, its next stop.

TAKING PICTURES

Saudis are sensitive about photo taking. If you do take photos, you may also be taking a risk. People, including one of the photographers for this book, have been thrown into jail for snapping pictures without holding the proper permits. Others have been jailed and held overnight just for carrying a camera. Yet others have taken all the photos they wanted and nothing happened. The law of the land is this: photo taking without a permit is against the rules and the source of permits that allow photos to be taken is not entirely clear. The only photo taking that is entirely legal is within someone's home.

Some of the photo subjects that would cause particular offence are obvious enough. Saudi Arabia is sensitive to its strategic position in the world. You would not be well advised, for example, to photograph military facilities. Taking photos of potential industrial targets such as oil refineries and port facilities will not be well regarded. Religious icons are off limits too—Saudis are sensitive about their religious beliefs. Whatever might be interpreted as showing the country in a bad light are risky photographic subjects. Snapping of *abaya*-clad women in the street is not recommended. Saudis know that the outside world views their treatment of women as regressive. There is an argument, too, that taking pictures of people or even scenery may violate provisions of the Qur'an concerned with recording images. Saudi art, which limits its subjects entirely to calligraphy, certainly seems to confirm that rendering natural objects as pictures is off limits. The safest photographic subjects are the country's most splendid non-strategic structures such as soaring city skylines. Street scenes inside expatriate compounds are acceptable subjects. So are the natural landscapes and subjects like camels. Whatever the subject, picture taking shouldn't be too overt.

ENTERTAINMENT AND LEISURE

Entertainment in Saudi Arabia is more restricted than in most countries. Activities such as gambling, drinking, cinemas, a wide range of literature, card playing, socialising with the opposite sex (other than family) and various sporting activities that display too much skin, are all off limits. Saudis rule makers regard life as a very serious business with a stringent behaviour code.

It was once said that the Puritans (a Christian sect prevalent in a past century in Europe) objected to bear baiting 'not because it gave pain to the bear, but because it gave pleasure to the spectators'. Likewise of the laws of Saudi Arabia might seem, to Westerners, targeted at banishing pleasure as distinct from advancing social justice. Having fun, while condoned on occasion, is not actively encouraged. Shariah Laws that seem to take the fun out of life for no obvious reason include banning music played over telephones that are on hold, banning sending of flowers by friends and relatives to patients in hospital and banning the children's game Pokemon.

Even chess is considered a questionable activity because of the possibly idolatrous nature of the pieces. According to one interpretation, the Prophet declared all forms of entertainment off limits for a Muslim except breaking a horse, drawing a bow, and amusing himself with his wives. Perhaps this is the reason for the prohibition on seemingly innocent pastimes, though it has to be said the Prophet was silent on the matter of Saudi Arabia's current favourite form of recreation—watching their national soccer team on TV.

SAUDIS AND SPORT

Camel racing is probably the only uniquely Saudi Arabian sport whose mass popularity has survived into modern times. For thousands of years the camel has been the *sine qua non* of desert life: the source of transportation, milk, meat, leather, wool, shade, shade-cloth as well as sport. Camels are one of the few animals that can keep hale and hearty on the meagre offerings of the desert. Though domestic camels show preference for more exotic foodstuffs, camels can survive on anything that is even remotely suggestive of being vegetable fare, such as spinifex and thorn bush.

The ship of the desert.

Though Saudi Arabia still contains plenty of camels living a traditional life as pack animals of Bedouin tribes, the country is now in the camel importing business. Some consider the best camels are those roaming in the wild over Australian deserts. These are the descendents of camels, originally from Arabia, that were brought to Australia in the 19th century to serve as pack animals to supply Australia's outback settlements. According to Australian folklore, only the most robust and healthy camels survived the long sea journey, thus culling the weak from the genetic strain. When road and rail displaced camel trains in Australia, the animals were released, thriving to become the largest camel population in the world, and the only significant herd that runs wild with no human owner. Being isolated on an island, this herd may also the most disease-free. Australian camels have been imported for racing in Saudi Arabia along with Australian know-how of improved husbandry and training methods.

Camel racetracks have been built in most of the kingdom's major centres. Races for prize money are held many weekends

Camel racing on the outskirts of Riyadh.

throughout the winter months. In the manner of racehorses, top dollar is paid for camels with breeding pedigree. Camels like horses go faster with lightweights on their backs. Sad to say, Saudis have been known to engage jockeys as young as four years old, obtained from underprivileged countries like Bangladesh.

Horses, now raced for sport, have also played a key part in Arabian history for a long time. Horses were first thought to have been domesticated in about 4,000 BC, in the area of present-day Ukraine. One Bedouin legend offers an alternative account, claiming that the Arabian horse was God's gift to Ismael, son of Abraham, as a reward for his faith. Whatever their source, after they were domesticated, horses later spread throughout Arabia, Central Asia and Europe. Civilisations became dependent on their horses for agriculture, transport and military activity.

Bedouins greatly treasured their horses, treating them as members of their household, thus ingraining in their horses a strong sense of loyalty towards their owners. Mares were especially prized because they were considered less temperamental than stallions and made less noise (thus not alerting the enemy during raids).

Arabian horses were bred for their fine features, speed and endurance, whereas the heavier European horses were developed for strength and carrying capacity. The Arabian horse was an essential aid to the spread of the Islamic Empire. With superior speed and endurance over other strains, Arabian horses have become the basis of the bloodstock industry worldwide.

Falconry, another sport with long traditions, is still enjoyed in the kingdom today. The apparently empty deserts offer sufficient small animals and birds to serve as prey, though overgrazing has reduced falcon populations in Saudi Arabia. Most falcons are now imported from neighbouring countries or further afield in Asia.

The falcon is a favourite mascot in the Middle East. For example Gulf Air's first class lounge is called the Falcon Lounge, in the UAE one of the brands of petrol is Falcon and the Arab Gulf Cooperative Council (AGCC) countries feature falcons on their bank notes and stamps.

At the falcon market in Riyadh, pure-bred falcons can be traded for millions of riyals.

Originally falconry served as a way for Bedouins to supplement their diet with wild game. As in the past, today's young falcons are taken from their nests, with the trainer becoming the surrogate mother. Once grown, the falcon is trained to perch on its trainer's arm. Since they make better hunters, female falcons are favoured over males. Female falcons are bigger and stronger than males, are more patient and less temperamental, and are thought to have better eyesight. Falcons can live up to 15 years.

With the influx of guest workers into the kingdom came sports some of which have made and impact on the Saudi scene and some of which haven't. The most popular imported sport is soccer, the world's most popular ball game, which has well and truly caught the imagination of Saudi public. Like many countries, the country has spent plenty of money developing its national soccer team, arguably the strongest in the region. The Saudi national team has reached three consecutive World Cup finals in soccer—1994, 1998 and 2002.

Basketball, introduced in the 1950s by guest workers from the United States is another imported sport. Though the game did not catch on for decades, basketball increased in

The Saudi Arabian national team before their qualifying game for the 2006 World Cup.

popularity after the introduction of a government programme encouraging participation among schoolchildren and the construction of hundreds of courts.

Despite these programmes, participant sport is still not all that popular in Saudi Arabia. One possible reason is the climate. Another is the traditional clothing that Arabs wear. While registered sportspeople, like the Saudi football team wear regulation equipment for their sport, casual players are often seen attempting to play sports in their street clothes—which are spectacularly unsuited to just about every sport ever invented. Injuries are commonplace amongst those who trip over the hems of their *thobes* while attempting to knock a ball around.

Clothing is even more of a problem for Saudis interested in beach sports. Despite a hot climate and warm water, Saudis are not known for their inclination to take a cooling dip. On beaches, normal Saudi dress code applies—a rule that sometimes leads to tragic consequences. A few years back, three Saudi women, who could not swim, drowned after getting into trouble at a beach north of Al-Jubayl. The women had entered the water fully clothed. They got out of their depth and were dragged down by their *abayas*, while

A Saudi family spend some time at a beach near the Red Sea.

their menfolk, similarly impeded, looked on helplessly from the beach.

The heat, the restrictions on displays of public enjoyment and the restrictions on dress code in public do limit the pastimes in which Saudis get involved. Since the Saudis are sociable people with strong family ties, a principal form of recreation for Saudi nationals is visiting friends and relatives and having family picnics. Bedouins leading urban lives take this idea a step further in maintaining their links with their traditional haunts. Families take vacations in the desert, setting up tents and spending a week or two reliving something close to the life of their parents or grandparents.

GUEST WORKERS AND SPORTS

Guest workers who enjoy participant sports will find plenty of opportunities to show their talents in Saudi Arabia, particularly if they live in compounds. Sporting facilities in guest workers' accommodations in places like Jubail, Yanbu and Dhahran are excellent. The full range of sports are catered for—playing fields (usually with a fine gravel surface), running tracks, tennis, squash and racquetball courts, swimming pools and gymnasiums.

Uniquely Middle Eastern-style golf courses can also be found in the kingdom. One of the authors was a member of the Whispering Sands club (logo: a camel with a golf club clenched between its teeth). This layout was constructed by an earthmoving contractor who turned an otherwise unused desert area into an 18 hole golf course. Facilities at the club were exceptionally basic. Greens were areas of the desert smeared with a bitumen solution. Tees were raised areas equipped with driving mats. Fairways were sand dunes that had been levelled. The rough was sand dune country left pristine.

Course architecture of this type has advantages and disadvantages from a player's point of view. The courses play long and, under the hot desert sun, arduously. An essential piece of equipment carried by golfers playing the sand belt courses of Saudi Arabia is a square piece of AstroTurf off which the ball is played wherever it lands. The principal advantage is that playing every shot on AstroTurf certainly improves the lies. One of the curiosities in playing golf in the sand pits of Saudi Arabia is that there are no bunker shots!

Not all golf courses in the Middle East are quite like the Whispering Sands. Championship courses, of which there are a few, particularly in the UAE, are completely irrigated grass layouts of a standard you would find anywhere.

Waters of both the Arabian Gulf and the Red Sea are suitable for swimming—though on the Gulf side of the country, the beaches tend to shoal very gradually. Despite the volume of oil being extracted and shipped, waters and beaches on both sides of the country are reasonably clean. Beaches are segregated into family beaches and men-only beaches. No women-only beaches are known to exist. Single men must not use family beaches. Women can only use family beaches. Both sexes should take care to establish the status of the beach they are intending to use.

Water sports other than swimming are also available. The Gulf, particularly the Red Sea, has a number of good dive sites where diving can be conducted hassle-free from the auhorities. Dive boats are available for hire. According to government websites, nautical activities such as sailing, windsurfing and waterskiing are permitted. But in the authors' experience, what is actually allowed may depend on the rules of the day as interpreted by local authorities. One of the concerns the authorities have about people messing about in boats is the opportunity for espionage.

The moral aspect, too, must be borne in mind. An enterprising Dutch guest worker at a job site in Jubail once started an off-the-beach yacht club at a secluded beach. After a few successful meets, the club attracted a visit from the Mutawa'een. The objection of the religious police was not that the sailing club represented a threat to national security, but more that the Dutch girls on the beach and in the boats were, in their view, indecently clad. The club was raided, disassembled and closed down. By contrast, other sailing clubs, on both coasts, have remained open for many years. What gets shut down and what remains open is at the whim of individuals of the Saudi regulatory authorities responsible for the general community level of virtue and vice.

LEARNING ARABIC

CHAPTER 8

MOST VEHEMENT AND
BLOOD CURDLING TERMS

'An intelligent deaf-mute is better
than an ignorant person who can speak.'
—Arab Proverb

SPEAKING ARABIC

Arabic, a Semitic language related to Hebrew and Aramaic is spoken by over 180 million people in North Africa, and most of the Middle East as their first language. As the language of the Qur'an it is studied by many millions more Muslims globally.

Arabic is thought by some Westerners to be a difficult language because it is written in an unfamiliar script and some of the sounds are made at the back of the mouth and throat (the glottals). But it has its redeeming features. For instance, it is a stress/timed language making its rhythm predictable and regular whereas English reduces and blends sounds together to fit its stress patterns. Intonation patterns of English and Arabic are similar: for example, questions are posed with a rising intonation.

The earliest copies of the Qur'an were written in a heavy monumental script known as Kufic but around AD 1000 this was replaced by Naskhi, a lighter cursive script joining letters together and widely used in Saudi Arabia today. Modern Arabic is not all that unlike other written languages. It has an alphabet and rules of grammar. The Arabic alphabet probably came into existence in the 4th century AD has 28 letters—22 consonants and six vowels. There are eight vowel sounds, including dipthongs, compared to 22 in English.

The three short vowels are:

- **a**   like the vowel in the word *hat*
- **i**   like the vowel in the word *hit*
- **u**   like the vowel in the word *put*

The short vowels are not written because they occur in predictable patterns, although encoding words into script when script is being translated from English into Arabic can cause confusion, especially when your name is being translated into Arabic.

The five long vowels are:

- **aa**   as the vowel in *father*
- **ii**   like the vowel in *keen*
- **uu**   like the vowel in *food*
- **oo**   like the vowel in *home* except the lips are rounder and tenser
- **ee**   like the vowel in *may* but with the lips more tensely spread

The consonants **b**, **d**, **f**, **g**, **h**, **j**, **k**, **l**, **m**, **n**, **s**, **t**, **v**, **w**, **y** and **z** are virtually identical to their English counterparts.

Pronunciation Guide

As nicely summed up by Lawrence of Arabia himself, transliteration of Arabic words is fraught with difficulties. Many letters in the Arabic alphabet do not have an equivalent in the English language. Here is a brief explanation of the pronunciation of the letters as they appear in transliterated text

Vowels

a   this is not normally written in Arabic, but does appear in transliterated text. Its pronunciation is somewhat similar to the *a* in *bag*.

u   is also not usually written in Arabic. Its pronunciation is similar to the *u* in *put*.

i   not written but pronunciation is similar to the *i* in *sit*.

aa (â)   this appears in Arabic and is often referred to as a long *a* like in *father*. It is sometimes transliterated as *aa*.

uu (û)   this sounds like a long *o* and is sometimes transliterated as *oo*. It sounds like the *oo* in *spoon*.

ii (î)   it's a long *i* and is sometimes transliterated as *ee*.

Pronunciation Guide (conintued)

Consonants

b	the pronunciation is similar to the English *b*
t	it is pronounced like the English *t*
r	rolled *r*, somewhat like the *r* in *road*
d	similar to the English *d*
s	similar to the English *s*
f	similar to the English *f*
h	similar to the English *h*
k	similar to the English *k*
l	similar to the English *l*
m	similar to the English *m*
n	similar to the English *n*
y	spoken like the *y* in the word *yes*
w	similar to the English *w*
q	it sounds like a *k* but is pronounced deep in the throat
kh	it is similar to the *ch* in the German name *Bach* or the *kh* in *khan*
gh	specific to Arabic, it sounds like a highly expressed rolled *r*
th	when written together in transliterated text, they denote one letter, pronounced like the *th* in the word *think*
sh	like **th**, *sh* denotes one letter and is pronounced like the *sh* in the word *ship*
dh	another combination that denotes one letter and is pronounced like the *th* in the word *that*. It has no sound and works as a pause in a word

---

Most of the 28 letters of the Arabic alphabet have similar sounds to those in English but Westerners often have difficulty in making some sounds. Some words like *la* meaning 'no' in Arabic require the speaker to make a sudden stoppage of breath at the conclusion of the word so that it sounds like 'la-huh'. Other words like *a'reed*, meaning 'I want' in English, require the *a* to be pronounced as *ah* far back in the throat. The greeting phrase *SabaHel Khair* meaning 'good morning' requires the *H* to be pronounced similar to the *h* in English but far back in the throat. The Arabic word for the numeral five, *khamseh*, requires the *kh* to be a guttural sound like the

Scottish *ch* in *loch* or the German *ch* in *nacht*. The metric weight gram is *ghram* in Arabic and the *gh* is as a guttural sound far back in the throat as the French pronounce the letter *r* in *Parisian*.

READING ARABIC

Arabic is read from right to left with the exception of the numbers which are read from left to right. Numbers in English are borrowed from the Arabic numeral system using one symbol each for 0 through to 9 and then adding new place values for tens, hundreds, thousands, and so on. A list of numbers in Arabic is found in the Glossary.

Arabic contains many references to God plus expressions of piety, courtesy and sociability. Bedouins infuse spoken Arabic with richness and emotion. The language has literary elegance, and a wide range of subtle meanings suit Arabic to poetry—a leisure activity of many Saudis. Formal poetry prose and oratory play a key role in Saudi culture. Bedouin poets passed on their history to following generations, recounting in their poems ideals of manliness, gallantry, bravery, loyalty, generosity and independence of spirit.

Reflections of a Bedouin

Sandra Mackey in her book *The Saudis* recounts the story of an old Bedouin man suffering from a chronic disease who launched into a perfectly constructed poem after being examined by an American doctor at the King Faisal Specialist Hospital. In his poem, he praised Allah for being allowed to come to this famous hospital but, in verse after verse, lamented the fact that he was not yet cured.

WRITING ARABIC

Non-technical business communications within the kingdom are most likely to be in Arabic, with English communications fairly widespread. Technical subjects are mostly in English. With the advent of computers, the written aspects of business tend to be conducted in English, with perhaps an Arabic translation. Since Arabic is an alphabeticised language, it can be typed on a normal 'qwerty' style keyboard. Word processing software usually incorporates a switch facility on the standard keyboard so that bilingual typists can switch from one language to the other.

Legal contracts tend to be written in English, or maybe both languages. Somewhat oddly, if the contracts are drafted in English, then translated into Arabic, the laws of the land require that in the event of conflict between the English and Arabic version, Arabic prevails; thus preserving any translation errors that have been made in the final agreement!

ARABIC AS SPOKEN BY ARABS

Saudis also use language as a means of aggression rather than physically fighting. When Saudis communicate in Arabic or English, they often do with exaggerated flattery. Threats are conveyed with a similar level of exaggeration. Through their love of language, Saudis are swayed more by words rather than ideas and more by ideas than facts.

As you go about your business, you will encounter shouting matches at incidents like motor vehicle collisions where the crowd of spectators become participants waving their hands around and making a great deal of noise. In the parking lot like the one at the Safeway Supermarket in Damman, you may see a Saudi sitting in his car blocking someone else who wants to get his car out. The blocking Saudi will not move until he has completed his argument with the other driver, or until assembled spectators to the disagreement force him to move his car.

Despite such shouting matches, it is most unusual to see a Saudi strike another Saudi. This carries through to the government who, for example, regularly condemns the State of Israel in the most vehement and bloodcurdling terms but rarely takes action.

Saudi commoners expect their princes to use poetic language in announcements to other nations. Western commentators may have trouble decoding the real message behind the words. Take for example the simple 'yes' or 'no'. To an American or another English-speaking Westerner, this is a definitive statement. Not so in the case of a Saudi. Because Saudis use flowery language and are accustomed to exaggeration and over-assertion, they find it difficult to respond to a brief simple statement. So when you hear a Saudi say 'yes' to a business proposition, you have to keep in mind that chances are he really means 'maybe'.

Like most languages, Arabic has regional variations, but not enough to prevent citizens throughout the Arab world from understanding each other. Classical Arabic and Gulf Arabic are the two main variants that are spoken in Saudi Arabia although there are five major dialects.

Classical Arabic spoken in Egypt is generally held to be Arabic's most prestigious form and is readily understood in most of the Middle East because of the massive export of popular Arab culture in the form of films, TV soaps and popular songs. Its grammar is more complex than dialect Arabic. Classical Arabic is usually spoken in formal discussions, speeches and news broadcasts, and is the only form of written Arabic.

Gulf Arabic is spoken by nationals in Bahrain, Kuwait, Oman, Qatar, Saudi Arabia, the UAE and Yemen, and is generally understood by Arabs living in Egypt, Lebanon, Jordan, Palestine, Sudan and Syria. Gulf Arabic is less understood by Arabs living in North Africa and Iraq, although one of the authors had few problems when he spoke Gulf Arabic in Baghdad.

LEARNING ARABIC

Arabic grammar is different from English grammar in quite a number of ways. In Arabic, verbs precede subjects. Adding *laa* or *maa* to a word makes it negative, rather in the same way as the English prefix *un*. Pronouns can be prefixed or suffixed to a verb which is always gender specific. Participles can be added to the beginning or end of words and can also be infixed or placed in the middle.

For those that are interested in learning it, Arabic is an interesting language. Those who make the

The attitude to learning Arabic varies with your role. If you are a diplomat, for example, mastery of Arabic may be highly regarded. If you are further down the pecking order, less so. Within the Western expat community there is an old school tie network centred on MEKAS which is a British Foreign Service-sponsored school in Lebanon that teaches Arabic to Western diplomats and senior executives.

effort to tackle the alphabet and acquire a basic vocabulary are likely to get more out of their visit to the Middle East than those that don't. For anyone wanting to try learning Arabic, plenty of tutorial classes are available.

One point to note: those who take the trouble to learn Arabic will need to exercise their Arabic language skills judiciously. If you know enough Arabic to understand a conversation in the language, you ought to do one of two things: either keep your language skills to yourself or announce them at the earliest possible opportunity. Arabs will generally assume that non Arab expatriates don't speak a word of Arabic. Arabs are accustomed to speaking among themselves in front of Westerners, confident that they are having a private conversation that cannot be understood. If they subsequently learn this assumption hasn't worked out, they may feel you have eavesdopped on their conversation.

COMMON ARABIC EXPRESSIONS

The following are few of the more common expressions used in base level conversation:

Hello	*Salaaam ali kum*
Response to 'hello'	*Wa alikum salam*
How are you	*Kay far lick*
Good	*Zane*
Praise be to God (I'm fine)	*Al humdallah*
Good morning	*Sabakl kair*
Good evening	*Sabakl noon*
My name is...	*Ismi...*
What is your job?	*Aish shtuggle*
Where is	*Wayne*
Why	*laysh*
How much	*Cham*
Please	*Min fadhlek*

Thank you	*Shookran*
Please take	*Tfadhal*
Come here	*Taal hini*
Yes	*Enaam*
No	*La*
Arabian coffee	*Gahwa*

SAUDI'S SECOND LANGUAGE

The second language in Saudi Arabia, like most places is American English, which is taught in all schools and widely spoken throughout the Kingdom. Signage around the countryside is in Arabic and English. In addition, English tends to be the second language of the guest workers from non-English speaking countries and over time, has crept into every day Saudi speech. For example Saudis are inclined to answer the telephone with a Saudi corruption of 'hello-hallas' and concluding their conversation with the Arabic word *yella* meaning 'let's go' and then say in English 'bye-bye'. English words that have crept into everyday Arabic speech include 'sandwich', 'bus' and 'radio'.

> English words which derive from Arabic include 'alchemy', 'alcohol', 'algebra', 'alkali' 'almanac', 'arsenal', 'assassin', 'cipher', 'elixir', 'nadir', 'mosque', 'sugar', 'syrup' and 'zero'.

BODY LANGUAGE

Saudi body language tends to be fairly forgiving. In fact, perhaps as you face your Saudi boss across the office desk and observe that under his desk, he has removed his sandals and is sitting on his foot placed on the seat of his chair, you may feel that in the area of bodily behaviour, anything goes. Like most places, Saudi Arabia does have a few prohibitions, though Saudis are not too pernickety in the unacceptable body language area.

But there are a few gestures that are considered insulting. Amongst these are the upward raising of a single finger, excessive pointing, fist clenching and clapping an open palm over a closed fist. One thing Saudis do not like to see is the soles of your feet. This is not a culture where you would put your feet up on your desk, or even use a footrest. Exposing the soles of the feet to another person is considered a mild insult. You should be careful how you arrange your limbs and try not to cross your legs.

WORKING AND DOING BUSINESS IN SAUDI ARABIA

CHAPTER 9

'Make your bargain before beginning to plough.'
—Arab Proverb

ECONOMIC DEVELOPMENT AND
THE LABOUR FORCE

During the 1970s, under King Faisal, Saudi Arabia embarked on a programme to apply its oil revenue to building an industrial infrastructure. The obvious industries to develop were those based on hydrocarbon feedstock (from the oil refining process) such as fertilisers and plastics. For good measure, Saudi Arabia also built a steel industry based on reduction of iron oxide by gas instead of coal.

Two fishing villages, Jubail on the Arabian Gulf and Yanbu on the Red Sea, were the selected locations for new industrial cities in which these industries were located. Both sites offered deepwater ports. Yanbu was strategically situated half way along the Red Sea coastline. Jubail lay at the centre of an oil/gas producing area and was the site of a major US naval base. From the basic industries it was hoped, the secondary and tertiary industries would also develop to transform Saudi Arabia into a manufacturing country.

The development plan was grand in its vision. But ultimately its effects have been marginal. The industrial cities did succeed in setting up some basic industries, but the effect on the national accounts has been minimal. Saudi Arabia has not turned itself into a manufacturing nation in the manner of Japan, Singapore and other Asian countries. The basic industries were built, but no commensurate programme was undertaken to develop the technical personnel to run them.

Saudis monitor share prices at a bank in Riyadh.

Despite its industrialisation programmeme, Saudi Arabia remains almost entirely dependant on its exporting oil and gas products.

After the second oil price spike of 1979, the price of oil went into a long decline and the fortunes of Saudi Arabia did likewise. As oil revenue declined, Saudi Arabia fell into deficit, financing its operations by borrowing. In the 1970s, Saudi Arabia had been a creditor country. By the 1990s, Saudi national debt was over 100 per cent of GDP.

But reprieve was at hand. A third boom for Saudi Arabia started at the turn of the century with rising oil prices. At time of writing, this boom was still in progress. Since the oil prices started rising in 2003, business in Saudi Arabia has boomed. The Tadwul All-Share Index (TASI) of the Saudi Stock Exchange doubled in value during 2004/2005.

During its ups and its downs, Saudi Arabia continued to hire foreign labour to look after both its day-to-day operations and its development plans. With the dramatic rise in oil prices since 2002, opportunities for a foreign labour force to participate in a new round of development look set to continue.

WHY CAN'T THE SAUDIS RUN THEIR OWN COUNTRY?

Despite two generations since the first commercial development of their own oilfields, Saudis of the present day seem to be no more capable of running their own country than they were when their industrialisation started in the 1940s. They still rely on a massive foreign workforce to get their day's work done. The question is often asked—why can't the Saudis run their own country? The answer seems to lie in a mix of cultural and historical reasons that have changed little in the two generations since Saudi Arabia first attempted to make the transition into a modern country.

One reason proposed is the absence of a traditional work culture. Agriculture, according to anthropologists such as Jared Diamond (and detailed in his prize winning book, *Guns, Germs and Steel: The Fate of Human Societies*), was the wellspring of the present work ethic of both the East and West. In the West, the idea that man was put into the world to toil is sometimes referred to as the 'Protestant work ethic'—an invention not merely of the Christian Church, but also of the lord of the manor of the feudal system during the Middle Ages. In times past, peasants were compelled to work in the fields from dawn to dusk. When the Industrial Revolution came along, the work ethic was transferred into town where workers toiled from dawn to dusk in the factories of the new industrial world. In societies with a culture of permanent agriculture and then of industrialisation, work was an essential part of life. Work filled people's lives. Sloth was listed as one of the seven deadly sins of economics— and still is.

Such a mindset never got underway in Saudi Arabia.

Around 3000 BC, the permanent agriculture of the Sumerians took root in the 'Fertile Crescent', centred around the Tigris-Euphrates confluence in present-day Iraq. Permanent agriculture then spread east and west, becoming the mainstay of both Asian and Western societies. But Sumerian agriculture ultimately failed. Major factors were salinity and climate change. The area became increasingly arid and depopulated as a result. Few large permanent settlements existed from which artisanship and innovation could spring. While agriculture prospered elsewhere in the world, and industry later followed, the region which invented permanent agriculture drifted back into nomadic animal husbandry.

After that, little changed for thousands of years. Bedouins lived a hand-to-mouth existence of driving their flocks between one patch of meagre grass and the next. While their flocks were grazing, there was little for Bedouins to do during the hottest hours of the day but shelter from the brutal sun inside their camel-hair tents. Conditions were too harsh over most of the country for crops. As a result, Saudi Arabia failed to develop a culture of working in the fields from which a tradition of working in factories flowed in other countries. Bedouin traditions were more in line with other hunter-gatherer societies—Australian Aborigines, Eskimos, most North American Indians and Khalari Bushmen—who were also fast-forwarded into the modern-day work culture without the time to adjust to the work ethic that gripped much of the rest of the world.

Despite the Arab advances of the Middle Ages, when industrialisation arrived in the 20th century, Saudi Arabia wasn't prepared for it. Unlike countries like the US, Saudi Arabia had no history of pioneering struggle to lay its foundations for a modern state. Unlike countries of Europe, and even Egypt, there were no generations of transition from agriculture to industrialisation. Unlike the nations further east—India and China—no complex administration was in place to handle commerce, trade and government.

With the advent of oil, the Saudis made a giant leap forward from Bedouinism to the consumer age in a single stride. The solution to the shortage of labour skills was promoted by oil companies themselves—hire a skilled foreign workforce to build an alien technocrat core within a technologically ignorant society. This was easily accomplished in just a few years. A society based on oil was an easier transition than other forms of industrialisation that revolutionised economies in other countries. Oil was simple. Oil companies drilled an oil well. Oil flowed to the surface all by itself, discharged into a pipeline and from there into an oil tanker. Everyone made money.

The influence of the Wahabbism sect of the Muslim religion was another factor that prevented Saudis from acquiring the skills needed to run their own country. Wahabbism is a highly dogmatic belief system that resists new knowledge. Wahabbism regards as sinful what other nations term as 'progress'. Nations with a more tolerant brand of Islam have done better reconciling their Islamic beliefs with the ideals and aspirations of the modern world. Malaysia, for example, has managed to maintain its religious core culture while building a successful modern economy.

But not Saudi Arabia.

The type of education Saudis receive is a related factor inhibiting the country's progress. The education system trains the new generation in theology not technology. A bachelor's degree in Islamic philosophy is not a qualification that finds employment in a job market that seeks engineers, skilled workers, technicians and business graduates. In the 1990s, over 6 per cent of the country's gross domestic product (GDP) was spent on education—much higher than most countries of a similar economic profile. But little of this expenditure had brought tangible benefits to the country.

Saudi Arabian Self Sufficiency: the UN Assessment

In 2002, the United Nations (UN) published the Arab Human Development Report which considered the question of Saudi Arabia's lack of labour self-sufficiency. The report found factors contributing to the kingdom's dependency on foreign labour were lack of personal freedom, poor education, government appointments based on factors other than merit and rules against employing women, particularly in small business.

Says the Arab Human Development Report: 'The barrier to better Arab performance is not a lack of resources, but the lamentable shortage of three essentials: freedom, knowledge and manpower. It is these deficits that hold the frustrated Arabs back from reaching their potential—and allow the rest of the world both to despise and to fear a deadly combination of wealth and backwardness.'

—Source: Arab Human Development Report, Nader Fergany, Egyptian sociologist and chief author of the report, 2000 published by the UN development programmeme.

Perhaps another reason for Saudi Arabia's failure to train up a labour force is simply habit. With its long traditions of slavery, Saudis were accustomed to having the guest workforce around. Peons were imported to perform low-grade tasks in Saudi Arabia, even before oil was discovered. Importing the highly-skilled workforce to build and operate oilfields and processing facilities was merely an extension of a habitual dependency.

Whatever the reasons, at the time of writing, Saudis have made little progress in taking over the running of their own country from their guest workforce. There are almost certainly more expatriate workers in the private sector workforce than Saudis, although reliable statistics are hard to come by. Saudis have allowed this situation to drift along for decades. They have been unable, one would have to say they haven't tried very hard, to educate their own workforce and develop their own expertise.

An interview in *The Economist* of 11 January 2003 recorded the thoughts one of Saudi Arabia's 5,000 princes on his country. "We are the most conservative country in the world," he said. Commented *The Economist* on the prince's remarks, 'with enforced Puritanism, medieval system of governance and culture of secrecy, the kingdom appears uniquely resistant to change.'

With change looking no more likely to happen than ever, bright prospects for the guest workforce look set to continue.

WILL YOU BE REPLACED BY A SAUDI?

One of the questions that might intrigue a visitor to Saudi Arabia is this: here is a country which has imported an alien workforce to perform tasks which in other countries provide employment to the average person in the street. Wouldn't this practice give rise to massive unemployment? What do people do for a living when three-quarters of society's normal occupations are removed and transferred to an imported workforce?

One immediate reply is that half the people who would go to work in most other countries are unable to do so in Saudi

Arabia for no better reason than they are women. But that still leaves an available indigenous workforce of about six million males aged 15–64, many of whom, according to the scanty statistics available, appear to be out of work. Which raises the question of how the local population spend their time and get money to live.

What is the rate of unemployment in Saudi Arabia?

The CIA World Factbook's convenient summary of the demographic statistics gives the 'official' unemployment figure for Saudi Arabia at 25 per cent. For comparison, a statement from the Sixth Development Plan (1995–2000) states that the 'participation rate [of Saudi nationals in the domestic labour market in the mid-1990s]... is only 30.2 per cent." Other sources give a similar impression of extremely high unemployment in Saudi Arabia.

It will almost certainly get worse before it gets better. With nearly half the population of Saudi Arabia under 16 years old, youth unemployment—already a considerable problem—seems likely to exacerbate in the future as the young population bulge is discharged from schools into the workforce. Saudi Arabia's chronic long-term unemployment problem would be overcome if the guest workforce were replaced with its own people.

Saudi Arabia has made desultory attempts to overcome this problem without really addressing the underlying issues that are causing unemployment in the first place. The policy to get Saudis into work is embodied in the phrase 'Saudisation of the workforce'. The Saudisation programme, which has passed into legislation, requires Saudi companies to increase the number of Saudi nationals on their payroll by 5 per cent per year. Another measure of the Saudisation programme is to offer free vocational guidance and financial assistance for anyone wanting to establish their own business. The Saudis have brought in legislation that only Saudis can work in designated industries such as selling gold and driving taxis. These laws were fairly quickly rescinded when the targeted industries degenerated, almost immediately, into chaos. But in tackling chronic problems of employability, the Saudi government has not yet summoned the will to implement the hard decisions to allow its Saudisation policy to be achieved.

Various conflicts between the five pillars of Islam and the modern world compromise successful Saudisation. Even something as simple as *salat*—the requirement to pray five times a day—seriously erodes productivity. *Inshallah* culture that God will take care of the smallest details breeds indifference to outcomes. The Wahhabi doctrine that no knowledge exists outside the Qur'an inhibits the learning of commercially useful skills. Only a massive change in the very cultural fabric of society—in particular religion—is likely to improve Saudisation performance. As long as religious studies remain the central theme in education, Saudi Arabia is unlikely to generate the skilled workforce it needs to run its own country.

The Wrong Skills for the Job

'"The companies who come to see us are looking for skilled workers, business grads, engineers and technicians," said Nassir Salih al-Homoud, director of an unemployment office in Burayday, a quiet farming centre of 350,000 in central Saudi Arabia. Few Saudis qualify. One of his clients is Abdulrahman al-Ali, 25. "I've been trying to find a job for a year," said al-Ali. "When I submit an application, people say they will call me, but they never do."

"The problem is his schooling." al Homoud comments. "Like many Saudis, al-Ali has a bachelor's degree in Islamic philosophy."'

—Source: 'Kingdom on Edge: Saudi Arabia', *National Geographic*, October 2003.

Another problem with getting Saudis into the workforce is a cultural aversion to certain categories of work. Saudis consider many occupations beneath their dignity. There are many jobs—sweeping the streets or collecting the garbage—that Saudis expect people of other nations to do simply because things have been that way in living memory. Saudis do not expect to fill such menial positions.

The entire service industry, the biggest sector of most economies, has proved difficult to staff from the local workforce. An international retail chain embarked on a programmeme to employ hundreds of Saudi Nationals.

After applications were received and processed, the company found itself unable to engage a single Saudi. Young Saudi men are culturally attuned to being served, not to serving.

Saudis are not normally interested in becoming truck drivers, factory hands, manual labourers, domestic servants, shop assistants and secretaries. And they do not qualify in sufficient numbers to take most of the jobs available as engineers, technicians, accountants and doctors. Guest workers from both ends of the job spectrum, are imported to the kingdom to fill these jobs. As a result, guest workers fill most of the labour market needs across the economy, from menial tasks that Saudis find undignified and too poorly paid to highly skilled tasks that are too technically demanding.

More pragmatically, employers have a number of other reasons for looking unkindly on the products of the Saudisation programme. One objection to hiring Saudis expressed by executives in a Jeddah-based company is that Saudi nationals take many more days off than their expat counterparts. Another objection is that, under employment legislation, unlike the foreign workforce, once hired, a Saudi is hired cannot be fired. Another has been the lack of obliging servility that is expected from employees in the service industry.

Such has been the level of protest from employers (who are as often as not either members of the Royal Family or have royal connections) that the government has had to back down on its attempts at Saudisation. When companies complained that they had to pay higher salaries to Saudis in return for poorer standards of work, the government relaxed the rules on hiring expatriates.

At the personal level, Saudis may feel a level of shame about the inability of their nation to get its day's work done without massive assistance. As a guest worker yourself, you may occasionally experience resentment expressed by your Saudi boss or your fellow employees. Saudis may get more than usually touchy about your performance of the job you have come to do. They may go to great lengths to explain to you why they need your services in the country instead of hiring a Saudi to do the job. This conversation is unlikely to touch on the real reason why your services are required—the clash of cultures between traditional Saudi beliefs and the skill requirements of the real world. In the opinion of most commentators, unless the Saudis fix their educational system, of which your boss is probably a product, the country's dependence on an expat workforce will most likely continue as will Saudi sensitivity on the subject.

PERPETUAL TRAINEES

Industrialisation projects originally initiated by King Faisal highlighted another aspect of Saudisation to one of the authors. These projects aimed not only to develop the physical infrastructure, but also the intellectual infrastructure by endeavouring to create a highly trained workforce of Saudis to take over future projects from the expatriate workforce. To facilitate the transfer of skills, guest workers were sat side-by-side with Saudi counterparts during their time on the project. The trainer was the guest worker and the trainee was a Saudi who, at some future period, was expected to take over the guest worker's job.

This aspect of the Saudisation programme moved at glacial speed since trainers and trainees shared a mutual disinterest in the training objective. The guest worker didn't come to Saudi Arabia to work himself out of a job. The Saudi trainee didn't have an overwhelming desire to join the workforce. At an individual level, the two parties could co-operate on a mutually beneficial policy of preserving the status quo.

The training programme also suffered through the lingering slave owner mentality of the trainees themselves. Saudi trainees saw themselves as the client. They saw the guest worker as the hourly hire. The slave-owner/slave relationship was not the ideal arrangement for passing on knowledge from the slave to the slave owner. Saudi trainees were no more interested in receiving their training than the expats were in providing it.

Trainees lacked an additional motivation to emerge from their trainee role. Many saw themselves as perpetual students. Given the opportunity to pursue a full-time career as a trainee, Saudi trainees were forever agitating to be sent overseas to undertake new university courses, preferably in the USA. One expertise the trainees did develop was in the area of training courses. Trainees queued up to participate in government-sponsored overseas study courses, seemingly more by a desire for an expenses-paid trip out of the country than to acquire needed qualifications. There was always another course to study, even for the trainee approaching middle age.

During your employment in the country, you may well find your employer earnestly explaining to you the importance of training a Saudi to take your place. Listen politely and say you understand. Your predecessor probably had the same conversation and so far nothing has happened. Thousands of Saudis have been sent to the best overseas centres of education that money can buy to acquire every piece of knowledge their country can possibly need to make it run like a Swiss watch. But guest workers continue to be imported to do the work in greater numbers than ever before. There are little signs at all that Saudis are becoming any more self-sufficient than they ever were. Which probably means, so far as the guest worker is concerned, the Saudi employment bonanza will continue.

INSHALLAH: PHILOSOPHY OR CRUTCH?

A word that you will hear repeatedly in conversations between Saudis is *inshallah* meaning 'if God wills it'. *Inshallah* embodies the Arab philosophy of fatalism in the same way that *mañana* embodies the Latin philosophy of procrastination. Unlike the Saudis themselves, the Saudi God is considered to be tremendously industrious, getting involved in the minutiae of every Muslim's life on the planet, making millions of decisions every second of the day of the most mundane aspects. Under the *inshallah* philosophy, believers may abandon all decision-making to God, neatly rationalising their own work avoidance as a possible violation of the Almighty will.

Inshallah thinking can be a tremendous irritant to the Western workforce. To holders of the Western work ethic, *inshallah* culture borders on intellectual laziness. But in its own context, *inshallah* thinking is a completely self consistent system of belief. If God has already pre-ordained every aspect of the future, planning ahead has no purpose. Why bother to plan if the outcome has already been determined by a higher being? In fact, planning ahead may be counterproductive. God might have cause to feel put out by the interference of man in the smooth unfolding of His future plans. On that argument, the puny efforts of man to plan ahead could be dangerous to one's spiritual health.

RELIGION IN THE WORKPLACE

The time that Saudis are obliged to devote to their religious needs is considerable. Of the five daily prayer calls, three are answered during the working day; the other two are before and after the working day. Competition between religious time and work time for Saudis at the workplace

Saudis will stop what they are doing in order to attend prayers.

can be exasperating for those from countries with a more structured work culture.

From the point of view of a guest worker in regular contact with Saudis, the call to prayer during working hours is a major disruption in the workplace. While it might seem practicable to schedule work around prayer breaks, in the manner of lunch breaks and meal breaks, this doesn't seem to happen, perhaps for no better reason than prayer calls are answered only by Muslims. Prayer calls leave the normal working day highly fragmented. As an alien guest worker you can be engaged is some deep and meaningful conversation with your boss, your friend or your bank manager when the *muezzin* or the loudspeaker announces the time for prayers. On a construction site you may be in the middle of a concrete pour. Whatever the situation, Muslims will answer the call, stop work and head for the nearest mosque, if there is one. (If there isn't, prayers will still be conducted, but at an alternative venue.)

Of the five prayer calls each day, the most disruptive from a business point of view are those in mid-morning and mid-afternoon. By the time participants have left the work site, made it to the mosque (which under law should never be more that 800 metres from every inhabited spot in the country), offered their prayers, perhaps stopped to chat with each other after proceedings in the mosque are completed, and made it back to work, half an hour to 40 minutes will have elapsed.

Praying on the Job

In the old days, before most of Saudi Arabia's 38,000 mosques were built, prayer time devotions would be performed from a prayer mat laid upon some level piece of ground. This is still the method for those out of range of a mosque at prayer time. Even in the middle of a business meeting, a prayer mat may be laid in a corner of the office, and the meeting adjourned while Muslims present perform their religious obligations and non-Muslims at the meeting look on. When prayers are complete, prayer mats will be rolled up, and the meeting will resume. (This arrangement takes less time and is less disruptive to the business of the meeting than having half the meeting attendees walk or drive to and from the nearest mosque.)

At whatever level you work in Saudi Arabia, the demands of religion on the workplace will be felt. If you work for a Saudi boss, religion will consume your boss's time. If Saudis work for you, religion will consume the time of your employees. From a business viewpoint, this aspect of religious practice performed twice or three times in every working day, must take its toll on the country's productivity and economic competitiveness.

The effect of the prayer call is felt further afield than the office. Prayers close down business operations across the country two or three times per day. If you are in a shop when the prayer call is heard, the shop may close and you may be discharged onto the street. If you happen to make a badly-timed visit to a restaurant and the prayer call is heard you may be bundled outside between courses, or even halfway through a course. If you are half way through a transaction at a bank, you may have to return to complete the other half about 45 minutes later. In addition to the massive loss of time each day to religion, Saudis are very often late for appointments anyway. So habitual is this practice it has earned its own sobriquet—*ma'esh* time—which loosely translated means late time.

All in all, despite occasional lip service to the contrary, Saudis, by and large, are not greatly impressed by the Western drive for getting things done in a hurry. Displays of exasperation by guest workers at breaks in the flow of work are not well regarded. It's not considered good form to show displeasure if the attention of your Saudi colleague strays from the subject under discussion. Stressed guest workers might take a leaf out of the book of the Saudi hosts at this juncture. It's not a bad idea to say to yourself as your work slips from dangerously behind schedule to critical: *inshallah*, this is the way things are in this part of the world. Life unfolds to a pattern determined by a higher being. Schedules that don't work out are not merely the fault of man: they are also the will of God.

EMPLOYMENT CONTRACTS

Arab culture is not really one that sets great store by the letter of the law. Arabs are unlikely to have quite such the same regard for contracts as their Western counterparts. This is one of the major cultural differences between west and east that has frustrated many a westerner more accustomed to a society that operates according to written rules.

In their negotiations Saudis expect to do lots of talking and lots of bargaining. They expect their negotiating partners to do the same. However even though an agreement is eventually reached, the terms of a written contract may mean little in the event of a conflict. In an arrangement that is not working out to the advantage of the Saudi partner, you are likely to find that your partner may try to change the terms of the contract without notice, and quite possibly without your knowledge. Saudis don't expect to expend their energies debating points of law about the changes they propose. Arabs are traders and have been for a long time. To them a written contract may be regarded more as an expression of the intention at a point in time rather than a hard and fast arrangement. After the written contract is signed, they will still be inclined to talk and bargain.

Whether your employment contract or business contract is worth the paper it is written on depends mainly on the

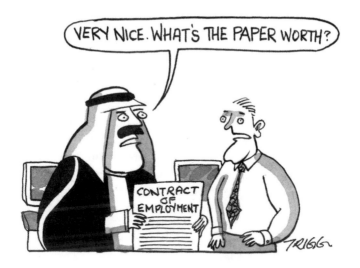

co-operation of the Saudi partner. In the event of a dispute, Saudi law may offer little protection to foreigners, either collectively or individually. Collectively, Saudi Arabia has refused to sign a number of international agreements, including labour agreements. Individually, a Saudi can generally rely on the courts to support his version of events in a disagreement with his foreign partner to the contract. The terms of a written contract are most likely to be upheld in Saudi Arabia if the contracting partner is a large foreign company. Next best is a foreign-Saudi partnership. If you have contracted to a fully-owned Saudi business, the smaller the business, the less the entitlements you feel are yours under your employment contract are likely to be understood by your Saudi partner or employer. In the Saudi Arabian small business world, written contracts are neither widely understood, nor highly regarded.

In addition, when argued in court, elements of the contract, particularly those relating to payment, may be illegal under Shariah Law if in the opinion of the judges it infringes on some interpretation of the Qur'an. In this case, provisions of the Qur'an will prevail over those of the contract.

People working in domestic duty are in the weakest situation of all. They may well be asked to work 16–18 hour days without holidays or days off. They may or may not be paid at the agreed rate. Whether they get paid at all is at the discretion of the employer. If they are female, or even if they are male, they may be pressured to grant sexual favours. The embassies of countries like the Philippines have had little success at protecting the rights of the citizens working in Saudi Arabia. Whatever goodwill the employees might enjoy from their employers is entirely based on the personal relationships that are forged.

Paying off the Agent

Workers from the Third World are particularly vulnerable to mistreatment by their Saudi bosses. Despite the hazards and discomforts, competition for jobs in Saudi Arabia is high, even though written contracts of employment are onerous. Workers are normally recruited in their home countries by employment agents who make their own arrangements with Saudi officials issuing work visas. According to a UN report on the subject, such agents typically charge their clients extravagant 'processing fees'. Cases have been cited of Asian nationals paying engagement fees of up to two years wages payable to their agent before they see any money of their own. Nevertheless, guest workers accept these terms. When they've paid off their agents, as often as not, they will remit most of their earnings to home base to finance their extended families back home. Such are the economic exigencies of the Third World that there is no shortage of applicants for positions carrying onerous terms of employment.

Occasionally people may wish to change employers while working in the country. Since work visas are issued by your existing employer, this is only possible with the cooperation of the three parties involved in the transaction—your existing employer, your new employer and the Saudi government. Not only do you need your employer's permission to leave the country, you need his permission to leave his employment—a process that can take months even with willingness on both sides. Switching employers in Saudi Arabia is difficult but not impossible.

Building Regulations and the Qur'an

After construction of the new Saudi city in Jubail was underway, the Mutawa'een paid a visit to the engineering drawing office. After inspecting the project drawings, the Mutawa'een ordered that all layout drawings of the project should also include an arrow showing the direction of Mecca, which happened to lie approximately WSW on this particular project. This direction arrow was duly added to drawings without too much difficulty.

However, trouble was to follow. A little while later, the Mutawa'een paid another visit to demand that no sewage could flow in the direction of the Mecca arrow (sewage flowing towards Mecca would have been considered insulting to Islam). The engineers then sat down to figure out how this requirement could be met without tearing up most of the work done so far.

Technically complying with the requirement wasn't possible. Streets and the pipes they contained ran in all directions. The engineers considered and rejected various arguments. That no other cities in Saudi Arabia complied with this requirement was rejected as a defence on the grounds that rules of precedent were a foreign concept to Saudi law. There was, of course, no point in disputing the relevant text in the Qur'an, the interpretation of which the Mutawa'een themselves were the world's leading experts. Instead, the engineers opted for the Non-Flat Earth Defence. The engineers argued that since the Earth was round and since Mecca was about 800 km from Jubail, nothing constructed horizontal or near horizontal could, on a three-dimensional view of the world, be considered as pointing in the direction of a town well over the horizon. Against most expectations, the Mutawa'een bought this explanation. Nothing in the Qur'an said the earth was flat! Engineers drew a collective sigh of relief and construction work continued.

But the Mutawa'een later returned. They had considered the three-dimensional view of the universe, they said, and were concerned about the orientation of toilets inside the houses of the new town. When pressed for details, the Mutawa'een explained their concern about the direction of flow of sewage in the act of using the toilets. They pointed out that, at some part in its trajectory would inevitably be in the direction of Mecca! They suggested that construction work be put on hold while engineers considered this problem.

A number of meetings were held at which the trajectory of urination was debated at some length, but no solution could be suggested. Cost engineers were summoned to estimate the cost of re-orientating the direction of those toilets in houses, which pointed WSW. Earnest discussions were held on what direction of toilet, in which the plumbing was vertical actually meant. No conclusion was reached. Construction proceeded cautiously while the next visit from the Mutawa'een was awaited. But they never returned, at least not to pursue this issue. They had made their point.

In Saudi Arabia, the Qur'an rules and the clerics interpret it.

COMMERCIAL LAW

Since the Qur'an was written in the 7th century AD, many of the matters the law has to interpret were not in existence when the basis of the law was written. When one considers what wasn't around when the Prophet lived his life—running water, sewerage, cars, telephones, paper and so on—it is some minor miracle that modern society run to the rules of Shariah Law can operate at all.

One of the difficulties with the commercial side of doing business in Saudi Arabia has been that Islam isn't really comfortable with the notion of paying interest on loans. Those lending money to Saudi institutions should be wary. Borrowers who default on their interest payments may escape their interest obligations on the grounds of that, under Shariah Law, the lender's loan was illegal in the first place.

Islam is also uncomfortable with the notion of insurance on the grounds that actuarial science can be interpreted as a form of gambling, which is against the tenets of Islam. The impossibility of hedging normal business risks can also increase the difficulty of doing business in Saudi Arabia.

The Saudi authorities recognise and are making some attempt to overcome the country's cultural conflicts between religion and normal business practice in the modern commercial world. The Government has created Special Tribunals tasked with the job of finding ways to circumnavigate the more restrictive aspects of Shariah Law and keep the wheels of industry turning. These Special Tribunals now hear most commercial law cases ranging from breach of contract suits to trade mark infringement and labour disputes.

To overcome the theological objection to insurance, a form of co-operative insurance known as *takaful* (under which resources are pooled to help the needy) has been around for centuries. *Takaful* casts the insured in the role of the potentially needy, and thereby overcomes the objection to acturial calculations by regarding the insured as a recipient of charity. Other forms of insurance are also gradually becoming accepted. For example, third party insurance to provide *diya* payments to road accident victims is now compulsory. A social insurance system was recently introduced, aimed at looking after the health care and other social needs of Saudi citizens in private business. Subscription under this scheme is voluntary, set at 18 per cent of the employee's salary, and shared 50:50 between employer and employee. A parallel compulsory insurance scheme for expat workers is also operating to oblige employers to provide health insurance for their employees.

INCOME TAX

The Shariah Law rules on income tax is good news for guest workers. The Qur'an, according to the clerics, prohibits the levying of income tax. But, as the kingdom sank deeper into deficit in the 1980s and 1990s, the interpretation of the Qur'an prohibiting income tax came under cautious scrutiny.

Saudi Arabia's objection to income tax was not merely religious. It was also political. Most people are quite aware of the extravagances of the House of Saud. If these extravagances were financed by oil money, that was thought to be one thing. If they were financed from the pockets of citizens, it might be quite another. To date, given their tribal cultural background, Saudi Arabians had not worried all that much about their lack of voting rights. But imposing taxes was thought likely to raise the argument: 'no taxation without representation'.

At the date of writing, Saudi Arabia is one of few countries which has never had to levy income tax. As a result of King Faisal's far-sighted policy in 1970 of wresting Saudi oil from the hands of major oil companies, Saudi Arabia owns its own resources. The country now lives almost entirely off the earnings of its oil company Aramco. Public revenue derived from this source has risen and fallen over the years with the oil price. After the oil price rises from 2003 onwards, pressures to increase government revenue through income tax abated. The government could once more finance its operations through oil revenue. Discussions about income tax were quietly shelved.

In terms of tax, as things stand at the moment, income earned by guest workers in Saudi Arabia remains untaxed and this arrangement looks likely to stand for the immediate future. Shariah Law states that one-fortieth of personal assets (*zakat*), an effective wealth tax of 2.5 per cent is meant to be given to charity. This is a voluntary arrangement based on religious beliefs and is not applied to the guest workforce.

NEGATIVE COMMENT

Issuing and receiving criticism is a tricky subject in any culture. The human race doesn't vary all that much in this area. No one, no matter what nation they belong to, enjoys being criticised. But it's probably fair to say that criticism of Saudis by members of their guest workforce has to be handled with unusual sensitivity. Candid criticism of a Saudi by a Westerner can quite easily be interpreted as a personal insult. A Saudi should never be criticised directly, or even to a third party. In the area of criticism and personal pride, Saudi culture is Eastern. Face matters. Face lost may never be regained. Criticism needs to be delivered indirectly, and never in front of others, and so circumspectly (amongst much praise and thanking for small favours) that it is scarcely noticeable.

If you have bad news to tell your Saudi boss, it should be delivered in such a way that there is no suggestion that a Saudi is responsible. A good technique is to first praise your Saudi boss for his business acumen and then to attribute the unpleasant news to bad luck. The more your boss convinces himself that your bad news is the will of Allah and not human error, the more easily the problem is likely to be resolved.

GETTING ON WITH THE BOSS

Those going to Saudi Arabia to run businesses inside Saudi Arabia with Saudi partners and subject to Saudi law are advised to check out their intended partners very carefully. If you're working for a Saudi Arabian company, obtaining and nourishing the goodwill of your Saudi sponsor is all important. Falling out with one's Saudi partners usually results in financial loss, whatever the legal rights and wrongs of the issue. Generally, if a contract is terminated, deportation from the kingdom follows, on the grounds that the reason for your being issued a visa in the first place is no longer valid.

Worse than deportation, in the experience of some, is the incarceration inside the country on some trumped up charge. Serious breakdown of relations between Saudis and their expatriate employees have led to some extraordinary escape stories when employers refused to return the passports of their employees or grant them exit visas. When all other avenues were closed to them, expat employees in conflict with their Saudi employers have been known to freight themselves out of the country as sea or air cargo—rolled up in a Persian rug, or nailed up inside a packing case!

Collecting from Royalty

In a widely publicised case in 1986, a US citizen and businessman Sam Bamieh went to Saudi Arabia to collect money owed to him by a business associate of the House of Saud. On arrival in Saudi Arabia, the Saudi creditors promptly had Bamieh thrown into jail in Jeddah without charge—and there he probably would have stayed except that he was able to get his plight known all the way up to the State Department who got him released.

On return to the US (without his money) Bamieh, a determined character, sued the Saudi Royal family for wrongful arrest and got enormous publicity. As the case moved through the courts, Bamieh managed to implicate the House of Saud in scandals as widely separated as the Nicaraguan Contras affair, the Bank of Credit and Commerce International, and financing political movements in Afghanistan, Somalia and the Sudan. Bameih had the money and resolve to make a nuisance of himself to both the Saudis and the US State Department. To avoid further unwanted negative publicity, the Saudis offered an out of court settlement which Bamieh accepted.

Employees can also fall foul of disagreements between governments. Despite long periods of residence, it is not easy for non-Saudi Arabs to become Saudi citizens. Saudi Arabia retains the right to deport its long-term immigrants back to their country of origin at a moment's notice. In the last ten years, this right has been exercised at various times when the policy of these other countries departed from Saudi policy.

During the first Gulf War, the Republic of Yemen supported Iraq. Approximately 850,000 Yemenis, many who had been in Saudi Arabia for decades, found themselves suddenly deported to a Yemen with which they had cut all ties. In Saudi Arabia, this action devastated the retail industry, where Yemenis tend to concentrate. In addition, the Republic of Yemen then had to cope with the sudden influx of nearly a million economic refugees it thought had left its lands forever. Palestinians and Jordanians, whose governments were also sympathetic to Iraq, faced similar problems for the same reason. Palestinians who had relocated their lives in Saudi Arabia were not welcome back after the war ended. Recruits from places like India and Egypt were admitted to fill the jobs that Palestinians had vacated.

WHO'S IN BUSINESS

The aristocracy of Saudi Arabia is one of the biggest in the world. If you operate anywhere near VIP level, you have a better chance of meeting royalty in Saudi Arabia than almost any other country. Some of the minor blue bloods operate at quite modest levels in the corporate and administrative hierarchies.

In Saudi Arabia, government and private ownership merges imperceptibly. Unlike other countries, no distinct boundary separates the private sector and the government. Since they have access to the almost unlimited funds of the Royal Treasury and are inclined to involve themselves in commercial activities, members of the Royal Family engage in all sorts of businesses. The Royal Family may own businesses in their own right, or in partnership with other people, either Saudi citizens or foreigners. Measured by extent of Royal Family shareholdings, in the mid-1990s, the Saudi government owned about two-thirds of the business interests of the country.

At the less regal level, people in Saudi Arabia tend to accept their lot in life to a greater degree than some other cultures. The frantic struggle to rise to the top of the heap is not quite as evident in Saudi Arabia as other parts of the world. However, there are exceptions. Despite the natural advantages in capital and connections of the aristocracy, heroic rise to fame and fortune of the workingman is not unheard of.

Pipeline Welder Makes Good

Sulieman S Olayan started his life as a pipe welder on a Saudi oil rig. In a chance encounter with a member of Aramco's senior management who was one day making an inspection of his company's oil rig, Olayan offered his services as a sub-contractor to Aramco. The Aramco manager gave Olayan his chance. From this small beginning, the Olayan Group of companies grew to what has become one of the largest and most diversified and profitable businesses in the country; among many other things, selling Coca-Cola and Burger King franchises throughout the kingdom. Olayan is a typical large diversified Saudi Arabian company with interests in everything from catering to heavy construction and petrochemicals. Wherever you go in Saudi Arabia, an Olayan company can supply you something. In a similar story, the bin Laden family, now the biggest contractor in Saudi Arabia with operations also in the US, started as a minor contractor after Osama bin Laden's father crossed the border as penniless emigrant from Yemen.

Until the mid-1980s, Saudi Arabia maintained controlling interests for all businesses operated inside the country. Foreign companies were permitted to operate in the country in partnership with Saudi firms, provided their partnership holdings were 49 per cent or less. In the mid-1990s, as the oil price plunged, the country needed increasing amounts of foreign investment to balance its books. Foreign ownership rules were relaxed. Areas identified as needing foreign investment were telecoms, utilities and financial services.

Changing Rules for Control of Hydrocarbons

In 2000, a Royal Decree was issued to allow 100 per cent foreign-owned businesses to operate in the country. Multinational companies including Exxon, Mobil, Royal Dutch Shell and Phillips Petroleum set up operations in the kingdom. This was a watershed event in a country that had previously wrested control of the country's oilfields back from the oil majors during the 1970s and 1980s. *The Economist* magazine, a fervent believer in free markets, commented at the time on the new measure: 'The most significant initiative is a US$ 25 billion scheme to attract oil majors into three huge natural gas projects...'

At a more personal level, Saudi Arabia remains a country where guest workers as individuals are denied the opportunity of embarking on a business for themselves. Guest workers are normally bound by their visa conditions which are specific to a particular employer and maybe to a particular job. For those determined to set themselves up in business, a Saudi partner will be required to organise permissions and lodge the appropriate paperwork.

Overseas businesses small and large have established operations in Saudi Arabia in large numbers in recent times. Investment attractive features of the Saudi business environment include generally good infrastructure, an entrepreneurial culture, minimal currency risk (the Riyal is tied to the US dollar), unregulated currency controls and a liberal tax system. Most businesses bring with them key members of their labour force.

CORRUPTION

In some quarters, Saudi Arabia has a reputation for corruption, but no more so than the average of many other countries. In its '2004 Corruption Index', Transparency International—the international organisation dedicated to fighting corruption—ranked Saudi Arabia as the 71st least corrupt country from 146 countries surveyed.

Handling the Critics

Saudi authorities are sensitive about corruption allegations whatever their source. In 2002, *Arab News* reported that the Saudi authorities arrested a Saudi poet, Abdul Mohsen al-Muslim, who had written a poem in which he alleged corruption of the judiciary. The editor of the Saudi daily *al-Madina*, which published the poem was fired from his job Abdul Mohsen was arrested and 'interrogated ... for a long time about his poem' by high ranking security officers. In 2003, the authorities conducted a major purge of clerics to weed out those who were critical of the administration.

An ongoing bone of contention between the clerics and the Royal Family is corruption in government, meaning the Royal Family itself. Allegations of corruption in the judiciary have also been raised. The most widely reported instances of major corruption are in relation to large arms purchases where payments of 'commissions' to princes holding ministerial positions are an accepted and expected way of doing business.

At the day-to day-level, our experience is that Saudis are pretty honest. Not much gets pilfered. Perhaps deterrence offered by the legal system is working. No one wants to lose a hand for an act of petty theft. An American guest worker in the kingdom has recorded on the Internet a typical experience of the culture of honesty regarding private property:

'Returning to Saudi Arabia after a vacation, my wife and I inadvertently left one of our many suitcases on the sidewalk outside the airport while we were loading them into the car. After the weekend, we asked a company driver to see if it had been turned in to lost-and-found. The driver returned with the bag. Airport security told the driver it sat on the sidewalk for two days. When no one picked it up, a policeman brought it to lost-and-found. Try leaving your bag on the platform in the New York subway for two days!'

FURTHER INFORMATION ON BUSINESS CONTACTS

For those who intend to do business in Saudi Arabia, advice can be obtained from The Saudi Chambers of Commerce and Industry which has offices in major urban centres of the kingdom. A list of Saudi distributors for most products imported into the kingdom can be obtained from these Chambers of Commerce. In addition, credit reports can be obtained on prospective Saudi business partners.

The Saudi Chambers of Commerce and Industry offices also offer an advertising service (for a fee) for those seeking Saudi representatives for their products or services. An Agent/Distributor Service is also available to identify the Saudi Arabian firms best suited to represent your products in the kingdom. In addition, the World Traders Data Report can be obtained to evaluate the performance of potential trading partners. After you have drawn up a short list of suitable representatives, you might be advised to visit Saudi Arabia to interview your candidates. For this purpose, you can obtain a short visit business visa, valid for one to three months, at your Saudi Arabian Royal Embassy or Consulate or Diplomatic Mission. For contact details for the Chambers of Commerce go to:

http://www.saudichambers.org.sa/index.html.

By law, prospective exporters of goods or services to Saudi Arabia, or firms or individuals wishing to do business in the kingdom need to appoint a Saudi Arabian partner, an import agent or a local representative to handle their business inside the kingdom. Since a great deal of the business in the kingdom is done through personal contacts rather than formal tender processes, such an arrangement is needed anyway to operate successfully inside Saudi Arabia. A local network of contacts is all important to realise exporters' ambitions.

It should be noted that companies that deal with Israel may be restricted from operating in Saudi Arabia. Two of the biggest brand names that found themselves unable to operate in Saudi Arabia for many years were Ford and Coca Cola.

Levi's is just one of the foreign companies that is allowed to operate in Saudi Arabia.

THE BUREAUCRACY

Saudi Arabia's bureaucracies are no better than many and quite a bit worse than some. Like many a developing country, Saudi Arabia has an insatiable appetite for documentation, and requires submission of a bewildering array of licence application forms to permit you to undertake the most trivial activities. You get a flavour of the bureaucratic culture on first entering the Saudi Arabia. Officials tend to be officious. Paperwork is extensive. Space provided on the many forms that need to be completed seems to bear little relationship to the volume of data requested.

An important function of the bureaucracy in Saudi Arabia seems is to provide employment for otherwise unemployable Saudi Arabians. The Saudi bureaucracy is the one area of the economy in which Saudis are isolated from competition from foreign labour for the simple reason that only Saudi citizens are permitted to work for the Saudi civil service. Guest workers who can work as consultants advising the Saudi government on their bureaucracy, cannot work within the bureaucracy itself. In fact, employment in the Saudi Civil Service is discriminatory even within Saudi Arabians. Members of the Shia sect, for example, are not normally hired for civil service positions.

From the point of view of the foreigner, Saudi bureaucracy is widespread, all embracing and on occasions, almost impenetrable. For example, while in Saudi Arabia, one of the authors decided to buy a windsurfer to sail in the fresh breezes of the Persian Gulf. This turned out to be no simple transaction of paying the money and collecting the goods. The retailer selling the craft explained (after the money had been paid) that the law required him to sight a copy of the boat licence before the goods could be delivered. In Saudi Arabia, he said, a windsurfer is treated like a boat and every boat must have a licence issued by the Department of Licences. He explained where the office issuing the licence was located. A trip to the designated office confirmed his account. Catch 22 was that the boat licence could only be issued after inspection of the boat, the boat could only be released by the vendor on presentation of the licence, and

the boat inspector was not permitted, or willing, to visit the premises of the retailer to carry out an inspection.

With matters gridlocked at this point, the author returned to the shop. After pleading with the retailer, and leaving a gold watch in the shop as security against proper issue of the licence, the goods were released into the buyer's custody on a temporary basis. The 'boat' was loaded onto the roof rack on the top of the car then driven to the Department of Licences. From there it was taken to the Harbour authority where it could be measured. A form was produced, written around a passenger-carrying vessel the size of QE2. The form asked about the number of crew, the number of engines and their size, the gross registered tonnage, the number of lifeboats and so forth. Legally registered sailboards in Saudi Arabia, according to this form, are meant to carry lights, flares and an impressive array of life preserving equipment!

The author filled out the form and submitted it to the official along with a fee (as always paid in cash). The official scanned the form, and didn't seem over-concerned about the absence of lifeboats and lifebelts, then asked where the boat was moored. Told that it was on the roof-rack of a car parked outside, the official shrugged. but co-operated and solemnly ran his tape measure over the boat and entered the results (2.5 m / 10 ft) as the waterline length of the boat. Back in the office, the official duly signed and stamped the form explaining it would need to be presented to the Department of Licences, as it wasn't the licence but merely a measurement certificate that would enable the licence to be issued!

The author had been in Saudi Arabia long enough to recognise the process. No one bureaucrat can explain the entire procedure. Each bureaucrat would explain a fragment and the customer would gradually piece the fragments together to make the whole picture. At each step of the procedure, a small amount of money (always cash) would change hands. Saudi bureaucracy isn't merely a licensing authority. It's an industry.

Back at the Department of Licences, the official accepted the measurement certificate and commenced filling out the licence form with the name of the vessel (which had to be displayed in letters at least 150mm high on both sides of the bow and across the stern). The official also explained that sailing a windsurfer legally in the waters of Saudi Arabia would also require issue of a master's licence issued by the Department of Coastguard! The author didn't bother with that. But occasionally, watchers at the security gate of the compound reported personnel from the coastguard en route to the beach to check the paperwork of the sailing fraternity. No one, to my knowledge, managed to complete the entire paper trail and most never even start.

SAUDI ARABIA AT A GLANCE

CHAPTER 10

'Ah, make the most of what we yet may spend,
Before we too into the Dust descend.'
—Omar Khayyam

Official Name
Kingdom of Saudi Arabia

Capital
Riyadh

Flag
The modern state of Saudi Arabia was created in 1932. The flag adopted on Saudi Arabia's assumption of nationhood was based on the banner of the Wahhabi tribe, and features

the Islamic inscription or *shahad* on a green field (the symbolic colour of Islam). The inscription read: 'There is no God but God and Muhammad is the Messenger of God'. The first Saudi king, Abdul Aziz bin Abdul Rahman Al Saud (Ibn Saud), added a sword to this flag in 1902 after he established himself as the King of Nejd in central Saudi Arabia. As a variation on this theme, the modern Saudi Arabian flag was introduced only in 1973. The inscription, which was unchanged from the previous flag, and its underlying icon of a sword encapsulates the essence of Saudi Arabia: this is a religious state supported by the power of the sword. Such is the deference to the message on the Saudi flag that when Fadh died in 2005 at the age of 83, though flags were dropped to half mast in many Arab capitals, they were not lowered in Riyadh on the grounds that doing so would have been tantamount to blasphemy.

National Anthem
Aash Al Maleek ('Long Live Our Beloved King')

Time
Greenwich Mean Time plus 3 hours (GMT + 0300)

Telephone Country Code
966

Land
Located in the Middle East, Saudi Arabia is bordered by Jordan, Iraq and Kuwait to the north; Bahrain, Qatar, the United Arab Emirates (UAE) and Oman to the east and south-east; and Yemen to the south. The Red Sea separates Saudi Arabia from Africa to the west while the Persian Gulf separates it from Iran in the east.

Area
total: 1,960,582 sq km (756,985 sq miles)

Highest Point
Jabal Sawda' (3,133 m / 10,279 ft)

Climate
Desert climate with extremes of temperature

Natural Resources
Copper, gold, iron ore, natural gas and petroleum

Population
26,417,599 including 5,576,076 non-nationals (July 2005 est)

Ethnic Groups
Arab (90 per cent) and Afro-Asian (10 per cent)

Religion
Predominantly Muslim

Official Language
Arabic

Government Structure
Monarchy

Adminstrative Divisions
13 provinces: Al Bahah, Al Hudud ash Shamaliyah, Al Jawf, Al Madinah, Al Qasim, Ar Riyad, Ash Sharqiyah (Eastern Province), 'Asir, Ha'il, Jizan, Makkah, Najran, Tabuk

Currency
Saudi riyal (SAR)

Gross Domestic Product (GDP)
US$ 310.2 billion (2004 est)

Agricultural Products
Barley, citrus, dates, melons, tomatoes and wheat

Other Products
Chickens, eggs, milk and mutton

A Saudi boy sits in front of his father's shop at a *souq* in Riyadh.

Industries
Ammonia, basic petrochemicals, caustic soda, cement, commercial aircraft repair, commercial ship repair, construction, crude oil production, fertiliser, industrial gases, petroleum refining and plastics

Exports
Petroleum and petroleum products

Imports
Chemicals, equipment, foodstuffs, machinery, motor vehicles and textiles

Airports
Estimated total of 201, of which 72 have paved runways. The main international airport is in Riyadh.

Weights and Measures
Saudi Arabia has adopted the metric system of measurement. Petrol is measured in litres (one US gallon = 3.86 litres), distances are measured in kilometres (one mile = 1.6 kilometres) or metres (1 metre = 3.28 feet) and weights are measured in kilogrammes (2.2 pounds). For those buying gold—a favoured pursuit in the *souqs* of Saudi Arabia—the conversion is one ounce = 28 grams.

FAMOUS PEOPLE OF SAUDI ARABIA
King Abdul Aziz bin Abdul Rahman Al Saud (better known to some as Ibn Saud)
Ibn Saud's achievement was to create modern day Saudi Arabia. The Al Saud family, originated in the Najd area around present-day Riyadh. As an adolescent, Ibn Saud saw his family bundled out of Riyadh by their rivals, the Rushidis, eventually finding sanctuary near present day-Kuwait. To Ibn Saud, then 21, banishment at the hands of the Rushidis was a matter of honour. In 1901, he set out to retake Riyadh from the Rushidis. Thirty years later, he had brought most of the Arabian Peninsula under his control.

World Leaders and Ibn Saud

Ibn Saud was a tall, strong, charismatic warrior with a reputation for mercilessness. Though uneducated in the modern sense, he learned the ways of the world from personal experience, meeting heads of state like President Franklin D Roosevelt—who he liked—and Winston Churchill whose drinking habits he couldn't abide.

Said Churchill, giving his take on his meeting with Ibn Saud, "My rule of life prescribed as an absolutely sacred rite smoking cigars and also the drinking of alcohol before, after and if need be during all meals and in the intervals between them." (from *Triumph and Tragedy* by Winston Churchill)

Apart from military campaigns, Ibn Saud employed more personal methods to unite the country. Under Islamic law, a man was allowed four wives at any one time and could divorce any wife of his choosing in less than a minute, no questions asked. Ibn Saud practised short term marriages and instant divorces on a grand scale. Before setting off on his military campaigns, he would divorce at least one of his wives—reducing his quota of wives left at home base to three or less and often taking concubines with him to assuage his grief for the loss of his least favoured wife. Later, after conquering a town or a tribe, he would summon the head of the newly conquered people to produce a suitable wife. In thirty years, after countless skirmishes with the many tribes of the country, opinions vary on how many women Ibn Saud married. Some authorities estimate the number at a modest 40 while others have it as 300–400. Ibn Saud himself probably didn't keep accurate records. From his wives, collected and discarded, Ibn Saud produced a great many children who, a generation later, created a Royal Family numbering thousands. Inclined to boast of his sexual prowess, (and, in his later years, attended by armies of doctors prescribing aphrodisiacs), Ibn Saud once proudly claimed that he had never seen the face of many of his brides. They would arrive in *abayas*, spend their one-night marriage in his tent, then depart before the first prayer call the next morning. During the course of his life, from 17 different wives, Ibn Saud fathered a known 44 sons—35 of whom were still alive on his death—and an unknown number of daughters.

Until he reached his mid-50s, Ibn Saud was perpetually short of money. He understood the potential of oil to change his country's fortunes and encouraged investment in the oil industry. In his last few years, oil made him extraordinarily wealthy. He died in 1953 at the age of 73. Ibn Saud is one of the few people in history to name a country after himself.

King Faisal

Faisal was born in Riyadh in 1905, the fourth son of Ibn Saud. Like his father before him, Faisal spent his early adulthood as a desert warrior. In 1925, Faisal and his supporters won a decisive victory in the Hijaz region of Saudi Arabia. He was appointed the Governor of Hijaz in 1926. When Saudi Arabia coalesced as a nation in 1932, Faisal was appointed Foreign Minister. The issue that most absorbed him in this role was the partition of Palestine, of which he disapproved. After Ibn Saud died, Faisal's older brother Saud came to the throne. Faisal continued to serve as a minister, gradually increasing his responsibilities. After a decade in which the country declined economically, the family engineered the abdication of King Saud who had proved to be a spendthrift and, in 1964, placed Faisal on the throne.

Before becoming king, Faisal became involved in arrangements for the pricing of oil. Over the last few years of the 1950s, the seven oil companies operating in the Middle East, nicknamed the 'Seven Sisters' had closed ranks to reduce their royalty payments to oil supplying countries. In his role as Foreign Minister, Faisal reached an arrangement with other oil exporting countries to control the production of oil. The five countries—Iran, Iraq, Kuwait, Saudi Arabia and Venezuela—met on 14 September 1960 in Baghdad and formed OPEC (the Organisation of Petroleum Exporting Countries). Later, other oil exporting countries joined OPEC's ranks. OPEC has probably been the only successful cartel the world has ever seen for a major commodity.

During the same period, back at home in Saudi Arabia, Faisal took one other measure to secure his country's long-term oil future. He progressively increased his control of Aramco from the international oil companies. These two measures have produced a very different financial situation in Saudi Arabia today than it otherwise would have been. Revenues from the Saudi oil company Aramco have been sufficient to finance most of the country's financial operations, without the assistance of taxes.

In 1973, the last of the Arab/Israeli wars was fought—the Yom Kippur War won by Israel. The US lent critical support to Israel during the war by emergency airlifting massive amounts of military equipment. King Faisal showed his disapproval of this US action by boycotting oil supplies. The price of oil rose 400 per cent almost immediately, in what economists of the West later termed 'the first oil shock'. (The second oil shock occurred six years later in 1979, during the revolution in Iran). Most economists consider the oil shock a major factor in precipitating a lower period of economic growth in the West in the 1970s, along with high inflation. From the Saudi perspective, the era of high oil prices had the opposite effect as inflated oil revenues flowed into the kingdom.

Faisal's other major economic measure has been to develop and modernise his country by investing its oil revenue in industrial development projects based on Saudi Arabia's advantage in obtaining cheap hydrocarbons from its oil and gas fields. A number of industrial plants have been built to produce petroleum derivative products such as synthetic fertilisers and petrochemicals.

Most commentators consider King Faisal by far the most capable of Saudi Arabia's kings. Faisal was named *Time* magazine's Man of the Year in 1974. But in 1975, his rule came to an end when he was assassinated—shot three times in the face from close range by one of his nephews.

Sheik Ahmed Zaki Yamani

Sheik Yamani was King Faisal's charismatic Oil Minister who became the face of OPEC during the 1970s and 1980s. He was born in Mecca in 1930, where he grew up. He obtained his first degree in law from Cairo University in 1951 and a master's degree in law from New York University in 1955. He then graduated from Harvard Law

School in 1956. In 1958, he became an advisor to the Saudi government. Working closely with King Faisal, Yamani was appointed as oil minister in 1962, an office he held with great distinction.

During the 1970s, when the price of oil was of interest to most people, Yamani became the spokesperson for OPEC. In this role, with his goatee beard, his diplomatic skills and his smooth delivery, he became one of the most recognisable people on the planet. The soft-spoken Yamani was a great favourite with the press.

OPEC, by its nature, was an organisation driven by the internal tensions of its various competing nations. Its operatons were based on member nations agreeing to production quotas that were unenforceable by the organisation itself as members frequently exceeded their production quotas. To the consuming countries of the world, OPEC was depicted as a malevolent force dedicated to undermining their economies. Despite the pressures, internal and external, the considerable diplomatic skills of Yamani maintained OPEC as a cogent economic force.

In 1975, in a bizarre escapade, Ilich Ramirez Sanchez, better known to the world as 'Carlos the Jackal', staged a highjack of OPEC representatives who were holding a regular meeting in the organisation's headquarters in Vienna. While Carlos issued death threats inside the plane, the OPEC representatives were taken on various flights back and forth around the Mediterranean, to Algiers, then Tripoli, then back to Algiers. After the event, Yamani stated he was sure Carlos meant to kill him, but at the end of the affair, Yamani was released unharmed.

After Faisal was assassinated, Yamani gradually lost his appeal to the House of Saud. The Ministry of Saudi Arabia was almost entirely composed of Al-Saud princes and Sheik Yamani was not of royal blood. In 1986, King Fadh sacked Yamani as oil minister.

At the time of writing, Yamani lives in Jeddah.

CULTURE QUIZ

SITUATION 1

You are an expatriate woman you are taking a shopping trip down town. Where do you sit in the car?

Ⓐ In the driver's seat.
Ⓑ In the front passenger's seat.
Ⓒ In the back passenger's seat.

Comments

Where you sit depends who else is in the car, and your relationship with them. Under Saudi law, women are not allowed to drive. So **Ⓐ** is not right. Depending on the circumstances, either **Ⓑ** or **Ⓒ** could be right. The golden rule is you should sit next to whoever is your natural male companion. If you are married, the most suitable person for this role is your husband. If the husband is unavailable, your brother or son, if they are over 12 years old. If you are unmarried, the closest member of your family is, in order, brother or father, then uncle or nephew. If you are riding in a taxi, you must have a male family member with you.

SITUATION 2

You are an expatriate woman who has been invited to a Saudi home. While you are there, you are offered alcohol. Should you:

Ⓐ Explain you are a teetotaller and decline.
Ⓑ Explain you are a reformed alcoholic and decline.
Ⓒ Say that you understand the rules of the country don't permit the consumption of alcohol and decline.
Ⓓ Accept.

Comments

Alcohol, being illegal, can be an awkward issue. The safest thing is not to drink while in the country, though most people who are not teetallers do. **Ⓒ** is probably the safest policy. However, plenty of people have accepted the hospitality as per **Ⓓ**, and lived to tell the tale.

SITUATION 3

You are in a conference with your Saudi boss and another Saudi walks in. The boss focuses his attention on the other person and ignores you completely. What should you do?

Ⓐ Quietly leave the room to allow the two Saudis to get on with it.
Ⓑ Sit tight and wait until the focus returns to you.
Ⓒ Offer the Saudis a cup of coffee.
Ⓓ Interrupt the Saudi conversation, saying that you have work to do and will return later to finish the conference.

Comments

Ⓑ is the correct answer.

SITUATION 4

You are invited to a dinner party, installed as guest of honour. Somewhere during the proceedings your host makes a great show of giving you a gift. Should you:

Ⓐ Decline to accept the gift and denounce the gift giver for attempted bribery.

Ⓑ Politely decline to accept the gift.

Ⓒ Accept the gift, but do not open it.

Ⓓ Open the gift in front of all the guests.

Comments

Gift-giving is widespread. Saudi attitudes to gift-giving are complex. Neither **Ⓐ** or **Ⓑ** is correct. If you reject the gift, however politely, the gift-giver will lose face. However, if you open the gift (**Ⓓ**), you may lose face, if the gift-giver has given you something that people think you should have already had yourself, or your family should have given you. Under the circumstances, you accept the gift, but do not open it. **Ⓒ** is the best policy. Having accepted the gift, the gift and the act of giving the gift should be quickly forgotten by both the donor and the recipient.

SITUATION 5

You are playing tennis and the prayer call goes up. Should you:

Ⓐ Keep playing.

Ⓑ Stop playing, and remain on court to resume after prayer call ends.

Ⓒ Go home.

Comments

It is in order to keep playing (assuming you are not a Muslim). Muslims do not expect non-Muslims to drop everything when the prayer call goes up. However, there is a fair chance, just to remind you who is boss of this nation, that if you are playing at night, the lights may be switched off.

SITUATION 6

You have invited a Saudi to your home and he asks for whisky, what should you do?

Ⓐ Say you don't drink.

Ⓑ Say you do drink, but don't have any whisky, and offer him some Sidiqui or home brew instead.

Ⓒ Give him all the whisky he wants.

Comments

Course **Ⓒ** is fraught with peril. If you give a drink to a Saudi, and he gets into trouble as a result of it, you are in trouble. In addition, Saudi-expat friendships tend to be fragile. If you fall out of friendship, the Saudi has the power to inform the authorities of your activities. If he does, the authorities will probably act. Option **Ⓑ** is not a good idea either for the same reason. Besides, Saudis don't regard the home brew industry going on their country highly, either as an activity or for the quality of its product. Likewise, Sidiqui is considered a low class drink. To offer it may be considered insulting. All round, **Ⓐ** is the best option.

SITUATION 7

You ring a business associate at his office and someone answers the telephone. You ask for the person by name. The voice answers, "Mr Mohammed has not come back yet." Should you:

Ⓐ Assume that Mr Mohammad is really there.

Ⓑ Leave a message for him to return you call.

Ⓒ Ask where Mr Mohmmad has gone.

Ⓓ Ask when Mr Mohmmad is likely to return.

Comments

Like in most places, the claim that someone you want to speak to is out could mean any number of things. Whether you are likely to a receive a call back in the event you adopt option **Ⓑ** depends on your status with Mr Mohammad. In most cases, the best option is to try again later.

SITUATION 8

You are interested in the Muslim religion and are invited to visit a mosque. Should you:

Ⓐ Accept.
Ⓑ Decline.

Comments

There is no rule in Islam precluding non-Muslims from visiting a mosque. A Western diplomat tells a story of an encounter at Riyadh Airport with a member of the al Saud family where he was invited to visit the Airport's ornate mosque. The diplomat asked under what circumstances a non-Muslim could visit a mosque in the kingdom. The short answer is that non-Muslims in the kingdom can visit a mosque so long as they are invited by an appropriate Muslim. Not all that many expats visit mosques, for fear of offending the sensibilities of Muslims, and perhaps this is a good rule to follow. If you do visit a mosque, be sure to observe the appropriate protocols such as the removal of shoes.

SITUATION 9

A public execution is to be held in your town. Should you:

Ⓐ Attend.
Ⓑ Stay away.

Comments

The answer to this one probably depends more on your own sensitivities than those of the nation. The national policy is that all and sundry are encouraged to attend public executions. But attendance is not compulsory. Executions are meant to be a deterrent. There are certain executions, such as stoning to death, where only Muslim males are meant to participate (apart from the victim who is more likely to be a woman). If you do go, you have a fair chance of being a minor attraction. You may be pushed to the front of the crowd so you get an unrivalled view of the events.

SITUATION10

You are introduced to a man wearing a white *thobe*, a red and white checked *gutra* and a black *egal*. What is his likely nationality?

Ⓐ Saudi.
Ⓑ Palestinian.
Ⓒ Jordanian.
Ⓓ Yemeni.

Comments

He is unlikely to be a Yemeni, since Yemenis do not wear *egals*. Although Jordanians do wear red and white *gutras* in Jordan, they are more likely to wear Western style clothing in Saudi Arabia—sometimes with *gutra* and *egal*. Palestinians working in Saudi Arabia also tend to wear Western dress—and if they wear *gutra* it is likely to be black and white check. So your new friend is likely to be a Saudi. But you can't be sure.

DO'S AND DON'TS

DO'S
- Do accept coffee and tea whenever offered.
- Display a positive attitude towards Saudis.
- Do tell the Saudis how much you enjoy their country.
- Dress conservatively—arms and legs of women should be covered in public.
- If you are a business visitor, carry your passport wherever you go.
- If you are long-term guest worker, carry an ID card.
- Refer to Saudi Arabia as the Kingdom of Saudi Arabia, or the KSA.
- Pronounce Saudi as 'So-wu-di' not 'Saw-di'.
- Ensure your company has a picture of the reigning monarch in the front office.
- Keep in touch with the diplomatic mission of your country.

DON'TS
Women
- As a woman, don't walk around Saudi-occupied areas unaccompanied by a male member of your family.

Men
- Don't wear shorts in Saudi areas.

Both Genders
- Don't go out of your way to press Saudi nationals with your friendship.
- Don't touch a member of the opposite sex in public.
- Don't take photographs without permission.
- Don't shake hands with Saudi women.
- Don't discuss politics or religion.
- Don't admit to any personal failings that might diminish your role as an employee.
- Don't carry any pornographic material, including newspapers with pictures of scantily clad females, into the country.

- Don't have Israeli visa stamps in your passport.
- During Ramadam, don't smoke, eat or drink during daylight hours in front of Saudi nationals.
- While sitting cross-legged, don't display the soles of your feet to anyone in the vicinity.
- Don't supply alcohol to Saudis.

GLOSSARY

> 'Arabic names won't go into English exactly, for their consonants
> are not the same as ours, and their vowels, like ours, vary from
> district to district.'
>
> —T E Lawrence to his proofreader
> on the various spellings of Arab names in his book,
> *Revolt in the Desert*, in 1926

USEFUL PHRASES
Pleasantries

Hello	*Marhaba*
Hello, peace be upon you	*As-salaam alaykum*
(Response)	*Wa alaykum salaam*
How are you	*Keef hal-ak*
Good	*Zane or Kowaies*
Praise be to God (I'm fine)	*Al-humdoolillah bikhair*
Good morning	*Sabaah al-khair*
(Response)	*Sabaah al-nuur*
Good evening	*Masaa al-khair*
(Response)	*Masaa an-nuur*
Good bye, go in safety	*Ma'a salama*
(Response)	*Allah yisullmak*
May God go with you	*Fi Amanellah*
Nice to meet you	*Tasharrafna*
Welcome	*Ahlan wa sahlan*
Excuse me	*Asif or Ismahlee*
Please	*Min fadlak*
Thank you	*Shukran*
You're welcome	*Af-wan*

Getting Around

Do you speak English?	*Tet kalam Ingleezi?*
Do you understand...?	*Fa-him?*
I don't understand	*Ana ma fehempt*
I don't speak Arabic	*Ana laa ta-kalam al-Arabiah*
My name is...	*Ismi...*
What is your name?	*Aish ismak?*
What is your job?	*Aish shoghol?*
Where...?	*Wain...?*
Why...?	*Lay'ish...?*
How much	*Kum*
Expensive	*Ghaalee*
Nothing, none, nobody	*Mafee*
Yes	*Enaam or aiwa*
No	*Laa*
Maybe	*Yimken*
Arabian Coffee	*Gahwa*
Water	*Moya or moy*
Hot	*Haarr*
Hotel	*Foon-dook*
Car	*Saiyara*

Colours

Black	*Aswad*
White	*Abyad*
Red	*Ahmar*
Blue	*Azrak*
Green	*Ahdar*

Numbers

Zero	*Sifr*
One	*Wahid*
Two	*Itnain*

Three	*Talata*
Four	*Arba'a*
Five	*Khamsa*
Six	*Sitta*
Seven	*Sab'a*
Eight	*Tamaniya*
Nine	*Tis'a*
Ten	*Ashra*
Eleven	*Ehd-ash*
Twelve	*Ith-nash*
Thirteen	*Ta-lat-ash*
Fourteen	*Aar-bat-ash*
Fifteen	*Kham-stash*
Sixteen	*Sit-ash*
Seventeen	*Sa-bat-ash*
Eighteen	*Ta-man-tash*
Nineteen	*Ti-sat-tash*
Twenty	*Ash-reen*
Thirty	*Thala-theen*
Forty	*Ar-ba-een*
Fifty	*Kham-seen*
Sixty	*Sit-een*
Seventy	*Sab-a-een*
Eighty	*Thaman-een*
Ninety	*Tis-a-een*
One Hundred	*Mee-a*

RESOURCE GUIDE

PHONE COMMUNICATIONS

Saudi Arabia's phone system is provided by a private company, Saudi Telecommunications Company (STC). Landlines cover all major centres in the country. In addition the Global System for Mobiles (GSM) covers 45 Saudi cities and towns and all major highways. Internet connections are widely available, though content may be censored more than most places. International Direct Dialling (IDD) is generally available. The kingdom's telephone country code is '966' while the main city codes are:

- Riyadh   01
- Jeddah and Mecca   02
- Al-Jubayl, Ad-Damman and Al-Khobar   03
- Yanbu   04
- Mobile   05

The following emergency contact numbers apply:

- Police   999
- Fire   998
- Ambulance   997

Finding a Phone Number

Saudi Arabia publishes an English language phone book, but extracting information from it is no easy task. The telephone book lists the name of the owner of the house rather than the occupant. This makes it almost impossible to find the telephone number of an expat.

In the classified section of the telephone book, there are some interesting entries. International consulting companies like British Aerospace are listed under 'O' for organisations whereas international companies like Seimens are listed under 'C' for companies. Organisations like the United Nations are listed under 'E' for establishments.

Using a Saudi phone book takes perseverance and imagination.'
—Source: Susan Mackay. *The Saudis*

Accommodation arrangements, including phone connection and payment of phone bills, for almost all guest workers staying in the country are almost always the responsibility of the employer. A guest worker would not normally be expected to or be authorised to arrange phone connections for landlines. Like other utilities, phone bills will normally be sent to and paid for by employers.

HEALTH

Most employers include full health care in the employment package. For those outside this arrangement, Saudi Arabia has a few top hospitals, but except for routine ailments, provision of health care services is expensive. Most embassies advise you to include medical insurance in your arrangements prior to entry in the country.

A list of hospitals in Saudi Arabia may be obtained at the following webpage:

http://www.gulfmd.com/hospitals/Major%20Hospitals%20in%20middle%20east.asp?id = #Saudi%20Arabia

Dental Clinics

Saudi nationals receive free dental treatment. Dental clinics are housed within general hospitals or as stand-alone clinics. Specialist dental hospitals are also available. For outlying districts and remote villages, mobile dental clinics are provided.

SCHOOLING

Most regions in the country have access to international schools. For a complete list of schools available in Saudi Arabia, you can consult the International Schools website:

http://www.isgdh.org/

Language Schools

Opinions amongst expats differ on the value of language schools for those who want to learn Arabic. Our general view is that most language schools are geared to teaching Classical Arabic, with a strong focus of interest on the Qur'an, not only for its language, but also for its general philosophy. Most likely, the mjority of expats would prefer to be learning conversational Arabic devoid of heavy religious overtones. An alternative to schools is to hire a private tutor. Skills of private tutors vary enormously. You will probably have to hire and fire a few to find someone compatible with your needs. Generally the recommended profile, at least for a start, is a non-Saudi Arabic speaker, either a non-Saudi Arab or an Arabic-speaking Third Country National. Details of people offering such services for your particular regional area in Saudi Arabia are liberally listed on the Internet and also in English-language newspapers such as *Arab News*.

EXPAT CLUBS
Expats visiting Saudi Arabia may obtain support from in-kingdom expat clubs. People, particularly women, who live in compounds tend to develop a large variety of common interest groups within their common living areas. Other expat groups are more widely spread. For those who wish to contact expat groups prior to travelling to Saudi Arabia and perhaps exchange some views in advance of going there, try:

http://www.expatexchange.com/net.cfm?networkid = 97

VOLUNTEER ORGANISATIONS
Opportunities for participating in volunteer work in Saudi Arabia are very limited due to the various restrictions on travel, working for anyone other than your designated employer or, if you are a woman, working for anyone at all.

NEWSPAPERS AND MAGAZINES
There are two nationally circulated English-language newspapers in the country: *Arab News* and *Saudi Gazette*. In addition, *Riyadh Daily* is an English-language paper of more restricted circulation.

A number of English-language magazines are in circulation as well, presenting the Arab point of view. It is worth taking a look at one or two of the English-language Saudi newspapers

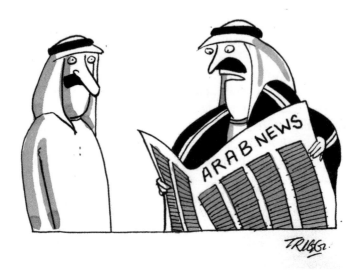

and the magazines to get a more Arab slant on the news than that presented by the pro-Israeli viewpoint of most of the Western press.

Copies of magazines imported into the country are scrutinised by censors. Girlie magazines of the *Playboy* ilk are banned in Saudi Arabia and thereby acquire scarcity value. Copies of *Playboy* and *Penthouse* may change hands for about US$ 100. Western magazines, particularly news magazines like *Newsweek* or *The Economist* are sometimes banned for carrying politically incorrect articles. For less serious misdemeanours, offending magazines may be allowed to go on sale provided that every copy of whatever article offends the Saudi censor is either cut out or blacked out by a marker pen-wielding minor bureaucrat. According to sceptics on this subject, thousands of such government salaried *imams* are employed on censoring magazines as a contribution to solving the unemployment problem.

The marker pen form of censorship is, incidentally, particularly ineffective. Not only does it draw attention to an article you might otherwise have missed, the text is quite legible if the article is held up to the light. If you find a magazine that contains a column that has been blacked out by a marker pen, you can assume that underneath the censor's handiwork lies an article of interest.

Bringing Information to Your Attention
Browsing through a library in Saudi Arabia, the author's attention was attracted by some Textra colour highlighting in the *Guinness Book of Records* under the heading 'The World's Biggest Bribe'. A Middle Eastern Prince taking his extraordinary dues on some defence company contract held the record. But for the activities of the censor, this snippet might have been missed.

Religious texts are also banned, particularly those that could be construed by Customs officials or the Mutawa'een as undermining Islamic faith. Books of Common Prayer and the Bible fall into this category. It is not a good idea to include Christian prayer books, bibles or other seditious material in your luggage when entering Saudi Arabia.

WEBSITES
General Information
- CIA Factbook
  http://www.cia.gov/cia/publications/factbook/geos/sa.html

Visa and Travel Information
- US Department of State: Consular Information Sheet
  http://travel.state.gov/travel/cis_pa_tw/cis/cis_1012.html
- Saudi Embassy
  http://www.saudiembassy.net/Travel/Travel.asp
  (For more detailed information, click on the relevant section in the menu on the left.)

Tourist Information
- US Department of State
  http://www.state.gov/r/pa/ei/bgn/3584.htm
- Lonely Planet Guide
  http://www.lonelyplanet.com/destinations/middle_east/saudi_arabia/

- Saudi Arabian Airlines (Saudia)
  http://www.saudiairlines.com

History of Saudi Arabia

- Library of Congress
  (Federal Research Division/Country Studies)
  http://memory.loc.gov/frd/cs/satoc.html
- The Middle Eastern Network Information Centre
  http://link.lanic.utexas.edu/menic/Countries_and_Regions/
  Saudi_Arabia/
- Arab Countries: Saudi Arabia
  http://www.hejleh.com/countries/saudi.html

Islamic Culture

- British Broadcasting Corporation
  http://www.bbc.co.uk/religion/religions/islam/
- Zawaj.com
  http://www.zawaj.com/links.html

Job Opportunities

- Jobs of Arabia (run by Professional Systems and Services)
  http://users.aol.com/saudijobs/saudijob.htm

Internet Filtering in Saudi Arabia

- Jonathan Zittrain and Benjamin Edleman, Berkman Centre
  for Internet & Society (Harvard Law School)
  http://cyber.law.harvard.edu/filtering/saudiarabia/

Human Rights Information

- Country Reports on Human Rights Practices (released by
  the Bureau of Democracy, Human Rights and Labour
  http://www.state.gov/g/drl/rls/hrrpt/2002/18288.htm
- Human Rights Watch
  Country Pages: Saudi Arabia
  http://www.hrw.org/doc?t = mideast&c = saudia
  (For an year by year overview of the Human Rights
  Development in the country, click on the respective year
  on the right of the page.)

- Amnesty International: Saudi Arabia
  http://www.amnesty.org/ailib/intcam/saudi/

FURTHER READING

Included here is a random selection of books that examine and extend some of the topics covered in *CultureShock! Saudi Arabia*, and look more generally at the Middle East as an area of compelling interest to most of the world. Since literally thousands of books have been written about the Middle East, so many worthy books will be omitted from the following short list. We have selected just a small sample of the literary offerings that we hope covers a range of viewpoints and subject matters. Most of the books we have listed take the outsider point of view, since this is the perspective from which *CultureShock!* is written. Our purpose is to detail the likely culture shock experienced by visitors to Saudi Arabia, not its own citizens. However, we have also included a sample of books displaying the insider, the Saudi, viewpoint of their own country. The books are roughly sorted by topics that do not coincide particularly with the chapter order of *CultureShock!*.

BOOKS ON HISTORICAL BACKGROUND

Seven Pillars of Wisdom: A Triumph. T E Lawrence. London: Penguin Books Ltd, 2000.

- The book is included in this section not only because it is a classic of its genre, but also because it contains some of the most acute observations of the physical conditions of Saudi Arabia from the viewpoint of a painstaking observer—the landscape, the weather, the living conditions and the food of the pre-oil Bedouin culture. Lawrence's role in Saudi Arabia wasn't all that well known until the blockbuster film *Lawrence of Arabia* portrayed him as the genius military strategist who 'went Arab', a role that some historians feel was exaggerated. The book, written by Lawrence, is an intensely personal account that may well embellish some of his own achievements. For that reason it has not been beyond controversy. Some historians also dispute the book's historical accuracy. For all that, for students of Saudi Arabia, this is an engrossing read.

The Kingdom: Arabia and the House of Sa'ud. Robert Lacey. New York, NY: Avon Books, 1983.

- This book is somewhat of a standard text. Though now a bit dated, it is an easy-to-read factual account of the history of Saudi Arabia through to about the 1980s. Covers the tribal aspect of the Saudi society as well as religion, politics, culture and economy.

A History of Saudi Arabia. Madawi Al-Rasheed. Cambridge, UK: Cambridge University Press, 2002.

- A complement to Lacey's book, *A History of Saudi Arabia* covers the same subject from a Saudi perspective. The book describes the history of this enigmatic country from inception to the present day, with special reference to the cultural and social life in the country from a female, Saudi Arabian perspective.

The Desert King. David A Howarth. London: Quartet Books, 1980.

- This is probably the most readable account of one of the most fascinating men of the 20th century, Ibn Saud, the first of the Saudi Kings, the man who spent the first half of his working life uniting his nation. It is an account of his origins, his battles, his marriages, his divorces, his many children and the birth of the oil industry. Though this is an old book and the story has been told many times by many different authors, for readability of a fascinating story, David Howarth's book sets the standard.

BOOKS ON CULTURE SHOCK

The Clash of Civilisations: And the Remaking of the World Order. Samuel P Huntington. London: The Free Press, 2002.

- This is a rather long and somewhat technical book written by a leading academic who is a Professor at Harvard University making the general point that 'east is east and west is west, and never the twain shall meet'. Huntington considers that the gap between western and eastern cultures is vast, and is not getting any narrower—a point that we have also tried to make in Culture Shock.

The Clash of Fundamentalism: Crusades, Jihad, and Modernity. by Tariq Ali. London and New York, NY: Verso, 2003.

- This recent book by UK-based academic, Tariq Ali, is a controversial, deeply personal and wide ranging description of the failure of nations to understand each other and therefore to wage wars of various sorts on each other. Ali had, by the time this book was published, established somewhat of a reputation as a radical thinker who generally opposed the established world order. This book ranges far and wide, well outside Saudi Arabia, in examining the interactions between the Islamic world and the rest of the world. It complements Huntington's book, and reaches similar conclusions via a different, more personal route. They say you shouldn't judge a book by its cover. This book is almost worth buying for its cover alone—a picture of George Bush, computer-enhanced to look like Osama bin Laden!

BOOKS PRESENTING A WOMAN'S POINT OF VIEW

Princess: A True Story Behind the Veil in Saudi Arabia. Jean P Sassoon. Minneapolis, MN: Econo-clad Books, 2001.

- This is the best selling book that lifts a corner of the veil of secrecy that shrouds women's issues in Saudi Arabia. It is (or purports to be) the autobiography of a rebellious Saudi princess living in opulent conditions in a palace in Riyadh. Princess Sultana writes under a pseudonym using a ghost author. So specific are descriptions, it's hard to believe that, if she really exists, she would not have been identified by her husband and close members of her family. One of the fascinating questions of the book is the degree to which it is true.

At the Drop of a Veil. Marianne Alireza. Costa Mesa, CA: The Blind Owl Press, 2002.

- The account of Princess Sultana has been contradicted by some in Saudi Arabia. Defenders of the Saudi Arabian way of life claim that *Princess* is a beat up, written by a woman's rights author for western consumption with the express purpose of making money. For those who want to hear the opposite viewpoint—that all is, in fact, well between womanhood and Saudi culture—an alternative is *At the Drop of a Veil* by Marianne Alireza, presents it. This book is a personalised description of an American women living in Saudi Arabia and married to a Saudi man; an arrangement that, according to the author, was generally satisfactory.

The Veil and the Male Elite: A Feminist Interpretation of Women's Rights in Islam. Fatima Mernissi. Trans. Mary Jo Lakeland. New York, NY: Basic Books, 1992.

- Women's role in Islam has received mixed reports. Muslims make the point that in principle, Islam is not a misogynist religion. However, Islam, as much as any religion, is bound not only by its holy scriptures but by those who administer the religion here on earth; and the

Muslim religion (like most others) is administered by men. Though women are permitted to enter mosques and are expected to worship the one true God, the administration of the religion is strictly the province of males. To date, there are no female *mullahs* in the Muslim religion.

CURRENT ISSUES IN POLITICS, OIL, ECONOMICS AND RELIGION

Forbidden Truth: US-Taliban Secret Oil Diplomacy and the Failed Hunt for bin Laden. Jean-Charles Brisard and Guillame Dasquié. New York, NY: Thunder's Mouth Press/Nation Books, 2002.

- We have included this somewhat radical book to present an alternative viewpoint. This is a highly controversial 'other side' account of the 9-11 attacks on New York, first written in French by French authors not known for their mindless obeisance to the US official version of the state of the world. The book offers clues to the answer of the intriguing question that was not generally allowed to be asked of the fatal attacks e.g. why did they do it?; and an even more intriguing question, did the US authorities know they were going to do it? The answers, according to the authors, lie in a murky mix of political intrigue, oil pipelines across Afghanistan and the ambivalence of Saudi Arabia in funding Islamic radical organisations on the one hand, while relying on US as a customer and defender of the regime on the other. Commercial links between oil companies associated with George 'Dubya' Bush and the Bin Laden family well prior to 9-11 are of particular interest.

BOOKS ON THE ISLAMIC RELIGION

Muhammad: A Biography of the Prophet. Karen Armstrong. London: Phoenix Press, 2001.

- Many books have been written on the Prophet Muhammad, rated by some as the most influential person in human history. Some are eulogies while others are scathing criticisms. In recommending a book on Muhammad, we have tried to opt for balance. Karen Armstrong's book is, we believe, a reliable 'warts and all' account of the life and times of this astonishing historical individual.

BOOKS ON ETIQUETTE

Living & Working in Saudi Arabia: Your Guide to a Successful Short or Long-Term Stay. Rosalie Rayburn and Kathleen Bush. Oxford: How To Books, 2001.

- Very similar to *CultureShock!*, this book is written with the purpose of advising those going to Saudi Arabia on how to learn the ropes. In *CultureShock!*, we have concentrated more on the cultural differences of Saudi Arabia and particularly for those coming from the West. Rayburn and Bush's book is more of a hands-on guide to operating in Saudi Arabia. A valuable adjunct to *CultureShock!* for those bound for Saudi Arabia.

Don't They Know It's Friday? Cross Cultural Considerations for Business and Life in the Gulf. Jeremy Williams. Dubai: Gulf Business Books, 1999.

- An amusing, practical hands-on guide to the pros and cons and quirks of doing business in Saudi Arabia. This book complements and reinforces some of the subjects covered in *CultureShock!*.

To Be a Saudi. Hani A Z Yamani. London: Janus Publishing Co, 1997.

- There are plenty of books looking into Saudi Arabia from a Western viewpoint. This is a book looking out of Saudi Arabia from a Saudi viewpoint, written by an author who clearly loves his country. It makes some interesting predictions (not shared by the authors of *CultureShock!*) as to where the country is likely to head to from here.

ABOUT THE AUTHORS

Peter North first started living and working in Asia about 25 years ago. He started writing for Marshall Cavendish about eight years ago and has now contributed six titles to the *CultureShock!* and business reference series. Peter is also a contributor of articles to various magazines, in particular *Pacific Ecologist*. He spends his time pursuing various interests in environment, current affairs, science and engineering. Peter's titles include *Success Secrets to Maximize Business in Australia*, *Success Secrets to Maximize Business in Britain*, *Countries of the World: Australia* and *CultureShock! Cambodia*—all published by Marshall Cavendish, and *Growing for Broke* and *State in Fear* published by Tomorrow Press.

Harvey Tripp is a graduate of the University of Melbourne and has spent most of his corporate life in international business, holding senior management positions in major international consumer goods companies including the management of their operations in the kingdom of Saudi Arabia. Harvey has lectured on international business, including how to do business in Saudi Arabia, at a number of universities in Australia and has been on the advisory boards of universities and other tertiary institutions to help develop their international business programs. Harvey has been a consultant to small and medium sized businesses and has had interim executive assignments with corporations whose primary focus is international business. He has also been a director of small to medium sized Australian companies. He is the co-author of *Success Secrets to Maximise Business in Hong Kong*, *Success Secrets to Maximise Business in the United Arab Emirates* and *CultureShock! Bahrain*.

INDEX

Titles in the CULTURE**SHOCK**! series:

Argentina	Hawaii	Pakistan
Australia	Hong Kong	Paris
Austria	Hungary	Philippines
Bahrain	India	Portugal
Barcelona	Indonesia	San Francisco
Beijing	Iran	Saudi Arabia
Belgium	Ireland	Scotland
Bolivia	Israel	Sri Lanka
Borneo	Italy	Shanghai
Brazil	Jakarta	Singapore
Britain	Japan	South Africa
Cambodia	Korea	Spain
Canada	Laos	Sweden
Chicago	London	Switzerland
Chile	Malaysia	Syria
China	Mauritius	Taiwan
Costa Rica	Mexico	Thailand
Cuba	Morocco	Tokyo
Czech Republic	Moscow	Turkey
Denmark	Munich	Ukraine
Ecuador	Myanmar	United Arab
Egypt	Nepal	Emirates
Finland	Netherlands	USA
France	New York	Vancouver
Germany	New Zealand	Venezuela
Greece	Norway	Vietnam

For more information about any of these titles, please contact any of our Marshall Cavendish offices around the world (listed on page ii) or visit our website at:

www.marshallcavendish.com/genref